Alaska
A Pictorial History

Alaska

A Pictorial History

by Claus-M. Naske and L. J. Rowinski

Design by Jamie Backus Raynor
The Donning Company/Publishers
Norfolk/Virginia Beach

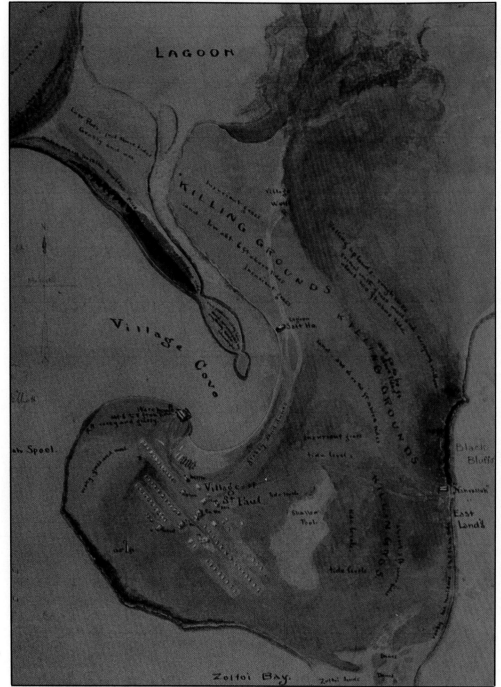

The village of St. Paul on the
Pribilof Islands is shown in this
1890 map by Henry W. Elliott.
Courtesy of the Alaska and Polar
Regions Dept., Rasmuson
Library, UAF

Contents

An oil painting by Ted Lambert depicts one of Vitus Bering's ships in the rough waters of the North Pacific. Courtesy of the University of Alaska Museum

Foreword

Dear Reader:

I'm proud to greet you at the beginning of this book—and to welcome you to a captivating visual adventure through Alaska's past.

For me, the trip through our history is both humbling and inspiring. Those early Alaskans faced many hardships, and they conquered them without the aid of the sophisticated technology and conveniences we enjoy here today. At the same time, it's exciting to see how far we have come in a relatively short time. So many challenges and opportunities remain.

Today, Alaska is home to a dynamic and diverse population approaching half a million. Alaska is alive—building and growing. I feel the special challenge of tomorrow: helping lead Alaskans who have one eye on the possibility of the international marketplace, the other eye on the peace of our mountains and streams.

So, this book is a gift to us all—Alaskans and Alaskans at heart—on the occasion of the 49th State's Silver Anniversary. I want to compliment the Anchorage Convention & Visitors Bureau for its efforts, and I hope you enjoy this history of America's "Last Frontier."

Sincerely,

Bill Sheffield

Bill Sheffield, Governor

The Golden Gate Hotel was one of the more elegant establishments in Nome in the early 1900s. Courtesy of the Norma Hoyt Collection

Nome in the early 1900s. Courtesy of the Norma Hoyt collection

Acknowledgments

Golden Gate Hotel, Nome, Alaska.

John J. Swenson Co.'s Cableway in operation unloading grain at Nome, Alaska.

The photos in this book have come from many sources. Large public collections have been particularly useful, for it is in these collections that the photographs taken or saved by individuals are preserved and made accessible to the public. The foresight and generosity of the donors to these collections must be recognized.

Many of the photos came from the Alaska Historical Library in Juneau, which has broad, well-organized collections. Phyllis DeMuth, Librarian, and Verda Carey, Photograph Librarian, offered valuable suggestions and made working in Juneau productive. Renee Blahuta, Library Assistant, made her familiarity with the collections of the Alaska and Polar Regions Collection at the University of Alaska, Fairbanks (UAF) an aid to finding useful material, and Dave Nelson saw that fine prints were produced. Diane Brenner, Archivist of the Anchorage Historical and Fine Arts Museum provided valuable assistance with its photo collection.

Evelyn K. Bonner made several photographs available from the Sheldon Jackson College. Other sources include the U.S. National Archives, the U.S. Army Corps of Engineers, the Library of Congress, the Smithsonian, and the University of Alaska Museum. We are grateful to Kent Sturgis, managing editor of the *Fairbanks Daily News-Miner,* for giving us access to the paper's photo file, and to June Pinnell Stephens, news room librarian, for helping locate material.

Norma Hoyt again made using her collection a pleasure, and Paul J. Sincic generously gave us the opportunity to use photographs from the extensive collection he has taken throughout Alaska.

We would also like to acknowledge the expert help Nancy Watkins Morgan, our editor, gave us, as well as the design artistry Jamie Backus Raynor contributed.

Introduction

Traditionally, Alaskan histories begin with the 1741 discoveries of Captain-Commander Vitus Bering, a Danish navigator in Russian service, and his fellow explorer Captain Alexei Ilyich Chirikov. Tsar Peter the Great, who had assumed the throne in 1689, had been curious to find out whether or not the converging continental land masses of Asia and America were joined or were separated by a body of water. After Peter's death in 1725, his widow, the Empress Catherine I, continued the inquiry. Not until 1741 did Bering and Chirikov answer the question when they discovered that the two land masses were separated.

Since the Russian occupation of Alaska there has been a quiet, steady interest in this northern giant. However, it was not until the beginning of the Second World War, with the Japanese surprise attack on Pearl Harbor in 1941; the Japanese occupation of the Aleutian Islands of Kiska and Attu, and the bombing of Dutch Harbor, both in 1942, that America paid extended attention to Alaska. And it was not until the postwar years that federal interest and involvement with Alaska reached a high pitch. Military planners, bureaucrats, and the American press discovered Alaska's strategic importance, not only from the military point of view, but also from the standpoint of its potential role as a cultural and commercial bridge between the United States and the Far East. In 1968 when Atlantic-Richfield discovered the gigantic Prudhoe Bay oilfield, with recoverable resources of 9.6 billion barrels of oil, America rediscovered Alaska as a storehouse of natural resources for the nation. ∎

This painting depicts the signing of the Treaty of Cession of Russian America to the United States. Secretary of State William H. Seward is seated at the left and Baron Edward de Stoeckel is standing with his hand indicating Alaska on the globe. Courtesy of the U.S. National Archives

Chapter 1

Geological
History

On the south side of the Brooks Range the forest of spruce thins as it reaches the northern limit of trees. In this picture a caribou stands among the low willows and dwarf birch. Photo by L. Rowinski

The Brooks Range separates the forested interior from the treeless North Slope. Bare ridges and tundra predominate in this view. Photo by L. Rowinski

Southeastern Alaska is a heavily forested strip of mainland and many islands. It is dominated by the sea and the mild wet climate it generates. Photo by L. Rowinski

Broad braided streams, seasonally filled to their banks, flow from the north side of the Alaska Range. Photo by L. Rowinski

Alaska is the largest state of the Union, encompassing 586,412 square miles. The state's east-west span covers a distance of 2,000 miles, and the north-south axis covers about 1,100 miles. Alaska has a coastline of 6,640 miles, and a shoreline of 33,904 miles. Of the twenty highest mountains in North America, seventeen are located in Alaska, with Mount McKinley the highest at 20,320 feet. The state has a number of large rivers, with the Yukon River the longest at 1,875 miles. For 1,400 miles the Yukon flows through Alaska before emptying into the Bering Sea. The upper reaches of the river flow through Canada's Yukon Territory. There are about three million lakes, including Lake Iliamna, the largest, covering 1,000 square miles.

Alaska's Several Regions

The Coastal Range and the Alexander Archipelago define southeastern Alaska. This part of the Pacific mountain system continues across the top of the Gulf of Alaska, there dividing into two spurs continuing to the west and south. The coastal one contains the Saint Elias Range as well as the Chugach and Kenai mountains, and finally, at its southwestern extremity, reappears near the ocean as Kodiak Island. The main spur continues inland and forms the crescent of the Alaska Range and the backbone of the Alaska Peninsula and Aleutian Islands chain. Between these two mountain systems lie the inland waterways of southeastern Alaska—the Wrangell Mountains, the Copper River Plateau, the Talkeetna Mountains, the Susitna lowlands, and Cook Inlet. Beyond these two mountain groups lies Alaska's interior, lowlands, plains, and rolling highlands, drained by the Yukon and its tributaries into the Bering Sea. Projecting from the northwest corner of this region is the Seward Peninsula which reaches out toward Siberia. To the north of this area lies the Brooks Range which divides the interior from the Arctic Slope.

Four major climatic zones exist. The maritime zone includes southeastern Alaska, the South Coast, and the southwestern islands. The transition zone between marine and continental influences consists of a very narrow band along the southern portion of the Copper River; the Chugach Mountains; Cook Inlet; Bristol Bay; and the coastal regions of the West Central division. The con-

The interior of Alaska, between the Alaska and Brooks ranges, is a land of spruce and birch forests with major rivers such as the Tanana and Yukon and numerous lakes. Photos by L. Rowinski

This high altitude aerial photo of Mount McKinley (with distorted color) was taken in July 1977 looking west over the Parks Highway, which is visible as a line just below the center on the photo. Mount McKinley, the highest peak in North America at 20,320 feet, is part of the 650-mile-long Alaska Range that extends in an arc across central Alaska. Courtesy of the Alaska Power Administration, State of Alaska

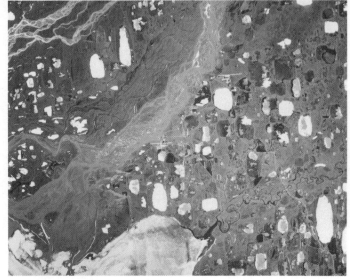

A satellite view shows the famous Prudhoe Bay oil field on the North Slope of Alaska. In 1968 Atlantic Richfield Company and Humble Oil and Refining Company (now Exxon U.S.A.) confirmed the discovery of a major oil find at Prudhoe Bay on the North Slope. The braided streams and rivers, ice-edged coastline, and numerous tundra ponds are typical of much of the area north of the Brooks Range. Courtesy of the U.S. Department of the Interior, EROS Data Center

tinental zone is made up of the remainders of the Copper River and the West Central division, and the Interior Basin. The fourth zone is the Arctic region north of the Brooks Range.

Climates range from moist and mild in the Panhandle to cold and windy on the Arctic Slope. Mean annual temperatures in the state range from the low forties in the south to a cool ten degrees along the Arctic coast. The greatest seasonal temperature fluctuations occur in the central and eastern portion of the continental interior. Here maximum temperatures reach the upper seventies, with extreme readings in the nineties, and winter temperatures average minus twenty to thirty, with occasional drops to minus fifty below and even colder. In other parts of Alaska, temperature contrasts are much more moderate. In the maritime zone the summer temperatures average near sixty, and the winter temperatures average in the twenties. In the transition zone, the range is from the low sixties to near zero. Except for the northern coastal region the west central part of the state is colder, with a range from the mid-fifties to nearly ten below zero. On the Arctic Slope the range extends between the upper forties to twenty below zero.

Earthquakes

Alaska's landforms are as varied as its climates, ranging from the rain forests of the southeastern Panhandle to the windswept and treeless islands of the Aleutian Chain, and from the valleys, mountains, forests, and streams of southcentral Alaska to the barren tundra of the North Slope. Alaska is geologically unstable. Citizens were reminded of this instability at 5:36 p.m. on Good Friday, March 27, 1964, when one of the greatest earthquakes of all time struck southcentral Alaska. Measuring between 8.4 and 8.6 on the Richter scale, it released twice as much energy as the 1906 earthquake which destroyed San Francisco, and it was felt over almost a half-million square miles. The motions lasted longer than for most recorded earthquakes, and more land surface was vertically and horizontally dislocated than by any previously known tremor. The earthquake left 114 dead or missing and Alaska's governor estimated property damages at between one-half and three-quarters of a billion dollars.

The tremors generated sea waves which traversed the entire Pacific, and the seismic vibrations indicated that a huge segment of the earth's crust had been dislocated along a deeply buried fault, the nature and exact location of which are still subjects for speculation. Not only was the land surface tilted, but an enormous mass of land and sea floor moved several feet horizontally toward the Gulf of Alaska.

A compilation by geophysicist T. Neil Davis of the Geophysical Institute of the University of Alaska at Fairbanks shows that between July 1788 and August 1961 some earthquakes measuring five points or more on the Richter scale occurred in Alaska. The foregoing examples make it obvious that Alaska's geological setting holds considerable peril. Despite the fact that geologists have worked in Alaska since the latter part of the nineteenth century, this huge land mass is not well known geologically. Complete geological mapping on a scale of four miles to the inch, comparable to that done in much of the lower forty-eight contiguous states, would require more than a century of intensive work.

Continental Drift

Alaska is a geologically young land and is constantly changing its geologic structure. In the last few decades scientists have discovered that the state is composed, in part, of land masses which have migrated to the northern Pacific rim from the far south. David B. Stone, a professor of geophysics at the University of Alaska in Fairbanks, is a proponent of the theory that the forces driving plate tectonics and continental drift have also created the unique land puzzle which is Alaska.

The plate tectonics theory has revolutionized geology in the last two decades. Plate tectonics holds that the earth's outer shell consists of a series of large plates, each moving independently over the relatively fluid portion of the earth beneath them. The earth's plates expand outward by extruding basalt from spreading zones along mid-ocean fractures of the oceanic crust. Thus plates, continually growing outward and moving independently, slide past each other and often collide and converge. Since it is unlikely that the earth is expanding, portions of the plates must be destroyed to balance their growth in the oceans. Scientists have found that plates are destroyed by diving under, or subducting, other plates.

The Aleutian Islands represent an example of a subduction zone in action today. In addition, southern Alaska and the Alaska peninsula show many examples of subduction zones existing through geologic times.

Scientists have determined that Alaska is a part of the North American plate. Alaska is situated between a fracture in the Arctic with the plates spreading outward, attempting to push Alaska south, and a northward-moving Pacific plate trying to push Alaska to the north. The combination of forces generated by these motions is responsible for the earthquakes and volcanoes. Professor Stone also thinks that, traced backward in time, the forces may well be responsible for the large curved systems of mountains, valleys, and major faults which dominate Alaska's landscape today.

The forty-mile long Columbia Glacier enters Prince William Sound on the south coast of Alaska about twenty-eight miles southwest of Valdez. It is one of many spectacular glaciers that flow from the Chugach and Saint Elias Mountains. Courtesy of the Heath Ives Collection, Alaska and Polar Regions Dept., Rasmuson Library, UAF

Tectonostratigraphic Terranes

Rocks from different geological environments are found close together in Alaska, but usually are separated by faults. This has led to the concept of tectonostratigraphic terranes, defined as areas that are bounded by faults and have internally consistent sequences of rocks which indicate a coherent geologic history within a block. The terranes are very different from their neighbors, so apparently there must have been motion between them. Geologists of the U.S. Geological Survey have subdivided Alaska into fifty of these terranes. Some of these may be subdivisions of very large major terranes. Scientists have studied the earth's magnetic force, as recorded by rocks when they were formed, and found from rocks from a number of Alaska' terranes that southern Alaska was far to the south about 200 million years ago. Between that time and the present, southern Alaska's terranes have migrated northward. Professor Stone states that the big questions needing answers are: how much of Alaska was involved in the plate movement, when did this land arrive, and what composed ancient Alaska? Obviously, much work needs to be accomplished before these questions can be answered.

This print, from the 1700s, shows the interior of a Tlingit house in southeastern Alaska. The proportions are distorted, but it does show the vertical plank walls, the fire pit in the center, and the drying racks overhead. Courtesy of the Historical Photograph Collection, Alaska and Polar Regions Dept., Rasmuson Library, UAF

Hunters of Unalaska in their small kayaks are shown wearing waterproof parkas and bentwood hats that shielded their faces, more likely from rain than sun in the Aleutians. The Russians pressed many of these hunters into their service to obtain the valuable sea otters which lived along the rocky coasts, coves, and inlets of the islands. Courtesy of the Historical Photograph Collection, Alaska and Polar Regions Dept., Rasmuson Library, UAF

Chapter 2

This drawing of a house on Unalaska is from an engraving by an early explorer. The artist has managed to give it the aspect of an English country cottage. Courtesy of the Historical Photograph Collection, Alaska and Polar Regions Dept., Rasmuson Library, UAF

The inhabitants of Norton Sound and their habitations are shown in one of the plates from Cook's *Voyages*, 1789. Courtesy of the University of Alaska, Fairbanks

Native Alaska

Prehistory

Alaska has a long record of occupation and settlement by her indigenous peoples. Although the exact time and circumstances of man's first arrival in North America remain uncertain, most agree that the route from Asia to America must have been by way of the so-called Bering Sea Land Bridge. The seas separating Alaska and Siberia in and near the Bering Strait are shallow, with water depths consistently less than 100 fathoms throughout the northeastern half of the Bering Sea, as well as the Bering Strait and the Chukchi Sea. Most scientists agree that in later geological times more than once, and perhaps during prolonged periods, there existed a wide terrestrial plain connecting North America and Asia. In 1937, the scientist Eric Hulten published his now classic *Outline of the History of Arctic and Boreal Biota During the Quaternary Period.* "Beringia" was the name he gave the vast arctic lowland that must have been exposed during the worldwide glacial epochs. An analysis of the distribution of living plant species indicated that Beringia had been a refugium in which most arctic and many boreal plant species were isolated while much of northern North America and parts of Siberia were covered with glacial ice. Applying the knowledge of Pleistocene glacial chronology which was just emerging in the 1930s, the author concluded that Beringia had been a land bridge during both the Illinoian and Wisconsin Glaciations when sea levels fell because water was stored in the form of continental glaciers.

And although the time and circumstances of man's first arrival in North America remain uncertain, the present consensus is that the first people who saw what is called America today were following ice-age mammals migrating east from Siberia into what is today Alaska. The animals were searching for food and fleeing their predators. The hunters, following the game, eventually wandered into the grasslands of the American interior, then east to the Atlantic shores of Canada, south across the deserts, through Central America, and finally to Tierra del Fuego, the tip of South America.

These early hunters entered Alaska via the Bering Sea Land Bridge. As the ice receded, the sea levels rose again, until, about ten thousand years ago,

This Tanana Indian was depicted by Frederick Whymper in 1868. Although the Hudson's Bay Company had established a post at Fort Yukon and the Russians had a redoubt at Kolmakov, these were austere outposts and there was a great deal of unexplored country in between. Gold miners, traders and exploring parties had small effect on the Native people until the late 1800s when the Klondike rush brought heavy traffic to the Yukon. Even then the Indians of the upper Tanana were, in many ways, isolated until well into the 1900s. The man depicted here is wearing a decorated moosehide shirt. His curved-handled knife is worn in a sheath in front. Whymper was an Englishman who was a member of the Western Union Telegraph Extension, sometimes also called the Collins Overland Telegraph. The vast engineering and construction project got underway in 1865. The plan was to direct a line north from Vancouver, British Columbia, to the headwaters of the Yukon River, and from there along the Yukon to Nulato, north of the Seward Peninsula, across the Bering Strait, and south across Siberia to meet the Russian line from Europe at the mouth of the Amur River. The 5,000 miles of line was expected to cost $1.5 million, or about $300 for each mile. In the summer of 1867 the Western Union Telegraph Extension terminated the project when Cyrus Field's leased ship, the *Great Eastern,* successfully laid the Atlantic cable. From *Travel and Adventure in the Territory of Alaska,* Frederick Whymper, 1868. Courtesy of the Alaska and Polar Regions Dept., Rasmuson Library, UAF

Alaska and Siberia parted once again. How long the Americas have been inhabited by humans is simply informed guesswork, but most agree that it has been at least fifteen thousand years. In any event, excavations south of Alaska have confirmed this approximate date. Perhaps it can be safely stated that long after mankind had settled the continents of Asia, Africa, and Europe, America was unknown to any human beings. At some point, fifteen to forty thousand years ago, humans began to live in the Americas after they had crossed the Bering Sea Land Bridge.

Today, a mere fifty-six miles of stormy waters separate Siberia's Chukchi Peninsula from the Seward Peninsula of Alaska, at the point where the United States and the Soviet Union confront each other most closely.

Ancestors of the American Indians apparently came to America through the northern part of the thousand-mile-wide Bering Sea Land Bridge, while the ancestors of the Eskimos and Aleuts probably took a southernly route along the shores of Beringia to the Aleutians where they established their coastal dwellings for sea mammal hunting.

One of the best known early sites of human occupation in Alaska dates back eleven thousand years. Onion Portage is located on the Kobuk River in northwest Alaska. Different cultural groups used it for thousands of years. Archeologists have excavated tools from the most ancient layers at the site which are similar to those found in Siberia. There are indications that man may have been on the upper Yukon River more than twenty-five to thirty thousand years ago, but these early occupants probably were not the ancestors of the present groups. There is evidence, however, that ancestors of today's Aleuts lived continuously in the eastern Aleutians for better than eight thousand years, and that the Na-Dene speaking peoples may have been in Alaska since before 9000 B.C.

Aboriginal Alaska

Captain-Commander Vitus Bering, a Dane in Russian service, discovered Alaska in 1741. Three separate ethnic and linguistic groups, named the Indians, Aleuts, and Eskimos, lived on the great peninsula on the northwest tip of North America at the time of Bering's discovery.

There were two groups of Indians,

both of whom spoke languages classified as Na-Dene. One, comprised of the Tlingits and the Haida, lived on the heavily wooded islands and mainland of southeastern Alaska. The other group, the Athapascans, lived in the interior of Alaska. The fourteen Tlingit subdivisions had a population of approximately nineteen thousand while the seven Athapascan divisions numbered about the same but they were distributed over an area about eight times larger.

The Aleuts and Eskimos spoke languages that had developed from the ancestral language of Eskaleuts about four thousand years earlier. The Aleuts lived on a long island chain that included almost one-third of Alaska's coastline and consisted of over one hundred islands larger than a half-mile long. It is estimated that the Aleut population in 1741 was between five thousand to sixteen thousand souls, while some Russian writers thought that it might have been as high as twenty-five thousand in aboriginal times.

The Eskimos occupied almost the entire Alaskan Coast from the Arctic Ocean to Yakutat Bay, including Kodiak Island, the Alaska peninsula, and Prince William Sound in southcentral Alaska. The Eskimos probably numbered between twenty-three to thirty-five thousand at the time of discovery. There are at least twenty Eskimo groups or divisions, but there may have been more than thirty autonomous political groups during the early 1700s.

Nine years before Vitus Bering, on his second voyage, discovered the Big Land, the Russian explorers Mikhail Gvozdev and Ivan Fedorov, together with a crew of thirty-nine, left the mouth of the Kamchatka River late in July 1732. They sailed to a point on the eastern face of the Chukotsk Peninsula from which they turned eastward to look for the Diomede island sighted by Bering in 1728. They found both of the Diomede Islands, probably landed on the larger one, and then sailed east to the Big Land, America. Their vessel, the *Sviatoi Gavriil*, anchored off the coast of Cape Prince of Wales at a distance of about three miles, but the Russians did not go ashore to investigate the area. Later, they coasted south along the land, then headed southwest, sighting King Island, and returned to the Kamchatka River late in September.

In the 1740s when Europeans arrived in Alaska in numbers after Bering's official discovery in 1741, Native settlement patterns had been stable for some

Petroglyphs are carvings in rocks, often of a geometric or non-realistic symbol, that are found in a number of locations in southeastern Alaska. Like many from other areas, this example from the Wrangell area cannot be dated or interpreted exactly. Petroglyphs are intriguing signs from the past. Photo by Paul J. Sincic

Nuklukayet was a trading camp and settlement near the junction of the Tanana and Yukon rivers. In the 1880 census the population was given as twenty-seven. Many of them seem to be here in this illustration from Allen's 1887 report. From *Report of an Expedition...*, Henry T. Allen, 1887, Alaska and Polar Regions Dept., Rasmuson Library, UAF

In 1885 Lieutenant Henry T. Allen made an exploratory journey up the Copper River to the interior and then down the Tanana and Yukon to Saint Michael. He visited Taral, a small Ahtena Indian village on the Copper River in the Chugach Mountains. There were two houses there at the time. One is depicted here. From *Report of an Expedition...*, Henry T. Allen, 1887, courtesy of Alaska and Polar Regions Dept., Rasmuson Library, UAF

The houses in the Indian village at Juneau in the late 1800s show a mixture of styles and modern features such as tall doors and windows. There is even a log cabin. However, several of the houses show smokeholes in their roofs rather than chimneys. Douglas Island is across the channel. Photo by W. H. Partridge, courtesy of the Alaska Historical Library

The interior of a Tlingit house at Klukwan, at the northern end of the Inland Passage, is shown in this photo from the late 1800s. The baby is suspended in a comfortable cradle. To the right are two elaborate camphor chests, used for storage, which traders brought from China. (Sea otter pelts and other furs were taken to China for sale.) Wide vertical planks form part of the wall. The board holding up the shelf on which the chests rest has been beautifully patterned with an adze. Courtesy of the Alaska Historical Library

time. The various groups occupied a diverse land, ranging from the desertlike tundra of the Arctic to rain forests, and from the seashores to Mount McKinley, at 20,320 feet the highest mountain on the North American continent. The many Native groups spoke different languages and developed their own social organizations, arts, and religions. But despite these many differences, they shared a number of characteristics. They were hunting and gathering peoples. They did not practice agriculture and had only one domesticated animal, the dog. They used Alaska's waterways as their main highways, and all, therefore, had boats of various sizes and shapes. They traveled over large areas, but few, if any, of Alaska's groups were nomadic. With a few exceptions, such as the Nunamint caribou-hunting Eskimos of the Brooks Range, all lived in permanent dwellings and villages but moved to summer camps for specific tasks, such as fishing. All tribes generally had well-defined concepts of group land boundary lines. They used various parts of their land separately from season to season. Almost all groups depended on fish as the mainstay of their diets, and the women collected as many berries and greens as the local resources permitted. Their religious beliefs were basically similar; they only had a vague concept of a supreme being; they respected the spirits of food animals and honored them with festivities; and the shaman, or medicine man, was the important interpreter of the supernatural. He also served as doctor for nonspecific illnesses. Most groups recognized the existence of an afterlife and cared for corpses and deposited personal goods in the graves. The Tlingits and Haidas practiced cremation. Ceremonial celebrations often inspired the carving of art objects and the composition of songs and dances. The myths everywhere included tales of the Raven, usually portrayed as the creator of the world. Their myths also included accounts of warfare and raiding, especially among the Eskimos and Indians who lived near each other.

The Indians of Southeastern Alaska

Among the first to migrate to the New World were the ancestors of today's Indians. Of particular interest were those who eventually made their homes along the shores of northwestern North America, from Trinidad Bay in northern California to Yakutat Bay at the northern tip of southeastern Alaska. These various Indian groups developed complex cultures based on the amazing wealth of the natural resources of the region. From the sea and the rivers they obtained the five species of Pacific salmon; in addition they caught halibut; cod; herring; smelt; and olachen, or "candlefish." (This last fish is so rich in oil that a dried one with a wick threaded through its middle burns like a candle.) They also utilized many other species of fish. The sea provided an astounding variety and quantity of edible mollusks. Marine mammals, such as the hair seal, sea lion, sea otter, porpoise, and whale were plentiful. Land game abounded, and even though vegetables were less plentiful, many species of wild berries provided a bountiful food supply, which, in most other parts of the world, man had to wrest from the soil through agriculture and the domestication of animals. This surplus of foodstuffs gave these groups an abundance of leisure to devote to the elaboration of their culture.

The Northwest Coast is not only a unit in its aboriginal culture patterns, but in a geographical sense as well. It possesses a moderate climate because the offshore Japanese Current prevents the occurrence of extreme and prolonged cold. It also releases huge masses of water vapor which the prevailing winds blow onshore, where they condense while rising over the coastal mountains, and produce the heavy rain characteristic of the region. Innumerable streams and rivers cascade from the coastal mountains and empty into the North Pacific Ocean. The heavy precipitation also produces a very dense, specialized vegetation consisting of stands of conifers, such as Douglas fir; a variety of spruces; red and yellow cedar; yew; and finally, at the southern tip of the area, coast redwood. Deciduous trees, such as alder, maple, and oak, occur as well.

Three Distinct Native Groups in Southeastern Alaska

Three distinct Native groups occupy southeastern Alaska or the "Panhandle," namely the Tlingits; the Northern Haida; and finally, the Tsimshian, in the community of New Metlakatla on Annette Island. The Panhandle stretches from

Dixon Entrance on the south to Yakutat Bay on the north. The area consists of a thirty-mile-wide strip of mainland bordered by an eighty-mile chain of islands, the Alexander Archipelago. The islands are mountainous and covered with a thick growth of spruce, hemlock, and cedar up to timberline. The mainland mountains are higher, less wooded, and mostly snowcapped, and numerous glaciers extend to tidewater. Although the coastline measures only 250 nautical miles along the ocean front, it is so convoluted and broken that there is a tidal shoreline of approximately nine thousand miles.

The Northwest Coast Indians adapted themselves superbly well to their coastal environment. Fishing constituted the basis of their economy, and they used a variety of fish traps, nets, and dip nets. For salmon and sea mammal hunting they used the harpoon, a spear with a detachable head connected to the shaft by a short line. For angling the Indians also used baited hooks of various shapes and sizes, particularly in fishing for cod and halibut.

All Indians built beautiful and utilitarian canoes for numerous purposes, ranging from fishing and hunting to warfare. All practiced limited land hunting, using snares, deadfalls, bows and arrows, and short hardwood pikes.

The Tlingits, the most numerous of the three groups, lived in various permanent villages throughout the region, from Yakutat Bay to Cape Fox. Consisting of fourteen tribal divisions, they spoke a language believed to be related to the Athapascans of the interior. In prehistoric times the various interior tribes immigrated from behind the mountains to the coast, and from the mouth of the Copper River eastward along the shore.

The Tlingits also extended northward from an area the Yakutat people called "the Southeast of Alaska," some coming along the shore or over the glaciers, or choosing the inland route over the Chilkat Pass and down the Alsek River to Dry Bay. Still others paddled canoes up from Cross Sound or even further south.

The Northern Haida also spoke a language believed to be related to Athapascan but differing from the Tlingit. These people lived on the Queen Charlotte Islands and the southern part of Prince of Wales Island. Legend has it that the Haidas of Prince of Wales Island, known as "hayani," drove out some southern Tlingit tribe or tribes a couple of hundred

years ago. Haida traditions maintain that some of their ancestors came from the mainland, and others had lived on the islands since the beginning of the world.

The Tsimshians, consisting of three major subdivisions each speaking a slightly different dialect, lived on the mainland. The three major subdivisions also differed culturally. There are linguists who classify the Tsimshian language with a linguistic stock they call "Penutian," but which has not, as yet, been defined with certainty. Fellow speakers are to be found in the south, in Washington, Oregon, and California. Tsimshian tradition has it that most of their divisions came from a legendary place called Temlaxam, "Prairie Town," somewhere up the Skeena River. When the Hudson's Bay Company built Fort Simpson in 1834, the nine tribes who wintered on Metlakatla Pass moved their winter quarters to Fort Simpson. In 1887 a large group of Tsimshians, led by the Anglican missionary William Duncan, moved to Annette Island in Alaska after some church-related quarrels.

These Eskimo men are from Icy Cape. The photo was taken between 1877 and 1881, and at that time labrets were still popular ornamentation for men. (Labrets were small decorated plugs of ivory or bone that were worn through the lower lip.) Photo by E. W. Nelson, courtesy of the Smithsonian Institution, National Anthropological Archives

Semisubterranean houses on Unalaska were photographed about 1888. These earth and sod covered houses had glazed windows with curtains. Courtesy of the Alaska Historical Library

On King Island, a precipitous rock in the Bering Sea, inhabitants built their walrus skin houses on posts since there was no level ground available. Although remote from the mainland and other people, the village survived on the rich sea life surrounding it. Almost everyone has now left the island to live in Nome, where schools and other services are available. This photo was taken about 1888. Courtesy of the A. Shattuck Collection, Alaska Historical Library

The Pribilof Islands are noted for the fur seals which come to the islands to breed and have their young. The Russians established Saint Paul about 1788 with Aleuts who were transported there to harvest the furs. The business continued after the United States purchased Alaska. Henry W. Elliott was a special agent for the Treasury Department when he drew this map of the Saint Paul area on June 6, 1890. It shows many features, such as the village with its houses and the killing ground. Elliott drew other maps and a series of watercolor scenes of the islands and the sealing activities. He went on to serve as a lobbyist for the Alaska Commercial Company in Washington where the company was trying to protect its monopoly in the seal trade. Courtesy of the Alaska and Polar Regions Dept., Rasmuson Library, UAF

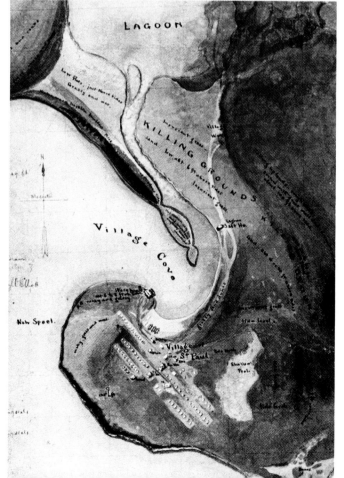

The Indians used wood as a primary construction material, building houses, canoes, storage vessels, dishes, cooking utensils, and cradles. Fine craftsmanship and elaborately carved and painted decorations distinguished many of their products. Their tools were rather simple, consisting of chisels made of nephrite, elkhorn, or the dense shells of deepwater clams, mounted in hardwood shafts. They used heavy chopping adzes for felling trees, and controlled burning to hollow out logs for canoes or their large trough-like feast dishes. They built large, rectangular gabled-roof houses, occupied by several families, in which the individual timbers were carefully notched to fit together snugly.

Dress varied among the groups. Only the northern Tlingit wore tailored garments. The Chilkats, who often visited the cold interior on trading voyages, wore one-piece trousers-and-moccasins made of buckskin, and fringed buckskin shirts trimmed with porcupine-quill embroidery, similar outfits to those worn by their Athapascan neighbors. Others wore breechcloths, and when weather permitted men went about almost nude, while women wore one- or two-piece skirts of buckskin over buckskin slips. Throughout the area both sexes usually went barefoot except when traveling into the mountains in the winter, when they wore crude moccasins. Raingear varied from conical capes made from shredded cedarbark to robes and rectangular rain capes of cedarbark matting. Fur robes were sometimes worn as well, especially by chiefs. In war, men wore various kinds of armor and elaborately carved wooden helmets.

Socially, the Tlingits, Haidas, and Tsimshians were organized along matrilineal lines where descent is traced exclusively through the maternal line. The Tlingits and Haidas were organized into two major moieties, or subdivisions, to one of which every individual was assigned at birth, and each individual had to marry a person of the opposite moiety. Tlingit and Haida moiety members also shared the right to use certain crests or representations of animals and supernatural beings reputed to have either assisted ancestors or to have been the original ancestors. In some tribes the moieties were subdivided into clans whose members traced their relationship from a legendary common ancestor. Unlike the Tlingits and the Haidas, the Tsimshians had no moieties, but several clans.

The photo says "A-Pat-Look and Wy-Ung-Ena, Cape Douglas, Alaska. Married at Teller, Alaska, April 10th, 1905." The couple show traditional face decoration markings. He had labret scars just below his lip. She had tattoo marks on her chin. Her parka was of reindeer or caribou skin while his was made of ground squirrel skins. Both had wolverine ruffs. Photo by F. W. Nowell, courtesy of the Smithsonian Office of Anthropology

This picture shows an Eskimo sod house and log storehouse on the Naknek River about 1890. The underground houses were warm, easily heated winter dwellings. In the warmer weather people would often move to other camps where tents or lighter shelters were used. The storage building was raised to protect the contents from dogs and wild animals. The space underneath was used for drying things. Courtesy of the Smithsonian Institution, National Anthropological Archives

Umiaks are the large seagoing boats of the Eskimo. Their wooden frames covered with walrus or seal hides are light and flexible enough to be used for hunting among the ice floes where they may have to be landed quickly. The crew here (about 1908) is using hand-carved paddles. The umiak has also been used with a sail in some areas, and those that are still in use are usually equipped with outboard motors. They are used for hunting

whales and walrus, as well as for transporting families and goods from place to place. Photo from the Lusk Album, Alaska and Polar Regions Dept., Rasmuson Library, UAF

Eskimo winter houses on Saint Lawrence Island were large elaborate structures based on houses used by Siberian Eskimos, to whom the Saint Lawrence people were closely related. The houses would often have a tent or other wall inside with insulation such as dried grass between the two, creating a snug interior that was capable of being heated with seal oil lamps. The meat drying on the rack above the door was probably walrus. Courtesy of the Call Collection, Alaska and Polar Regions Dept., Rasmuson Library, UAF

Totem poles towered over Fort Wrangell in this 1887 photograph. The term totem pole has been applied to many of the large carvings, such as house posts, mortuary poles, memorial poles, and potlatch poles of the northern Northwest Coast peoples. The large freestanding poles are probably relatively recent, dating only from the late 1700s. The symbols are generally heraldic, belonging to a particular family or group, and are very stylized, rather than being representational. The buildings show many traditional features such as posts and beams, vertical siding, and plank roofs. Courtesy of the W. H. Partridge Collection, Alaska Historical Library

The Chief Ka-ann totem pole stood in Ketchikan in 1905. Courtesy of the Historical Photograph Collection, Alaska and Polar Regions Dept., Rasmuson Library, UAF

In spite of variations, however, all these matrilineal societies were built up around basic units, the lineages, which were unilateral groups each having a nucleus of men related maternally. They were composed, for example, of a group of brothers and maternal cousins, their sisters' sons, and the sons of the sisters of the second generation. This social unit was usually politically independent, claiming fishing stations, hunting areas and berrying grounds. It had its own houses and chiefs, and operated socially as well as ceremonially as an independent unit. It also had its own crests and innumerable ceremonial prerogatives as well.

The Tlingits, Haidas, and Tsimshians also divided individuals into various classes, such as chiefs, nobles, commoners, and slaves. Actually, however, there was a good deal of flexibility and mobility between the various levels.

Warfare was well established and aimed at displacing or even exterminating another lineage, or family, in order to acquire its material possessions as well as lands. Religious beliefs also played an important part in everyday life. Certain fundamental principles combined to give the Indians' religion its distinctive cast. These were a lack of systemized beliefs on creation, cosmology, and deities; a vague belief in a remote, disinterested Supreme Being or Beings; a belief in the immortality of certain economically important species of animals; together with ritual practices designed to insure the return of these creatures; and belief in the possibility of lifelong assistance by a personal guardian spirit.

All three groups had a rich oral literature of myths and legends. Each lineage or extended family claimed some myth or mythical episode, and incorporated it into the official family tradition explaining the origin of the kin group.

The shaman, or medicineman, played an important part in community life, curing or causing illness, and the shamanistic regalia and gear varied greatly from group to group. All groups developed highly complex art forms. The famous carved "totem poles" are perhaps the best example. Actually, the term is a misnomer, because they are comparable to crests. There were several varieties of totems with differing functions. The heir of a deceased chief usually erected a memorial pole as a part of the process of assuming the title, duties, and prerogatives of his predecessor, and mortuary poles were erected alongside the grave of the deceased chief. House portal poles were built onto the fronts of houses, each rising high above, with a large opening which formed the doorway near the base.

In short, over long periods of time the Northwest Coast Indians developed complex cultures made possible by an abundance of food.

The Athapascans

The Athapascans inhabited the great expanse of Arctic and Sub-Arctic lands stretching across the northern edge of the American continent. In contrast to the Northwest Coast with its rich natural resources, the land of the Athapascan is as difficult and demanding to man as any in the world. Greatly varied in topography, the region forced the Indians to search for the scant resources on which to survive.

The Northern Athapascans inhabited the drainage of the Yukon River just short of where it empties into the Bering Sea, and also those parts of northern Canada drained by the MacKenzie River. Mountainous, and with much of its area covered by northern coniferous forests, the region varies greatly in its topography, and its climate is characterized by long, cold winters and short, hot summers.

The Northern Athapascan groups all speak languages belonging to the Athapascan branch of the Na-Dene speech family, the most widespread linguistic phylum in North America. It includes the whole Athapascan family, divided into three subgroups—the Northern, Pacific, and Apachean Athapascans.

Archeological evidence suggests that the ancestors of the Athapascans had crossed the Bering Sea Land Bridge into Alaska approximately ten thousand years ago, at the end of the last great glacial period. In time these people moved east and south through the Yukon Territory and into interior British Columbia as far down as the present state of Washington. As the Athapascans moved, they were greatly influenced by the cultures of the people they encountered. In time, this culture change resulted in three distinctly different types.

Unlike the coastal Indians, the Athapascans had no tribal organizations and possessed only a limited tribal consciousness. Anthropologists, therefore, have described Northern Athapascan culture as continuous and carried on by a series of interlocking groups whose lifestyles differed only in detail from that of their neighbors.

This shows the Chief Johnson pole in Ketchikan. Courtesy of the Woods Collection, Alaska and Polar Regions Dept., Rasmuson Library, UAF

Some Chilkat dancers at a potlatch in Angoon pose about 1902. Potlatchs were ceremonial occasions given by some prominent person and his group to mark some significant event such as a marriage, a birth, or the assumption of a title, among others. They involved the host group giving gifts to the guests and were marked by speeches, dances, and performances, as well as feasting. Groups would come long distances to attend. Courtesy of the Soboleff Collection, Alaska Historical Library

This photo is titled: "After the dance of welcome to the Sitkas." It was taken in 1900, possibly at Klukwan. This crowd scene is interesting because it is an informal photo from a time when most pictures were posed. The many carved canoes, the mixture of ceremonial clothes and western suits and hats, the American flags and the painted standards, and the conversing women all convey the excitement of the occasion. From the Pinneo Album, Alaska and Polar Regions Dept., Rasmuson Library, UAF

Sitka dancers pose at a Klukwan potlatch in the early 1900s. Courtesy of the Historical Photograph Collection, Alaska and Polar Regions Dept., Rasmuson Library, UAF

Athapascan chiefs of the Indian villages in interior Alaska gathered in Fairbanks in 1915 to discuss the problems of their people with James Wickersham, Alaska's delegate to Congress. At the meeting they affirmed their desire to continue to use the country as they had traditionally. From left to right, they were: bottom row, Chief Alexander of Tolovana, Chief Thomas of Nenana, Chief Evan of Koschakat, and Chief Alexander William of Tanana; top row, Chief William of Tanana, Paul Williams of Tanana, and Chief Charlie of Minto.

For this picture the chiefs posed in their best garments, "chiefs' jackets" of moosehide decorated with beadwork and beaver fur. Note the dentalium and bead decorations at their necks and supporting the knife sheaths in which their curved-handled knives were carried. Courtesy of the Bunnell Collection, Alaska and Polar Regions Dept., Rasmuson Library, UAF

CHIEF WILLIAM OF TANANA   PAUL WILLIAMS, TANANA.   CHIEF CHARLIE OF MINTU.
CHIEF ALEXANDER OF TOLOVANA.   CHIEF THOMAS OF NENANA.   CHIEF EVAN OF KOSCHAKAT.   CHIEF ALEXANDER WILLIAM OF TANANA.

Chief Mitlakatle and his wife, of Basket Bay, pose at Angoon. He wears a Chilkat blanket woven of mountain goat wool and cedar bark, and a carved and painted hat with basketry rings. He is holding a carved Raven rattle. Courtesy of the Soboleff Collection, Alaska Historical Library

Athapascans made their living by hunting and gathering. Some groups depended largely on the caribou, a migratory animal abundant at certain times of the year. Athapascans drove the animals between two long, converging rows of wooden sticks which led to large enclosures of branches where the caribou were caught in snares or could easily be killed by the hunters with bows and arrows. At times caribou were also driven into lakes or rivers, and there lanced or stabbed from canoes. The larger moose were tracked down and shot or caught in deadfall traps. Other game animals, such as bears, wolverines, and smaller fur-bearing animals, were also caught in traps, shot with bows and arrows, or captured in rawhide nets. Snares were used for small game animals.

Depending on the locality, the Athapascans fished for salmon with dip nets, gill nets, and basket-shaped traps; and they also caught other fish, such as trout, whitefish, pike and other species, by spearing them from canoes. Fish were also hooked. In addition, they gathered bird eggs, hunted a variety of birds, and also gathered the berries and roots which supplemented their diet. In times of game scarcity, starvation was common.

In aboriginal times, the men hunted on foot in the winter since dogs were not yet used for pulling sleds or toboggans. Snowshoes, therefore, were important and the Northern Athapascans made two types, one for hunting and walking over fresh snow, and the second for walking over a previously broken trail.

The Tanaina Indians in the Cook Inlet-Susitna River basin area were the only Athapascans to live on the coast, and the hunting of sea mammals, therefore, occupied a good portion of their time. Much of the technology for coping with coastal life these Indians readily adapted from the neighboring Eskimos.

The dwellings of the aboriginal Northern Athapascans reflected their mobility— they were among the simplest found in North America. Structures reflected the climatic conditions at various times of the year, as well as the subsistence activities characteristic of the season. Basically, there were two types of houses; the semipermanent and the temporary. In the former category belonged the circular winter house made of a frame of long, curved poles. The lower ends were stuck in the snow while the upper ends did not meet, leaving a smoke hole. The framework was reinforced by two horizontal poles, and the whole was covered with sewn moose skins or caribou hides. Summer houses were often rectangular in shape and also constructed with a series of poles driven into the ground to make inside and outside walls, while the strips of spruce or birch bark were laid between the walls. And although the dwellings differed widely, they all used wood, a readily available material.

Most aboriginal Athapascans spent at least a part of the year in small groups. If food supplies were sufficient, small groups might combine into bands, rarely more than one hundred individuals. Because of their mobility, the material culture of these people was simple and portable, consisting mostly of food-getting equipment.

Formal leadership was minimal, and usually advisory. Adult males often reached decisions together, although at times leaders emerged who attained prestige and influence through demonstrating superior abilities, such as hunting skills. The Northern Athapascans also knew both offensive and defensive warfare. They used a variety of weapons, including knives, spears, and bows and arrows, and in places a specialized adze. War leaders usually were aggressive men of exceptional physical strength. Leadership in both peace and war, however, rarely was hereditary, and once a leader lost his special abilities he also ceased to exert any particular influence.

The nuclear family constituted the basic unit of social organization, consisting of a man, his wife (or wives), and their natural or adopted children. Furthermore, throughout much of the Athapascan area, extended kinship was characterized by the matrilineal sib (blood kinship) organization. These sibs acknowledged a bond of common descent on the maternal side, and were tied together in a network of reciprocal obligations. Members usually had to find mates outside their own sibs. The number of sibs varied among different groups, but there were usually three.

The potlatch, a ceremony in honor of the dead, played an important part in the social organization of many Athapascans. At the potlatch there was much feasting and merry-making, climaxed by a distribution of gifts. This helped in assuaging grief, but also served as a means of gaining prestige.

As with their social institutions, anthropologists have had difficulties reconstructing the religious belief system of the Northern Athapascans. It is clear that the supernatural world was vague and poorly defined. They lived in a world of many

spirits influencing every aspect of their lives. The only religious practitioners were the shamans, individuals with the greatest amount of personal power. The shaman, usually a man, used magico-religious practices to influence and control the spirit world, prevent and cure disease and bring good as well as bad luck.

The Athapascans' belief in reincarnation in animal form blurred the distinction between animals and humans, and there existed a reciprocal relationship between men and the animals on which they were dependent for a living. The spirits of the animals used for food had to be placated in order for men to continue to hunt these

"Old Mary" of Orca was a basket maker. Tlingit spruce root baskets were finely woven with elaborate stylized patterns. They were made in various shapes and sizes to fit household needs. Long after many other crafts were given up, basket making continued, as there was always a market for the beautiful and useful objects. From the Wheatley Album, courtesy of the Anchorage Historical and Fine Arts Museum

This shows a bear trap of the Athapascans. The bear was lured into the log enclosure, where he tripped the mechanism that dropped the heavy log cover. The cover killed or imprisoned him. The Indians were dependent on fur and game animals for subsistence and later for trade. They devised a variety of traps and snares, which, with their knowledge of the country and animal habits, made it possible to use whatever was available in their territory. Courtesy of the U.S. Forest Service Collection, Alaska Historical Library

The people of Fort Yukon pose, probably in the early 1900s. The group is all in western clothing, except the older man in the right front who wears a shirt of small skins that resembles the old traditional garments. Courtesy of the Historical Photograph Collection, Alaska and Polar Regions Dept., Rasmuson Library, UAF

"Nakeeta's camp on the Matanuska, 1906" (as this photo was labeled) was probably a temporary hunting camp. The picture shows a semipermanent shelter, as well as a canvas wall tent equipped with a stove. There are moose antlers on the left, probably from the previous year's hunt. On the right is a large (but light) sled which could be used to move the family, its goods, and the meat supply to their winter home. From the Wheatley Album, courtesy of the Anchorage Historical and Fine Arts Museum

"Old Silas" was an Athapascan whose portrait was made by A. J. Johnson, a photographer in Fairbanks in the early 1900s. Courtesy of the Alaska Historical Library

An Athapascan man constructs a birchbark canoe. The birch tree provided many of the needs of the interior people. Containers of various kinds and canoes were handsome products. This view of the canoe shows the careful light framing and the neat binding of the bark to the frame with split spruce root. The canoes were extremely light and could be portaged easily. Courtesy of the Richards Collection, Alaska and Polar Regions Dept., Rasmuson Library, UAF

An Athapascan Indian woman scrapes moose hide. After the hide was carefully cleaned it was often smoked to preserve it and help make it supple. The complex process produced material for clothing, containers, dog harnesses, and other uses. The village at Circle City was near a trading post established by Leroy N. "Jack" McQuesten in 1887. Photo by Paul J. Sincic

creatures. Religious individualism was another characteristic of their belief system. Survival depended on individual fitness, and in religion this meant that much emphasis was placed on individual rather than community rites.

Their mythology was quite complex and provided answers for most questions concerning the origins of the world and man. Since European contact, however, most of the old beliefs and practices of aboriginal Athapascan life have been abandoned or have changed greatly.

The Aleuts

Thousands of years ago an Eskimoid people, the ancestors of the Aleuts, settled on the island chain eventually named for them. And like other Native groups, the Aleuts adapted themselves well to life in the marine environment of the islands. They developed a rich culture and secured a good livelihood from the sea. But they were also the first people to be colonized by the Russians, in the 1740s, and within a short time their aboriginal culture had nearly disappeared. Early eighteenth century explorers left only scattered reports of Aleut life. In 1778, the famous British navigator Captain James Cook visited the Aleutian Islands and recorded his impressions. Carl Heinrich Merck, a German physician, visited Alaska in 1790 and 1791 and wrote about his ethnographic observations. It was Ioann Veniaminov, an Orthodox missionary who spent ten years on Unalaska Island (from 1825 through 1834), who made the only thorough and systematic ethnographic study of Aleut culture before it deteriorated.

Estimates of the aboriginal Aleut population vary between fifteen to thirty thousand, the latter figure seemingly very high. But since no exact figures exist, the estimates cannot be refuted. In any event, major diseases such as tuberculosis, measles, pneumonia, and smallpox, to mention but a few, drastically reduced the population after contact. Margaret Lantis, an American anthropologist, has concluded that at least 80 percent of the Aleut population was lost within the first two generations of contact with the Russians.

Much remains to be learned about Aleut social structure, although early observers left fairly good acounts of Aleut life. According to these accounts, the islanders lived in many small settlements, then, as now, mostly situated on the northern side of the islands facing the Bering Sea. This was because of the more abundant fish life, the availability of driftwood, and the occasional whales cast upon the beach. The typical Aleut house, containing several related nuclear families, was spacious and built underground. In addition to their permanent settlements, the Aleuts occupied temporary dwellings for seasonal occupations.

A typical household consisted of a man and his wife (or wives) and his older married sons and their families. Sometimes it also might house a younger brother and his family. The young sons of the household's head were raised by their mother's older brother in her village. A head of a household also might have a nephew working for him who might marry one of his daughters. And although anthropologists so far have been unable to determine the Aleut role of descent, many assume that matrilineal descent existed. Aleuts were permissive in sexual matters, and both polygyny and polyandry were permitted. Transvestism was accepted openly, but, as among other peoples, incest was clearly defined and prohibited.

The Aleuts mummified the bodies of highly honored individuals, included many grave goods, and on occasion killed slaves to accompany the master or also to show the grief of the principal survivor.

Chieftainship was sometimes inherited, although the leader for a group of villages or a larger island was chosen from among the lesser leaders.

Wealth was important, both in the form of dentalium shells and amber, and it was also exhibited through acts of generosity, such as the freeing of slaves. But there is no evidence that the Aleuts had anything like a potlatch.

In short, much needs to be learned about Aleut culture. It is clear, however, that the Aleuts, like other Native groups, developed highly functional societies which enabled them to live well in their environment. It is also clear that much of the aboriginal Aleut culture disappeared quickly after initial contact with the Russians.

It is difficult, therefore, to make any general statements. Many experts today agree, however, that the Arctic-Mongoloid peoples first arrived in the Bering Sea area from ten to fifteen thousand years ago. These arrivals were the progenitors of the Eskimos and Aleuts, as well as various paleo-Siberian groups.

The Eskimos

An immense amount has been written about the Eskimos, probably more than about any other Native people. This is particularly true of the Greenlandic and Canadian Eskimos because of their adaptations to an environment where it is nearly always cold. Most of Alaska's Eskimos, however, did not face such rigors because they inhabited a great diversity of environments. These ranged from barren, ice-bound coasts to the edges of great coastal forests, while some lived so far inland that they never saw the sea. For some, fish constituted the bulk of their diet, while others depended on caribou, or still others hunted great whales from skin-covered boats and hunted seals at their breathing holes.

It may be said that Eskimo culture developed first in western Alaska. Linguistic evidence indicates that in Alaska the Eskimos flourished. It was also here that the division into the Eskimo and Aleut stocks occurred. And while the Aleut stock remained limited to Alaska, the Eskimo stock became more diversified in western Alaska than in any other region they occupied. In time, the Eskimos developed an economy adapted to the exploitation of the arctic seas. The Arctic Small Tool Tradition, dating to 3000 B.C., represents the technological base for Eskimo culture, reaching back to Siberia. It eventually spread across the Arctic from Alaska to Greenland. It did not penetrate the Pacific drainage, and had been drastically modified by the time it reached Bristol Bay. By that time, Eskimo hunting devices had become so flexible that they allowed members of the culture to utilize both sea and land resources. In time, various subcultural forms of the Arctic Small Tool Tradition developed in the coastal zone, ranging from whale hunting in the north, salmon fishing along the river systems, and caribou hunting inland.

Eskimo social life centered around the nuclear family as the primary unit. In order to survive economically, Eskimo culture placed an overwhelming emphasis on subsistence activities on the part of the men. So individuals had obligations not only to their own households and immediate family members, but also to various voluntary associations, such as the whale hunting crews. Yuit nuclear families apparently possessed less cohesion than Inuit families. Perhaps the primary difference in their living patterns

was the importance of the men's or ceremonial house among all Yuit except the Chugach. The men's house, or kashgee, was within a community, and Yuit husbands resided in the kashgee and were visitors in their wives' households. Most Yuit boys started to live in the kashgee while still quite young. Closely-knit nuclear family ties did not develop where fathers and sons lived in the kashgee, separated from mothers, daughters and young children.

Since game animals played such a large role in survival, it is not surprising that they also occupied an important place in tribal religions. The Bladder Feast, for example, focused on the seals. The whale played an important role amongst the whaling people. Eskimo supernaturalism was based, to a great extent, on charms which aided individuals. There were also many taboos, such as combining land and sea products.

In short, Eskimos shared many traits found among other peoples. The term "Eskimo," in fact, stands for much subcultural diversity. ■

The Ahtena Indians along the Copper River used the fish wheel to catch the abundant salmon that ran upstream each year. Prospectors and traders introduced the fish wheel. It had been used earlier in the Pacific Northwest. To harvest the salmon runs the Indians of the interior have used it effectively in many variations and built of many materials. It is still commonly seen on Alaskan rivers. Courtesy of the Ives Collection, Alaska and Polar Regions Dept., Rasmuson Library, UAF

An Ahtena Indian girl fishes in the Copper River with a traditional dip net. She stands on a small platform built out into the river where the migrating salmon can be most easily reached. The salmon runs in the Copper River still attract fishermen from other parts of Alaska as well as the local people. Courtesy of the Anchorage Historical and Fine Arts Museum

This fish wheel in the Yukon at Eagle Village in 1958 shows a modern variation of the device. The baskets use wire mesh rather than wood strips and it is probably nailed and bolted together. Courtesy of the U.S. Forest Service Collection, Alaska Historical Library

An Ahtena Indian poses with his two children. Courtesy of the Anchorage Historical and Fine Arts Museum

An Ahtena family is shown in this photograph, taken about 1930. The man carries his gun over his shoulder in a moose hide or canvas scabbard. Two of the dogs are carrying packs. Courtesy of the Norma Hoyt Collection

Doc. Billum Of Copper River

"Doc Billum of Copper River," a proud Native man, poses with his flag and top hat. Courtesy of the Norma Hoyt Collection

Meat is hung to dry on this improvised rack in the Copper River area. The sun and wind will dry the meat so it will keep over an extended time. Courtesy of the Norma Hoyt Collection

This 1866 photograph shows the people of an Auk village that was close to the new mining town of Juneau where gold was discovered in 1880. Courtesy of the Alaska Historical Library

William Duncan came to Fort Simpson in Canada as a missionary to the Tsimshian Indians. With his converts he left Fort Simpson in 1857 to set up a new community, Metlakatla, where, under his guidance, the people set up a model community which prospered for many years. Finally, because of conflict with his mission superiors, he moved many of his followers to Annette Island in southeastern Alaska where they established New Metlakatla. In 1891 Congress established the 86,000-acre Annette Island Reservation. William Duncan lived until 1918. His house still stands as he left it. Courtesy of the Anchorage Historical and Fine Arts Museum

New Metlakatla soon became just Metlakatla. The church that Duncan built (shown in 1938) is an imposing structure. There is little of the Tsimshian culture in the town. Photo by Ray B. Dame, courtesy of the Anchorage Historical and Fine Arts Museum

The Alaska Native Brotherhood gathered to pose in front of the new hall in Sitka in 1914. The organization was a strong voice in defining and defending the rights of Native people. Seated, from left to right are: unknown, Frank Mercer, unknown, Chester Worthington of Wrangell, Peter Simpson, Paul Liberty, Edward Marsden, Haines DeWitt of Juneau, Mark Jacobs, Sr., unknown. Standing, in the middle row are: John Willard, unknown, William Kootz, Steven Nicholis, Harold Bailry, Ralph Wanna-maker, Charlie Daniels, unknown, Ralph Young, unknown, Rudolph Walton, William Jackson, and Frank Price. In the top row are: unknown, Andrew Hope, un-known, Thomas Williams, un-

known, and Sergus Williams. Courtesy of the Merrill Photo Collection, Sheldon Jackson College

For many years the people of the interior used a trading site at the confluence of the Tanana and Yukon rivers. Later, a trading post, mission, and army fort were established in the area. Today an annual celebration is held to commemorate the old days when the peoples of the rivers would gather here. Called "Nuchala-woyya," or "between the rivers," the informal celebration lasts for several days. Young celebrants raise flags of greeting on the riverbank to greet arriving guests. Courtesy of the *Fairbanks Daily News-Miner*

Chapter 3

This illustration, entitled "Sea Horses," shows crews of the ships of the Cook expedition hunting in the pack ice. The *Resolution* and the *Discovery* are in the background. Whalers later turned to the walrus to fill their holds when whales became scarce in the north Pacific. They depleted the animals so badly that the Eskimos who depended on them for food became desperate. From plates to *Cook's Voyages,* 1784, Alaska and Polar Regions Dept., Rasmuson Library, UAF

The Russians in Northern North America and Voyages of Discovery

The Russians and Northern North America

Within the space of a man's lifetime the Russians swept eastward from the Ural Mountains to the Pacific. This feat of land occupation was as remarkable as that accomplished by Spain in America. It was the river pirate Ermak and his cut-throat Cossack companions who initiated the push. After Ermak had been driven from the lower Volga River by the soldiers of Tsar Ivan the Terrible, he led a horde of Cossacks north along the western slope of the Urals to salt mines being operated by the remarkable frontier merchant family, the Stroganovs. Perhaps uneasy in the company of such uninvited guests, Grigorii Stroganov rid himself of these intruders by telling them of vast and rich fur grounds beyond the mountains.

Ermak and his Cossacks crossed the Urals in 1581, the year after Francis Drake brought his treasure-laden *Golden Hind* back to England. Ermak and his companions attacked the Tartars of the "godless sultan Kuchum" and utterly overwhelmed him. Kuchum abandoned his capital, the city of Isker or Sibir. Within fifty years the city of Sibir had given its name to the vast region. In the van of this invasion went the promyshlenniki, the wild and reckless counterpart of the American mountain men.

Close behind them came the fur merchants, accompanied by the collectors of Yasak (the annual tribute in furs to the tsars). All three mercilessly oppressed the natives they encountered. If a tribe did not meet its quota of furs, hostages were tortured and killed, and villages destroyed. In fear, therefore, the Natives delivered the sable, ermine, and marten furs to their oppressors. And as fast as the animals were exploited in one area, the promyshlenniki hurried on to the next.

In the meantime, the eastern wilderness of Siberia, including the gigantic Kamchatka peninsula, remained an unknown land. The Chukchi of the northeast Asian coast did not know, nor care, that a continent ended in their territory. And as long as the promyshlenniki found a profitable fur supply, they did not care where they were.

Toward the close of the seventeenth century, however, the Russian throne had passed into the hands of a man who

Gregori Shelikhov was a leading Siberian fur merchant who did a great deal to organize the Alaskan fur trade and make it profitable. He was unsuccessful in getting a trade monopoly from the Russian Government but he was responsible for sending Aleksandr Baranov to manage his enterprises in Russian-America. Courtesy of the Historical Photograph Collection, Alaska and Polar Regions Dept., Rasmuson Library, UAF

Before his death in 1725 Tsar Peter the Great instructed Vitus Bering, a Dane serving in the Russian Imperial Navy, to undertake an expedition to determine whether Asia and America were connected. Bering went on two expeditions, the first to determine whether Asia and North America were connected, the second to explore the American coast. Both expeditions were ill equipped and encoun-

did. He was Peter the Great, the energetic westernizer of his nation, and almost the first Russian to have any interest in creating a navy and providing an attractive environment for men of science.

Peter the Great and Vitus Bering

Peter's importance for northern North America lies in the fact that in 1723 he began importing European scholars for the purpose of starting an Imperial Academy of Sciences. On his visit to Europe, Peter had greatly enjoyed his contacts with European men of science. At that time, the geography of the North Pacific was a field for heady speculation, and map makers projected lands that did not exist. They also debated whether or not America and Asia were joined. Peter became interested in this question himself, and in 1719 he sent two men to Kamchatka to settle the dispute. Nothing was learned from that expedition, but apparently Peter's curiosity had been awakened to find out more about the mysteries of that distant part of the world.

One of the last acts of Peter, as he lay dying from the effects of his enormous debaucheries, was to bring a forty-four-year-old Dane named Vitus Bering out of self-imposed retirement late in 1724. Bering, one of Peter's numerous foreign naval officers, was a heavy-set, methodical man. Peter ordered Bering to travel across the continent to Kamchatka, build a vessel where neither shipways nor supplies existed, and discover whether a land bridge connected Asia to America. He then was to explore the coast of the neighboring continent. If Bering found the Northwest Passage, that would be even better.

Bering spent nearly three and a half years of backbreaking labor and suffered dreadful privations before he at last launched his sixty-foot vessel, the *Sviatoi Gavriil,* from the eastern coast of Kamchatka and sailed northward close to the shoreline. After a month of sailing, the hitherto north-trending coast turned sharply westward. Bering guessed that he had passed the farthest reach in Siberia, but it was a guess only, and in order to quiet his scientific conscience he sailed northward until he reached 67°18′ north. He saw no land, and afraid that unfavorable winds might detain him he turned back, convinced that America and Asia were not joined. Staying well out to sea on his return journey, Bering failed to sight the new continent he was supposed to examine because of the prevailing dense mists.

On March 1, 1730, five years after his departure from the capital city, Bering returned to Saint Petersburg. There the academicians, from the comfort of their studies, pointed out how inconclusive his findings were. Bering, intensely annoyed, thereupon proposed another expedition be dispatched to check his findings.

Considering his previous failure, it is surprising that Bering was given command of not only this new expedition but of three more interlocking ones as well. With his lieutenant, Alexei Chirikov, he now was supposed to study the natural resources of Siberia, chart the entire Arctic Coast, and explore Kamchatka southward toward Japan and eastward toward the mythical continent of Gamaland. Finally, he was to determine once and for all whether or not Asia and America were connected.

Some 580 men, including laborers, mechanics, soldiers, and scientists, among others, were assigned to assist Bering in his task. Many, including Bering, took along their wives and children. As the caravan moved across the continent, hundreds of reluctant natives were recruited for transporting the mountain of supplies, including food, clothing, books, instruments, and building materials. Barges had to be built at each river, and thousands of pack horses readied at the portages. Local officials, whose help was needed, had to be flattered to lend support or forced to help when all else failed. Bering's men fought with each other, oppressed the natives, sought his ear, and complained bitterly about one another, and intrigued behind his back.

Finally, eight years after leaving Saint Petersburg, Bering crossed the Sea of Okhotsk to the new port of Petropavlovsk on the eastern coast of the Kamchatka Peninsula from whence he hoped to sail for America. Along the way Bering lost one of his supply barges. As a result, his ship, the *Sviatoi Petr,* and Chirikov's ship, the *Sviatoi Pavel,* left Avatcha Bay in 1741 with only five months' supply of food instead of the two years' quantity on which the explorers had counted.

On Bering's ship was the German scientist, Georg Wilhelm Steller, while Louis Delisle de la Croyere, one of two map-making brothers in the Imperial Academy of Sciences, accompanied Chirikov on the *Sviatoi Pavel.* Croyere's map, as well as others of the period,

tered severe weather and difficult conditions. Bering died during the second expedition. Survivors of the expeditions brought back furs, including the sea otter pelts which prompted the development of the fur trade. An oil painting by Ted Lambert, an Alaskan artist, depicts one of Bering's ships in the rough waters of the North Pacific. Courtesy of the University of Alaska Museum

showed a continent known as Gamaland, and it was one of Bering's assignments to find out whether or not this continent existed.

The two vessels sailed southeast to latitude 47°, approximately even with the mouth of the Columbia. At that point Croyere had to admit that Gamaland did not exist. Finally, a storm separated the *Sviatoi Petr* and the *Sviatoi Pavel.* For a few days the two captains looked for each other. Then Chirikov sailed northeast.

On July 15, near the present Sitka, Chirikov sighted land. Two days later he sent a watering party ashore, but the men did not return. Another party was sent after them, and when it likewise disappeared, Chirikov sailed on. The fate of these men has intrigued historians. It is probable that they were killed by the Natives.

The weather turned bad, with storms and fog enmeshing the *Sviatoi Pavel.* At last, however, Chirikov returned to Kamchatka but had to summon rescuers to get into the harbor. Not enough able-bodied men were left on his ship, and among those who had died was Croyere.

In the meantime, Bering had his difficulties as well. After the separation he also had sailed northeast. On July 16, 1741, a crewmember sighted a towering, snowy peak rising above islands, inlets, and glaciers. Bering named the mountain Saint Elias, the name it still bears. But rather than feeling elated like the scientists on board, Bering merely felt weary. He was sixty years old and nearly worn out. He also suffered from the initial stages of scurvy which induce a general lassitude and sense of depression.

However, George Wilhelm Steller, the scientist on board the *Sviatoi Petr,* felt overjoyed. Seldom in history had a scientist been presented with the opportunities given to the young Bavarian whom Russian officials had appointed to the second Kamchatka expedition. He was the first trained individual to view a vast region hitherto unknown, the first scientist to describe the rich and varied mammal life of the Bering Sea, and the first to observe the customs of the aboriginal peoples of the Aleutian Islands. He was also the first to examine the flora and fauna of Saint Elias Island, today's Kayak Island. He classified scores of unknown plants, and gave posterity the only full description of the now extinct giant manatee, or sea cow. He made careful notes on northern seals, sea otters, various birds, foxes, and other animals. Most of this he accom-

Captain James Cook's famous voyages brought him to the Northwest Coast and Alaska in 1778. He mapped much of the unknown coast and named many familiar geographical features. Cook Inlet commemorates his explorations. From plates from *Cook's Voyages,* 1784, Alaska and Polar Regions Dept., Rasmuson Library, UAF

Aleksandr Baranov first came to Russian America in 1790 as manager for Shelikhov's enterprises. He later became chief manager for the Russian-American Company, which combined the efforts of the various Russian trading companies under a charter granted by Tsar Paul I in 1799 which gave the company almost complete control over Russian America. He was relieved of his duties in 1817 and died on his way back to Russia. Courtesy of the Historical Photograph Collection, Alaska and Polar Regions Dept., Rasmuson Library, UAF

Nikolai Rezanov, well-connected at the Imperial Court, helped in the formation of the Russian-American Company and its charter for the fur trade monopoly in Alaska. In 1805 he joined Baranov in Sitka, where they often disagreed on policies and procedures. He died while on his return to Saint Petersburg. Courtesy of the Historical Photograph Collection, Alaska and Polar Regions Dept., Rasmuson Library, UAF

This illustration of Russian America from about 1828 shows an early view of Novo-Arkhangelsk (New Archangel), which later became Sitka. Baranov established it as his headquarters in 1804. The fortified "castle" on the hill commanded the harbor and the area in which the town developed. From an atlas: *Voyage Autour du Monde...*, *1836*, by Frederic Lutke, with drawings by Alexandre Postels, Alaska and Polar Regions Dept., Rasmuson Library, UAF

This view of New Archangel's harbor from Castle Hill shows a large warehouse in the foreground. Courtesy of the Historical Photograph Collection, Alaska and Polar Regions Dept., Rasmuson Library, UAF

This view near New Archangel (Sitka) shows the area outside the stockade with Tlingit houses and the stumps of the clearing. The woman at the left is dressed in a French peasant costume of the period. (Native people in illustrations often resembled the people with whom the artist was most familiar.) From an atlas: *Voyage Autour du Monde...,* *1836,* by Frederic Lutke, with drawings by Alexandre Postels, Alaska and Polar Regions Dept., Rasmuson Library, UAF

plished in the incredible short period of ten hours, the time Bering allowed him to spend on Saint Elias Island. He did have months, however, to investigate Bering Island, where he and his shipmates were wrecked. Steller used his opportunities exceedingly well.

He was born on March 19, 1709 in the free imperial city of Windsheim in Germany. In 1729 he enrolled at the University of Wittenberg as a student of theology, but switched to natural sciences. After moving from university to university, he finally settled at the University of Halle in 1731. Examined in Berlin, Steller was found proficient to fill a professional chair in botany.

In 1734 Steller offered his services to the Russians, who engaged him as a physician caring for their wounded soldiers. At the end of 1734 he arrived in Saint Petersburg, poor perhaps, but healthy, with a splendid education and a full supply of hope and energy.

In 1737 Steller was appointed as an adjunct in natural history to the second Kamchatka (or Great Northern) Expedition, at a salary of 660 rubles a year. Assigned to Vitus Bering's ship, the *Sviatoi Petr,* where he acted as ship physician as well as expedition scientist, he was short-tempered and arrogant, and soon was at odds with the ship's officers, which hindered the endeavors of the expedition.

It was Steller who first sighted land on July 16, 1741. The highest peak, part of the coastal range which loomed up out of the sea, was christened Mount Saint Elias. Steller landed on Saint Elias Island, which lies a few miles off the mainland, midway along the great arc of the Gulf of Alaska. On this island Steller accomplished an incredible amount of work. A Cossack hunter assigned to him brought the naturalist a colorful bird which he recognized as an American species of blue jay, later to be called Steller's Jay. The bird proved to Steller that they were really in America.

The *Sviatoi Petr* left Saint Elias Island on July 27, 1741. On August 30 Steller and others landed on Nagai Island, one of the Shumagin Islands southeast of the tip of the Alaska Peninsula. Steller gathered a number of antiscorbutic herbs with which he hoped to cure Bering's scurvy, and observed clouds of birds, including swans, pelicans, auks, ducks, snipes, gulls, sandpipers, puffins, and sea parrots. A few days later they landed on another of the Aleutian Islands where they observed their first Native American, whom Steller carefully described.

Then the weather became foggy, and rain turned to sleet. Scurvy spread among the members of the crew, and a dozen men died. Finally, early in November, the weather cleared and the men detected land in the west. During the night, however, conditions worsened again when heavy winds broke the shrouds of the main mast and the scurvy-weakened crew found itself unable to carry out repairs. At the request of the officers, Bering called a meeting, and the group decided to head for the land. At four in the afternoon, the *Sviatoi Petr* anchored in view of a sandy beach in calm water. Soon, however, the wind came up again, snapped the anchor cable and carried the ship onto the reef which the outgoing tide had uncovered. Suddenly, a huge wave lifted the *Sviatoi Petr* over the reef into the quiet channel between it and the beach. There they dropped anchor, and nearly all believed they had arrived back in Kamchatka.

But it was not Kamchatka, all soon realized, and before long waves rolling in before the arctic wind parted the anchor cables and hurled the vessel into a quiet cove. Here the remaining crew made preparations for landing. Steller and Sven Waxell, one of the officers, scouted ahead. They observed blue foxes everywhere, and offshore in the kelp beds Steller discovered huge animals, now extinct, which, like the jay would be named after the scientist—Steller's sea cow, *Rytina steller*. These animals were about twenty-five feet long and weighed up to three tons. There were no trees, so the men dug pits in the sand for primitive shelter. These they lined with driftwood and sailcloth and chinked with mud and fox skins.

Some of the men were so sick that they did not survive the transfer. The foxes were a nuisance, eating the hands and feet of the corpses before they could be buried. Captain-Commander Bering was brought ashore on November 9 and died on December 8, on what was to be named Bering Island.

The survivors of the crew slowly recovered from the scurvy and hunted sea otters, seals, and sea cows for food, and also used a whale which was cast up on the beach. Steller, who had used antiscorbutic plants, did not get sick. He used the months he spent on Bering Island to closely investigate the newly discovered land. He dissected and described the sea cow, which would assure his fame for perpetuity. He also devoted much attention to the bird life, and, among many others, described the large cormorant, unable to fly, which followed the sea cow to extinction. Other birds he was the first to discover were Steller's Eider, the rare Steller's Eagle, and Steller's White Raven. In addition, his botanical work was of equal distinction to his observations of marine life, birds, and land animals.

By the spring of 1742, the crew set about building a smaller ship from the *Sviatoi Petr,* which had been wrecked beyond repair the previous fall. The carpenters had all died, but fortunately Waxell found a Cossack who had once worked in a shipyard. They built their escape vessel, and although it leaked, it held together long enough for them to reach Avatcha Bay in Kamchatka.

Bering's initial estimate of the cost of the expedition had been far too low. Eventually, the human cost was to be very expensive as well, because only a few of those who had been members survived the years of hard labor, privations, and sufferings. Even those few who did return were broken in health and died soon thereafter. Among those who had survived all hardships was Steller. On his way back to Saint Petersburg, however, Steller died in Tyumen on November 12, 1746 after having become infected with a fever. Thus, the promising career of one of the most outstanding naturalist explorers came to an untimely end. Chirikov reached the capital to submit his report, but lived only a short time afterwards. Moreover, death had removed the sovereign under whose orders the expedition had been undertaken. The Empress Elizabeth, while intelligent and devoted to the interests of her land, had come to power by invoking native patriotism, largely against foreigners in government circles. The inevitable reaction against foreigners involved the Academy of Sciences, and for twenty years that institution was inactive. Some of the scientists returned from Siberia and began compiling the results of their research, but no steps were taken to publish them. It was not until two members of the academy published their findings abroad that the Russian government allowed some of the vast collection of material assembled by the expedition to appear in print.

Historian Frank A. Golder in his book *Russian Expansion on the Pacific, 1741-1850,* republished in 1960, summed up the results of Bering's last voyage well. Many points about the geography of the region which had been in doubt had been settled. A northeast passage was found to be impracticable, and Terra de Jeso, Company Land, and Gamaland, as pictured by cartographers of the day, did not exist. The American Coast ran in a northwesterly direction from Cape Blanco. The question of whether or not the two continents were separated or united was not answered to the satisfaction of all; however it was generally believed that they were separated.

The Quest for Furs

The Russian court, as already stated, was indifferent to the results of the expedition. But news of the results of the expedition leaked out unofficially, and in eastern Siberia the knowledge that the survivors of Chirikov's ship had brought back sea otter skins spread rapidly.

The Russians called the animal bobri morski, or sea beaver. The five-foot long animal had a beautiful, dark brown fur with underlying silver which gave it a lustrous sheen. The Chinese merchants highly prized the fur and were willing to pay top prices for it.

Soon the promyshlenniki, freebooters who hunted on their own account, stampeded for Bering Island in craft modeled after the barges used on the rivers. These crude, so-called "woven" boats or "shitika," consisted of flat-bottomed log frames covered with green planks. The whole was held together with raw deerhide thongs, caulked with tallow and moss. The men who sailed these craft could hardly plot a course. Casualties among the promyshlenniki quickly mounted. Yet the promise of easy riches lured these men to continue risking their lives in these unseaworthy vessels.

The results of successful voyages were sometimes spectacular. Emelion Basov, an army sergeant in partnership with an Irkutsk merchant, sailed for the second time to the Aleutians in 1745. He and his crew accumulated 1,600 sea otters, 2,000 fur seals, and as many blue foxes. He returned to Siberia in July of 1746, "showing his countrymen a new road to a vast and rich trade." The value of Basov's cargo amounted to 112,220 rubles, in today's currency perhaps as much as one million dollars.

The Russian contacts with the Natives were disastrous for the latter. The exploiters treated the islanders brutally, and introduced diseases, such as syphilis, tuberculosis, and whooping cough, among others, which soon took their toll.

The promyshlenniki first landed at

The Russians established a stockaded post at Saint Michael, near the mouth of the Yukon River, about 1833. The blockhouse which remained on the site for many years was eventually dismantled and brought to the University of Alaska Museum. Courtesy of the Eva Alvey Richards Collection, Alaka and Polar Regions Dept., Rasmuson Library, UAF

Another Russian redoubt, the stockaded fort at Kolmakof, on the Kuskokwim River, was built in 1832. The location was later used by a mission and an American trader. The blockhouse from this fortification was also dismantled and shipped to the University of Alaska Museum. Courtesy of the Bunnell Collection, Alaska and Polar Regions Dept., Rasmuson Library, UAF

Bering Island where they slaughtered the sea cows and cured the meat for their provisions. So efficient were the Russians that the animals were soon extinct. Next the hunters steered for the Aleutian Islands, stripping each one methodically of its furs, then moving on to the next. As the promyshlenniki moved farther and farther from their base, their ships of necessity grew larger and their piloting improved as well.

At first, the Russians themselves hunted, but soon they had the Aleuts perform the task in their seaworthy little skin bidarkas in return for mere trinkets. When the Aleuts demanded more compensation for their labors, the promyshlenniki used methods of persuasion originally developed among the Siberian natives. They took hostages, mainly young women, and held them as an incentive to production. The Aleut men trapped the foxes with traps supplied by the Russians, and strung nets across tidal channels to catch the sea otters. Another method of bagging otters consisted of a number of bidarkas surrounding an otter and keeping it diving until its oxygen supply ran out and it had to surface. Then the Aleut hunters killed the animal. Still another method was to wait until the frequent violent storms drove the otter herds onto the reefs for shelter. The Aleut hunters followed the animals through the surf and clubbed them from their bidarkas, or disembarked and ran up on the otters undetected and killed them.

Four Phases of Russian Occupation

The Russian occupation of northwestern America proceeded in four distinct phases. The first period was from 1743 to 1799. It was characterized by the long fur-trading voyages undertaken by numerous private companies. The promyshlenniki fully explored and hunted the Commander, Kurile, Aleutian, and Pribilof islands, as well as the coast and islands of the Gulf of Alaska.

By the 1770s, diminishing fur supplies necessitated longer voyages and better ships. Fierce competition reduced the number of companies, while the warlike Tlingits of the Alaskan mainland made life for the Russians much more difficult than had been the case with the more passive Aleuts of the Aleutian Islands. By 1781 there were only seven companies, while

by 1795 that number had been further reduced to three. In 1797 two of these, the Northeastern American Company of Gregori Shelikhov and Ivan Golikov on Kodiak Island, and the Irkutsk Company of Nicholas Mylnikov and his partners on Prince William Sound, amalgamated and formed the United American Company. The latter, in turn, became the nucleus of the Russian-American Company. Granted a charter for twenty years by Tsar Paul I in 1799, it monopolized Russian activity in America.

Permanent Settlements

Between 1743 and 1799, the Russians also established a number of permanent settlements, usually situated atop promontories at the mouths of rivers or at the heads of bays along the insular coasts. These locations reflected the necessities of maritime hunting as well as Native hostilities.

It was the Northeastern American Company, founded in 1781 by Gregori Shelikhov and Ivan Golikov, which established the first permanent settlement at Three Saints Bay on the southwestern coast of Kodiak Island in 1784. During the summer of that year, Shelikhov, with approximately 185 men in three galiots, went to work at the settlement site, and by 1786 there were 113 Russians at Three Saints Bay. Shelikhov also had forts built on neighboring Afognak Island and on Kenai Inlet, later called Cook Inlet.

Three Saints Bay remained the headquarters of the company until 1791 when Alexandr Baranov, the new colonial manager, founded Saint Paul's Harbor and moved the headquarters to the new location in 1792. Built on a steep and rocky beach, the new settlement contained barracks; ships; smithies; houses; an infirmary; a school within a wooden, semicircular stockade; and a church outside the walls.

Other settlements followed, but the Russian population remained small and scattered. In 1788 the Spanish captains Martinez and Lopez de Haro learned at Unalaska that there were between 450 to 500 Russians with twenty ships at seven settlements. The consolidation of companies halved this total by 1799, when there were about 225 Russians in Alaska.

For most of the first phase, the Russians met little foreign competition because rival European fur traders did not appear until the middle 1780s. Without Aleut hunters, and lacking established posts, the competitors had to obtain furs through trade and barter. The Russians, however, keenly felt the disadvantages of being barred from Canton, the best entry port for the lucrative Chinese fur market. Instead, they had to use the inland border town of Kyakhta, as agreed to in the Treaty of Nerchinsk in 1689.

In time, news of Russian expansion across the far North Pacific reached Spain. After the discovery of the largest and most populous Aleutian Islands, Unalaska and Unimak, became known in Saint Petersburg in the early 1760s, the Tsarina Catherine in 1764 ordered an official and secret government expedition sent under the command of P. K. Krenitsyn and M. D. Levashov. The two were to delineate the discoveries more precisely and make subjects of the Aleuts. The Spanish quickly learned of these plans, and, partly to counter this advance, the Spanish king instructed the viceroy of New Spain to extend the garrisons (or presidios) and missions northward. San Diego was founded in 1769, followed by Monterey in 1770, and San Francisco in 1776. In 1768 the Spanish established a naval base at San Blas, and between 1774 and 1792 twelve naval expeditions examined the Northwest Coast of America. Several of these went as far as Unalaska, entered Sitka Sound, sighted Mount Edgecumbe, gazed upon Iliamna Volcano on the far side of Cook Inlet, and saw the massive Mount Saint Elias.

In the meantime, England had also taken part in the explorations of the North Pacific. The British already had searched for new lands in the South Pacific, but the desire to find a northwest passage motivated the undertaking in 1776 spearheaded by the famous navigator, Captain James Cook. In his two sloops *Resolution* and *Discovery*, Cook explored the Northwest Coast between Cape Fairweather and Icy Cape. His crew obtained sea otter pelts from the Indians very cheaply and subsequently sold these for fabulous profits at Canton. This captured the attention of British and American traders, and in 1785 the *Sea Otter*, under the English Captain James Hanna, was the first trading vessel to appear on the Northwest Coast. Soon the Russians complained to their government about the increasingly stiff competition offered by the British and the Yankees.

It was not long before English and Spanish rivalries climaxed in the Nootka Sound Controversy of 1789-90, removing Spain, the weaker nation, from the area. Competition between the British and Yankee traders continued, and by the end of the century the Yankee traders had constructed such a superior trading system between the Northwest Coast and China that they had all but eliminated the British.

Russia's Second Phase

A remarkable individual dominated the second phase, indeed gave his name to it. Alexandr A. Baranov was born in the northwestern Russian town of Kargopol in 1747. The son of a storekeeper, he had run away to Moscow at the age of fifteen and gone to work for a German merchant. After ten years he returned to Kargopol, married, had a daughter, and established a business. But he soon left for Irkutsk in Siberia where he interested investors in establishing a glass-making factory. Bored after a few years, he left the business and went north to the Okhotsk sea in the Anadyr country where he became a fur trader among the Chukchi natives. Within a year misfortune befell Baranov in his new venture, and he decided to accept a previous offer by Shelikhov, to manage his business in Kodiak. Baranov left for America in the summer of 1790 but was shipwrecked at Unalaska where he and the men wintered. Not until the summer of 1791 did Baranov reach Kodiak.

The Baranov phase, from 1799 to roughly 1818, coincides with the first charter of the Russian-American Company, modeled after the East India Company, and empowering the company to monopolize Russian settlement, exploitation, and trade in America. Intended, in part, to curb foreign expansion on the Northwest Coast, many of its shareholders were high government officials, among them the Tsar himself. By 1801 the headquarters of the company had been moved from Irkutsk to Saint Petersburg. With government involvement, the Russian-American Company now acquired more prestige and capital, as well as men. This enabled Governor Baranov (a new title he acquired in 1799 and kept until the end of his tenure in 1818) to expand southward. In 1799 he founded Archangel Saint Michael on Baranov Island in the Alexander Archipelago. Established to offset American and British trade with the warlike Tlingits, the location also had abundant timber and deep water, favoring the construction

КАРТА
Северной части
СЬВЕРНАГО
ТИХАГО ОКЕАНА
Ново-Архангельскъ
1849

From 1845 to 1850, Captain Mikhail Dmitrievich Tebenkov was in Russian America as director and governor. During that time he developed a series of charts of Alaskan waters. They were published as an atlas in 1852, and were more accurate and detailed than those done before. From Tebenkov's *Atlas*, 1852, Alaska and Polar Regions Dept., Rasmuson Library, UAF

of ships. New Archangel, as it came to be called, quickly became the center for the company's operations. In July of 1802, however, the Tlingits destroyed the settlement and killed some of its inhabitants. It was not until 1804 that Baranov, accompanied by two crude new sloops, two schooners and 300 bidarkas, and reinforced by the Russian frigate *Neva*, defeated the Tlingits and rebuilt the settlement on the site originally occupied by the Natives.

In 1808, New Archangel became the colonial capital, and by 1817, it had a population of 190 Russians, 182 Creoles, and 248 Aleuts. Not only did New Archangel become a substantial settlement, but Baranov also reached farther south in 1808 when he dispatched an expedition to make a reconnaissance of California. Led by his assistant, Ivan Kuskov, one of the two ships came to grief near Gray's Harbor, and the survivors did not return to Sitka until 1810. Kuskov in the *Kodiak* reached Bodega Bay in California. There he successfully hunted sea otter, and returned to New Archangel in the late fall of 1809. Kuskov told Baranov about the riches and opportunities of that land, its suitability for cultivation and the breeding of cattle. Baranov thereupon proposed to the company main office that a settlement be established in California for the production of food.

By 1812 the company had built Fort Ross, some miles north of San Francisco Bay. The Russians used their new settlement for growing foodstuffs and as a hunting base. The Russian holdings in California eventually included Port Rumyantsev on Bodega Bay, several farms, and a hunting camp on the Farallon Islands off the Golden Gate.

Seemingly not satisfied with this extension, the Russian-American Company, between 1815 and 1817, pushed as far south as the Hawaiian Islands and established several enterprises with half-hearted company support. The first Russian visit to the islands occurred in June of 1804. The sloops *Nadezhda* and *Neva*, under the command of Lieutenant-Captain Ivan F. Lisianskii, stopped at the Island of Hawaii on their round-the-world voyage aimed at providing supplies and naval support to the Russian-American Company. Kamehameha I, however, was not at his residence, but on Oahu with his army preparing to crush his lesser rival, Kaumualii. Hearing that an epidemic had beset Kamehameha's army, the Russians bypassed Oahu and visited Kaumualii's capital on Kauai. The latter asked the

Russians for protection from Kamehameha I. Although unable to grant this request, the Russians sailed away impressed by the king's character and the justice of his claims to the rest of the islands. Eventually, a modest trade developed between Baranov's agents and those of Kamehameha I, but Russian attempts to gain concessions and a site on the islands were unsuccessful.

In November of 1817, the frigate *Suvarov*, under the command of Captain Leontii A. Hagemeister, entered Sitka Sound. The captain was under orders to replace Baranov if his investigation found him unfit to continue in office. Baranov, during the last few years, had run into trouble with various naval officers who resented his authority because he was only a commoner. Russia was a very class-conscious society, and the navy officers belonged to the elite. On a number of occasions trouble had arisen when officers refused to obey Baranov's orders and banded together to protect one another, complaining to company headquarters about Baranov. There also had been the unfortunate mission of Dr. Georg Anton Schaeffer, whom Baranov had dispatched to King Kamehameha to gain help in retrieving the cargo of a Russian ship which had been seized by the ruler of Kauai. Schaeffer totally botched the mission, and wasted well over a quarter of a million dollars of company money to boot.

In 1818, Captain Hagemeister relieved the old governor of his duties. After putting his affairs into order and going over the company books with the accountant K. T. Khlebnikov, Baranov left for Russia. After a stormy ten-week passage unbroken by any stop, the *Kutusov* stopped for thirty-six days at Batavia on the island of Java. On April 14, 1819, by the Russian calendar, while the *Kutusov* lay idly in the Strait of Sunda which separates Java from Sumatra, Baranov died and was buried at sea.

His accomplishments had been many. He left twenty-four establishments ranging in size from simple hunting stations to New Archangel, a sizable settlement. Some 391 Russian men and 13 Russian women inhabited the colonies, together with 244 creole men and 111 creole women, while 8,384 male Natives heeded Russian orders. One hundred and ninety-eight Russians lived at New Archangel and twenty-seven at Fort Ross, together with approximately sixty Natives, and twenty-seven lived on the Pribilof Islands. Some hunting stations had but one or two

Russian residents. The company's estimated worth was seven million gold rubles, an increase of five and a half million in twenty-one years. Baranov had directed the construction of nine vessels, bought five from foreigners, and purchased four frigates in Europe. During his twenty-one years in the colonies, Baranov had realized net profits of seven and a half million gold rubles. Of that amount, four and a quarter million were distributed as dividends to stockholders.

Russia's Third Phase

The departure of Baranov initiated the third phase of Russian occupation, characterized by corporate reorganization, a reorientation of settlement northward and inland, and better relationships with the Natives. In 1821, the Imperial Government granted the company a second twenty-year charter. The old days of independent management by traders such as Baranov had ended, and henceforth naval officers provided a conservative administration of company affairs. Instead of shares, employees received salaries, and with the arrival of more missionaries, doctors, and teachers, the needs of the inhabitants were better taken care of. Most famous among the clerics was Father Ioann Veniaminov, a man of considerable intellectual gifts.

Veniaminov arrived in the Aleutian Islands in 1824 and was brought to New Archangel by Governor Ferdinand von Wrangell. There he established an ecclesiastical school, later converted into a seminary for training Native priests to conduct services in their own languages. As previously mentioned, he also recorded his observations of physical phenomena, and devised an alphabet and grammar for the Aleut language.

In 1868, long after Veniaminov departed Alaska, when he was seventy-one years old and losing his sight, he was elected Metropolitan of Moscow, and thus became his country's foremost prelate.

The Russian reorientation of exploitation and settlement to the north and the interior was triggered by strong American and British competition to the south and on the coast. It was the Hudson's Bay Company, strengthened by a merger with the North West Company in 1821, which offered stiff competition to the Russians. Ably led by George Simpson, the Hudson's Bay Company entered the coastal trade in the 1820s. The

Russian-American Company's shift to the north and the interior was caused, among other factors, by the depletion of fur resources along the coasts of New Albion and Alta California.

From the late 1810s, the company began a series of expeditions along the Bering Sea coast and into the interior of Alaska; and ventures into the Kuriles in the mid 1820s, the Kolosh Straits in the mid 1830s, and Kamchatka and the Commander Islands in the late 1830s and early 1840s. These expeditions culminated with the famous venture of Lieutenant L. A. Zagoskin into the Yukon and Kuskokwim valleys between 1842 and 1844. In the course of these expeditions in search of new fur resources, the Russians founded numerous new stations, among them a station on the Kuskokwim River in 1832 (known as Kolmakov Redoubt from 1841 onward), and Saint Michael Redoubt on Norton Sound in 1833. Another of their

A view of Sitka in 1851 has the steeple of Saint Michael's Cathedral as a distinguishing landmark. Baranov's "castle" is at the right, and at the left some of the fortification of the town is visible. From Tebenkov's *Atlas*, 1852, Alaska and Polar Regions Dept., Rasmuson Library, UAF

In its early years, Sitka had a mixture of frame and log buildings and narrow streets and boardwalks. The Cathedral of Saint Michael, which dominates the town, was begun in 1844 and dedicated in 1848. The original building burned in 1966, but the Orthodox Church constructed a replica. The original icons and furnishings that had been saved were reinstalled. This scene was photographed in the late 1880s. Courtesy of the Anchorage Historical and Fine Arts Museum

settlements was established on Stuart Island in Norton Sound in the 1830s. Its purpose was to tap the fur trade of the Alaskan interior and the coast of the Bering Sea near Siberia.

All this activity required more people. By 1833 there were 627 Russians in the colonies, 991 Creoles and 9,120 Natives. Earlier the colonies had been subdivided into counters (higher order units) and districts (lower order units). By 1833, the colonies consisted of five counters, namely New Archangel, Kodiak, Unalaska, Atka, and Ross and two districts, Northern and Kurile. New Archangel counter predominated because the seat of the governor was located in New Archangel, and concentrated there were the colonial administration, shipping, manufacturing, fishing, and lumbering. Ross counter (Russian California) offered the most comfortable living conditions, and also was the most diversified economically, with hunting; farming; shipbuilding; lumbering; manufacturing, such as tanning and brickmaking; and a little trading and fishing. Atka counter, the rawest and bleakest, was rocky, windy, rainy, and foggy. Provisioning this counter, which included the Andreanof, Rat, and Near Islands of the Aleutians, and the Commander Islands off Kamchatka, always proved to be difficult.

During the third phase, company trade with Alta California stabilized. The relations between Russian America and the United States and Great Britain were regulated by formal treaties in the 1820s. These treaties were the result of a decree which Tsar Alexander I issued in 1821. It forbade foreign ships to approach within 100 Italian miles of the coast of Russian America north of 51°N latitude, making this the southern limit of Russian America. The measure had been supported for years by the Russian-American Company in order to prevent poaching and smuggling by foreign (mainly American) traders. The United States and Great Britain quickly protested this unilateral claim by the Tsar. Soon, discussions got under way between the three powers, and Russia relented and signed two conventions with the United States and Great Britain, in 1824 and 1825, respectively, permitting foreign ships to trade along the coast of Russian America. It also fixed the southern boundary of Russian America at 54°40′N latitude, thereby excluding Russian California. These agreements ended Russian expansion in North America and legitimized foreign competition in the fur trade. Both agreements were valid for ten years,

The Princess Maksoutova was the wife of Prince Dimitri Maksoutov, the last governor of the Russian American Company. Under the last governors some effort was made to establish settlements and missions and to provide education for some of the population. Photo by R. Alberstone, courtesy of the Alaska Historical Library

and neither was renewed, although the U.S. government requested renewal.

While American traders left the region because of a scarcity of furs, British interest remained strong. During the 1830s the Hudson's Bay Company established several posts on the straits and maintained a couple of vessels along the coast. This policy eventually led to the famous Stikine or Dryad affair. It developed in 1834 when the Russian-American Company refused to allow the Hudson's Bay Company ship *Dryad* to proceed up the Stikine River to establish a post. Britain claimed that this action had violated the Anglo-Russian Convention of 1825 and demanded compensation for damages amounting to 22,150 pounds sterling. Not until 1839 was the incident resolved.

Russia's Fourth Phase

The fourth phase lasted roughly from 1840 to the sale of Russian America to the United States in 1867. It was a period characterized by readjustment, contraction, diversification, and finally, deterioration. In 1841 the Imperial Government renewed the company's charter for another twenty years. The company became even more an extension of the government, ruled by bureaucrats and naval officers. On the new board of directors only Nicholas Kusov was a merchant; all the rest were government officials. The company flew its own flag and its employees wore uniforms.

During this period, the company's financial difficulties increased. The fur trade was changing because of dwindling suppy and demand. This called for cost reduction and a search for new sources of revenue. The first readjustment consisted of a ten-year agreement with the Hudson's Bay Company in 1839. Under its forms the latter leased the continental portion of the Alaska Panhandle for hunting, with a yearly rent of 2,000 river ottters; and, perhaps more importantly, with the delivery of goods from England and foodstuffs from the Oregon country to New Archangel, assuring the Russians of a reliable source of supplies. Assured of a supply source, the Russian-American Company sold Russian California to General John Sutter of New Helvetia for $30,000. The decision to sell was an easy one, because Fort Ross had always been a political problem, first with the Spanish and later with the Mexicans, and it had never

produced the expected food supplies. The Russians also realized that the United States probably would absorb California fairly soon. In addition, the agreement allowed the Russians to discontinue their trade with the ruthlessly competitive Bostonians. But no sooner had Yankee trading ships disappeared from colonial waters when they were replaced with Yankee whaling and sealing vessels. As early as 1842, up to 200 American whalers pursued their prey in the far North Pacific.

While Russia contracted its North American activities, it used the Russian-American Company from 1851 onward to help explore and develop China's Amur Valley. In 1853, Russia gained jurisdiction over Sakhalin. Russia long had coveted the Amur Valley, and China, plagued by internal unrest and foreign intervention, was unable to resist. The shift to the Asiatic continent also was caused by the disastrous decline of the maritime fur trade with the near extermination of the sea otters and fur seals, despite conservation measures undertaken by the company. The fur market further collapsed as silk hats replaced felt hats in fashion, and the Chinese demand declined as a result of internal disorders.

Attempts to market furs elsewhere were unsuccessful. This prompted the company to diversify economically. In the early 1850s it began the ice trade with San Francisco, a successful venture for more than a decade. The company also began selling fish and timber in Hawaii and California; attempted whaling and coal mining; and marketed walrus hides in England. All of these efforts temporarily increased dividends in the 1840s and 1850s. Still, it was not enough to reverse company fortunes. Company critics called into question Russia's ability to defend the colonies from attack and questioned the wisdom of government subsidies for the company. Most importantly, perhaps, Russia was plagued by domestic difficulties, brought about by the disastrous Crimean War with Great Britain and France. The conflict demonstrated that Russia had gained an inflated reputation during the Napoleonic wars and was unable to wage modern warfare. It also made clear to the Imperial Government that the construction of a modern industrial society was not possible while serfdom still existed. In March of 1861, Tsar Alexander II signed the decree abolishing serfdom.

When the charter of the Russian-American Company came up for a third renewal in the early 1860s, it was not renewed. By that time the very existence of the company, and even of the Russian colonies in America in general, had become troublesome problems for the Imperial Government. Besides the declining financial fortunes of the company, there was fear among some Russian statesmen that Russian-America might be lost to Great Britain or an expansionist United States in the course of time. After all, the colonies were noncontiguous and the Russians had always experienced difficulties in supplying their North American possession. Furthermore, many influential Russians desired to continue the exploration and development of the Amur region, a contiguous area and in much closer communication with the government. This region, many felt, was Russia's true sphere of interest and there she did not have to contend with the ambitious Western powers.

Even if Russian America was not to be forcefully alienated by either the United States or Great Britain, there always existed the threat of peaceful economic penetration which Russia was in no position to resist. The example of how Mexico had lost Texas, California, and other territory to the United States clearly demonstrated to the Imperial Government the dangers from that quarter. By 1857 rumors had also reached the Russian diplomatic representative in the United States that the Mormons, under Brigham Young, planned to move north to Russian America. Even though there was no basis for such a rumor, it did worry the responsible Russian officials.

Anatole B. Mazour, an American historian, observed that the Imperial Government had three courses of action open to it: it could try and maintain an unsatisfactory status quo; it could make the colony the full responsibility of the government, placing too great a strain on its inadequate financial resources; or it could get rid of Russian America altogether. But perhaps it was the Soviet historian S. B. Okun who best summed up Russia's adventure in North America:

Having seized a foothold on the western shore of North America, Czarist Russia aimed to proceed further into the Western Hemisphere. However, in her expansions she met a strong rival—England—and later on, crossed the way of also another great growing power the United States—and then she renounced, in the long run, the struggle for strengthening of her influence on the North American Continent.

RUSSIAN CHURCH AND SCHOOL, UNALASKA, ALASKA

A glance at the map suffices to make us realize that large [armed] forces and [financial] means were required in order to protect and maintain these remote and too exposed advance posts. But the attention of Russia, beginning with the 1840s, was centered upon her tasks to be accomplished first on the European and Asiatic continents. Russia had to renounce any further expansion in the Western Hemisphere; she also had to renounce her American settlements which were created as footholds for this expansion. The expansion stopped on the Western shore of the Pacific. On this natural frontier, where there was access to the open sea, Russia has defended its vital interests. ■

The interior of the Russian Church at Unalaska is pictured. Courtesy of the Bunnell Collection, Alaska and Polar Regions Dept., Rasmuson Library, UAF

The Russian church and school at Unalaska is shown circa 1910. Father Ioann Veniaminov, in charge of religious work in Russian America for many years, stated that the first church was built here in 1826. Courtesy of Selid-Bassoc Collection, Alaska and Polar Regions Dept., Rasmuson Library, UAF

This is the interior of the Russian church at Belkofski, on the south coast of the Alaska peninsula, in 1888. Father Andronik, the priest, is at the right. Courtesy of the A. Shattuck Collection, Alaska Historical Library

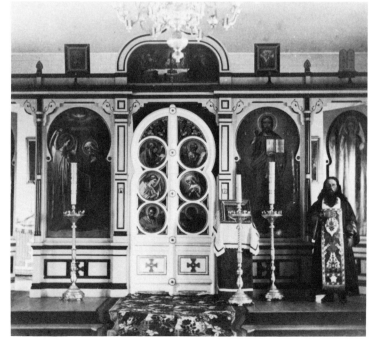

The Russians established Nulato as a trading post in 1838. That post and succeeding ones the Indians destroyed. About 1854 the Russians built a stockaded fort at the village's present location. Frederick Whymper sketched the village in 1866, depicting it at night with an aurora overhead. From Frederick Whymper's *Travel and Adventure in the Territory of Alaska,* 1868, Alaska and Polar Regions Dept., Rasmuson Library, UAF

This sketch shows Fort Yukon, the Hudson's Bay Company post as seen by Whymper. The Company established the post elsewhere in 1847 and moved it to the present location of the town about 1864. The Hudson's Bay Company knowingly built the post on Russian territory, and Americans took over the post after the purchase of Alaska. From Frederick Whymper's *Travel and Adventure in the Territory of Alaska,* 1868, Alaska and Polar Regions Dept., Rasmuson Library, UAF

The Western Union Telegraph Company idea of placing a line across Canada, Alaska, and Siberia to establish communications between Europe and North America led to some of the early exploration of the Yukon River area on into Canada. In 1865 Robert Kennicott led his party from Saint Michael to Nulato, where he died in May 1866. Others continued the exploration of the Yukon. This drawing shows one of the exploring party's camps. This project, under a concession from the Russian government, was the last major exploration effort before Russia sold Alaska to the United States. Courtesy of the Historical Photograph Collection, Alaska and Polar Regions Dept., Rasmuson Library, UAF

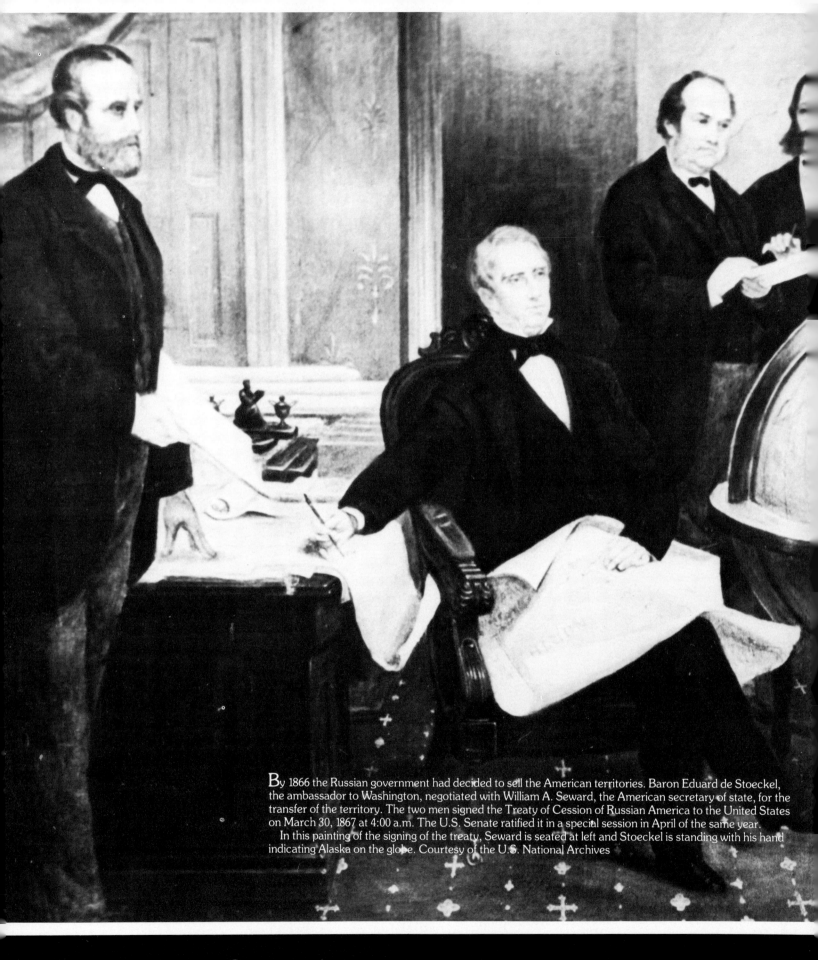

By 1866 the Russian government had decided to sell the American territories. Baron Eduard de Stoeckel, the ambassador to Washington, negotiated with William A. Seward, the American secretary of state, for the transfer of the territory. The two men signed the Treaty of Cession of Russian America to the United States on March 30, 1867 at 4:00 a.m. The U.S. Senate ratified it in a special session in April of the same year.

In this painting of the signing of the treaty, Seward is seated at left and Stoeckel is standing with his hand indicating Alaska on the globe. Courtesy of the U.S. National Archives

Chapter 4

The United States
Purchases Russian America

Secretary of State William H. Seward was the principal American in the negotiations which led to the purchase of Alaska. In later life, when asked what he considered to be his outstanding contribution to his country, Seward stated that he considered the purchase of Alaska to be his most important act, though he thought that it would take the American people a generation to find it out. Seward did not err in his estimation. Indeed, it was not until World War II that the United States fully recognized the value of Alaska.

It is also safe to assume that President Andrew Johnson and his cabinet favored the purchase, for at least they did not oppose it. They seemed to feel that the secretary of state knew what he was doing. In his message to Congress in 1867 and 1868, Johnson noted why he had approved the Treaty of Cession of Russian America. It was his belief that the United States should have the territory because of the need for naval bases in the North Pacific, and because the acquisition would spread republican institutions.

Treaty Drafted

In any event, after negotiating for three weeks, Seward and Baron Eduard de Stoeckel, the Russian minister to the United States, met at Seward's home in Washington, and during a long night of phrasing and rewording, they finally completed the Treaty of Cession. Early in the morning of March 30, 1867, the two weary men signed the document. That same day, the treaty was sent to the Senate with the president's message of transmittal. Since the Senate conducted its review of the affair in secret session and refused to allow its debates to be published, little is know regarding what the senators thought about the annexation. There were, however, some leaks to the newspapers, and a fair amount of what happened can be gleaned from the newspapers of the day.

The general feeling in the Senate seemed to be to vote against any administration measure in those bitter days of reconstruction following the Civil War. Many senators opposed the president and Seward and were resolved to vote against the measure. Seward, recognizing that his treaty was not faring well, began an intense campaign of education. He sent all available information on Alaska to friendly newspapers, including reasons for the annexation. It soon became apparent that many of the arguments voiced

against the acquisition were the same ones which had been used when the Louisiana Purchase was being discussed. Seward had the old Louisiana debates collected and published. In his campaign before the Senate and in the newspapers, he saw to it that the people were made aware of the importance of Alaska. Its climate compared favorably with that of the Scandinavian countries, and it held vast natural resources. Above all, immediate action was necessary, because what would prevent Russia from selling the territory to another power? The argument that seemed to have the most weight in the Senate called for acceptance of the treaty so that friendly relations between Russia and the United States could be preserved. The senators clearly were put in a position of insulting the Tsar and injuring their country's relations with Russia if they refused to ratify the treaty.

Seward's greatest success, however, was the early conversion of the powerful chairman of the Senate Foreign Affairs Committee. He convinced Senator Charles Sumner of Massachusetts that he should support the cession. Personally, the senator did not seem to be too enthusiastic about the purchase, for, as he wrote to a friend, he opposed further acquisitions of territory unless they occurred by the free choice of the inhabitants. In the case of Alaska, considerations of politics and engagements already entered into by the government complicated the picture. He therefore hesitated to take the responsibility of defeating the treaty. After Sumner decided to support the purchase, he was unstinting in his efforts. It was probably due to his labors that on April 8, 1867, the committee which he chaired reported the treaty favorably without amendments. In the debate which followed the next day, Sumner delivered the principal address which became the highlight of the discussion. He used all available information on Alaska, including translations of works in foreign languages. He covered Russian America thoroughly. His three hour speech was published later and still remains a valuable source of information on Alaska.

Sumner basically cited five reasons why he thought that the United States should acquire Alaska. First, there was the desire on the part of the Americans on the Pacific Coast to be granted hunting and fishing privileges; secondly, Great Britain should not be allowed to acquire Alaska; thirdly, there was the friendship between the United States and Russia which had to be preserved; fourthly, the acquisition of the region would increase American trade with Japan and China; and lastly, republican institutions would be further extended in North America. The last point was illuminated by Sumner when he stated that with the acquisition of Alaska, one more monarch would be dismissed from this continent. The upshot of it all was that when the vote was taken on April 9, 1867, the Senate approved it by the necessary two-thirds margin.

The United States Takes Possession

On October 18, 1867, the United States took possession of Alaska even though the House had not yet appropriated the purchase price of $7.2 million. House action on the appropriation was delayed in 1867 and 1868 because members were interested solely in the impeachment of President Johnson. Not until the summer of 1868, after the trial had been dismissed, did the House consider the money bill. In the following debates, the majority of reasons given both for and against the purchase were the same ones which had practically been exhausted before the public in the previous year.

Those representatives favoring the treaty extolled Alaska's marvelous natural resources and the commercial, economic, and political importance of the territory. Above all, the treaty had already been negotiated, and to keep Russia's friendship the money would have to be voted. N. C. Banks, the chairman of the House Committee on Foreign Affairs, led the forces favoring the appropriation of the purchase price. He talked in glowing terms about Alaska's mineral resources, agricultural opportunities, fisheries, and the timber of Alaska which was the best in the world for shipbuilding. Alaska would add to the industrial product of the country and provide employment to fishermen, lumbermen, miners, colliers, mariners, shipbuilders, trappers, hunters, farmers, ice-cutters, and traders. When the resources of the territory were fully developed, he stated, a quarter of a million people would be gainfully employed, representing a population of one million people. Besides, refusing to carry out the binding provisions of the treaty would constitute bad faith on the part of the United States.

Expansionists in the House favored the treaty because it increased the size of the United States. Others wanted Alaska simply to keep Great Britain from getting it. Expansionists were also convinced that with the purchase of Alaska, British Columbia would, as a matter of course, enter the Union as a state. Some House members with vision believed that Alaska was important to the United States because of the future importance of the Pacific Ocean.

Representative Cadwallader C. Washburn led the opposition in the House. He essentially opposed the purchase on five points. First, he maintained that there had been no one in the country before March 30, 1867 who had wanted to purchase Alaska or had even thought about the territory; secondly, the treaty had been negotiated secretly; thirdly, he maintained that by existing treaties the Americans could fish and trade in Alaska without having to go to the expense of buying the region and governing savages. Fourthly, the territory was absolutely without any value. To prove this point he cited the opinion of a Russian authority who pictured the country rather bleakly. Alaska would never attract settlers. It was a land of permanent fogs and dampness, and lacked sunlight. Agriculture was made impossible because of the climate, and that would force people, because they lacked bread, salt, and meat, to live upon fish, berries, shellfish, sea cabbages, and other products of the sea. These foods would have to be profusely soaked in the grease of sea beasts in order to escape the dreaded scurvy. His fifth point dealt with the danger inherent in manifest destiny, one which Washburn did not elaborate. Finally, one representative stated that if it was so important to keep Russia's friendship, why did the United States not pay her the purchase price and let her keep Alaska? He thought that $7.2 million was a small sum to give for friendship's sake if only the United States could get rid of the land, or ice, which it was going to get by the payment of the money.

While the House debated, the country's newspapers condemned the delay in passing the appropriation. Finally, on July 4, 1868, the House passed the measure by a comfortable margin.

Congress, once it had purchased Alaska, showed very little interest in the new territory. In July of 1868, it extended to Alaska the laws of custom, commerce, and navigation, legislation which, once amended, remained the only law effective over all of Alaska for seventeen years. Congressional refusal to provide a civil government, together with the region's

difficult physical geography, made Alaska an anomaly, namely an unorganized, non-agricultural, noncontiguous colony in a nation whose colonial system was designed for self-governing agricultural, contiguous, settler colonies.

Without an authorized government, the president faced the task of administering the first colony of the American oceanic empire without legal authority or adequate funds. Lacking legislation and a bureaucratic machinery, the federal government sought a solution to governing without law by calling successively upon the Army, the Treasury Department, and the Navy to serve as extralegal colonial agencies until 1884, when Congress passed Alaska's first Organic Act, principally sponsored by Indiana's Senator Benjamin Harrison.

The Army Takes Over

In 1867, however, all of that still lay in the future. On September 24, 1867, two companies under the command of Brevet Major General Jefferson Columbus Davis, 23rd Infantry, sailed from San Francisco to occupy the first overseas dependency and assert United States authority over Alaska. On October 10 of that year the steamer *John L. Stephens,* with troops and supplies aboard, dropped anchor in Sitka Harbor. Eight days later, the American and Russian commissioners arrived on the U.S.S. *Ossipee,* and that afternoon the official transfer took place. General Lovell H. Rousseau of Kentucky repre-

sented the United States government in the ceremonies, and Captain Aleksei Pestchurov represented the Russian government. The Russian flag was lowered and the Stars and Stripes went up, and after a few remarks by both commissioners, Alaska became an American posession. It would be administered by the new Department of Alaska, a branch of the War Department.

Next, the commissioners inventoried buildings and designated them as public, private, or church property. Soon, the troops occupied their new quarters and the post quickly fell into a normal garrison routine.

Early in 1868, Major General Henry W. Halleck, Commanding General of the Military Division of the Pacific to which Alaska was attached, ordered the construction of four new army posts; at Wrangell, at the mouth of the Stikine River; on Tongass Island; at Saint Paul, Kodiak Island; and on the Kenai Peninsula. All posts, with the exception of the Kenai one, were constructed. The latter was delayed because the bark carrying the troop contingent for Kenai, the *Torrent,* struck a reef in English Bay. Although all hands on board were rescued, the loss of supplies necessitated a delay. It was not until April of 1869 that construction of Fort Kenai began at the site of the old Russian post, Fort Saint Nicholas.

The army constructed its last post in the Department of Alaska in the same year, 1869. In 1868 the Pribilof Islands, long a major source of profits for the Russians, had been infested with free-booters who indiscriminately slaughtered

This check was issued for the purchase of Alaska, for $7,200,000, in August 1868. Courtesy of the Historical Photograph Collection, Alaska and Polar Regions Dept., Rasmuson Library, UAF

On September 6, 1867, Major General Henry W. Halleck, Commanding General of the Military Division of the Pacific, issued instructions to Brevet Major General Jefferson Columbus Davis, Colonel, Twenty-Third Infantry, for the occupation of the first overseas dependency of the United States. Davis, thirty-nine years of age, had had a checkered, but generally successful, career before his assignment to command in Alaska. Volunteering for duty in Mexico in 1846, he earned a battlefield commission at Buena Vista. He remained with the regulars after the Mexican War and was at Fort Sumter when the Civil War began. Returned north after the surrender of Fort Sumter, he raised a volunteer regiment and soon became a brigadier general of volunteers.

During the war Davis participated in twenty-one engagements, winning successive brevets from major to major general. In 1862 he gained some notoriety when he killed Major General William Nelson after a heated quarrel over Nelson's alleged mistreatment of Davis. Despite arrest and indictment, he escaped prosecution largely because of favorable public opinion. He rose to command a corps in Georgia during which time he became the object of a Congressional investigation for abandoning 6,000 fugitive slaves to Confederate cavalry. Still holding the permanent rank of captain at the end of the war. Davis received a colonelcy in the reorganization of the army in 1866.

When Davis was sent as the military commander of Alaska, he had a few hundred soldiers and several forts under his command. The Army ruled Alaska until 1877 when the troops were withdrawn. Courtesy of the Historical Photograph Collection, Alaska and Polar Regions Dept., Rasmuson Library, UAF

the fur seals. In July of 1868 Congress prohibited the killing of fur-bearing animals in Alaska except with the permission of the Secretary of the Treasury. Early in 1869 Treasury Secretary Hugh McCulloch requested the Army to station troops on the islands to help Treasury agents enforce the law. The army complied and erected what proved to be the most isolated post so far established. These six posts completed the Army's structure in Alaska, and although there were plans for various others, they were never realized.

The Army soon found that there was little challenge to United States sovereignty in the new region, and it acted swiftly to expel the Hudson's Bay Company from its Fort Yukon post. In 1847 the company had built the fort at the confluence of the Yukon and Porcupine rivers, just north of the Arctic Circle, with full knowledge that it was located in Russian territory. At the Army's insistence, the Hudson's Bay Company left American soil in early 1870. The Army found, however, that it was totally out of its normal element in Alaska, where at that time it was necessary to get around by boat. Basically a land service, with inadequate transportation the Army had to rely on occasional merchant steamers for transportation, and on visiting naval and revenue vessels for inspection trips.

It soon became apparent that the Department of Alaska was doomed. In the Congressional belt-tightening following the Civil War, Army appropriations dropped from $123 million in 1868 to $58 million in 1870. And when the Treasury Department reported in early 1870 that it had cost $330,000 more to maintain posts in Alaska than having the same in the continental United States, it was only a matter of time before cutbacks would occur. In April 1870 the War Department discontinued the Department of Alaska and attached its posts to the Department of the Columbia as an economy measure. In July of 1870, Secretary of War William S. Belknap ordered that all Alaskan posts, except Sitka, be closed. By October only Sitka remained as an active military post.

The closure of Army posts coincided with a decline of American interest in the new region and the economic decay of Sitka. For while there had been a rush of speculators to Sitka in 1867, all hoping to get rich quickly, an economic decline had already begun in 1868. In that year, population dropped as Russians and disappointed Americans went home. And although Sitkans had formed a municipal

government in 1867, this could not stem the decline. Population statistics illustrated the drop. In 1870 Sitka had 394 non-Indian inhabitants. In 1872 their numbers had declined to 314, a loss of 20 percent. More telling of the business climate was the drop in the number of prostitutes from a high of 34 to a mere 18. School attendance and church membership had declined even more alarmingly. The customhouse receipts perhaps best illustrate Sitka's slump. Between late 1867 and July of 1869, marine traffic had produced more than $21,000 in duties. In 1870, the duties came to a mere $449.28, and three years later amounted to only $155.25. No wonder that on February 18, 1873, the Sitka city council held its last meeting.

Gold Discoveries

In 1874 miners discovered gold in the Dease Lake region in British Columbia. As news of the discovery spread down the Stikine River, it sparked a minor gold rush. Fort Wrangell, at the mouth of the Stikine, boomed as a transfer point from oceangoing vessels to river steamers and smaller craft. In 1874 about 3,000 people called at Fort Wrangell, and it soon became a popular wintering place for miners, resulting in the construction of stores, bakeries, restaurants, and a saloon and a dance hall. Because of some lawlessness, the Army sent a small detachment to Fort Wrangell to suppress illicit distilling and liquor smuggling. The small Army detachment remained, and Fort Wrangell became a subpost of Sitka until August of 1875, when an infantry company took over and made Fort Wrangell a regular military post.

The Army Leaves Alaska

As early as 1875, General O. O. Howard, in his annual report, pointed out that federal courts had questioned the Army's authority in Alaska and recommended that Congress either bestow the necessary powers on the Army to govern the area, or provide for a civil government. The following year he recommended the appointment of resident United States commissioners and deputy marshals, the establishment of courts, and the assignment of a gunboat to cooperate with these civil functions. Clearly, the Army wanted out, and it only needed an opportunity to withdraw gracefully. A fire in the officers' housing in Sitka on February 8, 1877, provided the opportunity. Replacement was estimated to cost $15,000, and the Chief Quartermaster of the Military Division of the Pacific reported that if the troops were withdrawn they could be replaced cheaply with naval vessels. On April 10, 1877, John McCrary, the new secretary of war in the Hayes administration, ordered the abandonment of the Sitka and Fort Wrangell posts upon the arrival of a new cutter. In June of 1877, the troops left Alaska.

During its ten-year stay in Alaska, the Army hardly ruled the great land. Throughout its decade in the north, the military never possessed legal authority to govern, and Army officers assumed the duty of enforcing an arbitrary order near their posts in the absence of civil authority. They conscientiously attempted to enforce the laws they believed applied to Alaska. Burdened with a task they neither expected nor desired, the military authorities struggled unsupported by money and law to furnish at least a semblance of government for Alaska. By nineteenth century standards, the Army's Indian policy in Alaska was a benevolent one, attempting primarily to restrict the liquor traffic. In this they failed, and liquor contributed significantly to the degeneration of Alaska's Native cultures. The Army can hardly be blamed for failure in the liquor suppression, because physical and legal obstacles made this an impossible task. In retrospect, land forces are unsuited for law enforcement in a marine environment, especially if lacking water transport.

More Settlers and Economic Advances

The nation at large may have lost interest in Alaska, but hardy individuals continued to trickle north after the acquisition. As early as 1869 the *Yukon,* a small sternwheeler, was the first steamboat to ever appear on the mighty Yukon River. In 1873, Leroy Napoleon McQuesten and his three partners arrived at Fort Yukon by canoe, having paddled downriver from Canada. McQuesten, Arthur Harper, and Alfred Mayo went to work for the Alaska Commercial Company in the early 1870s, supplying trappers and staking an occasional prospector.

Although the fur trade dwindled after 1867, salmon fishing, which had merely provided for local needs under the Russians, expanded into a thriving business. The first American saltery was established in 1868, and the first cannery began operating at Klawock on Prince of Wales Island in 1878. By 1898 there were fifty-nine canneries in Alaska.

Prospectors discovered gold in the Sitka region in the early 1870s, and in 1880 Joseph Juneau and Richard T. Harris made a strike at the present site of Juneau. In that same year the two men entered a townsite which they named Harrisburg. Although the economic development was modest, it resulted in an influx of white fortune seekers. The first official census of the territory in 1880 recorded 33,426 inhabitants, of whom all but approximately 430 were Native Alaskans. The 1890 census showed an increase of 3,868 whites and a decline among Alaska's aborigines of 7,642, due to the traumatic collision between Caucasian and Native cultures.

The Navy in Alaska

It was not until August 10, 1877, that the *Corwin,* commanded by Captain J. W. White, an old Alaska hand, arrived at Sitka. Although White found conditions peaceful, he discovered that the abandoned government buildings had been plundered. There was also much drunkenness. After spending a few weeks in Alaskan waters, White sailed south again in September. But despite White's report that all was well, reports about possible trouble continued to circulate. On October 17, the *Oliver Wolcott,* commanded by another old Alaska hand, Captain J. M. Selden, arrived in Sitka. He also discounted possibilities of troubles. Unfortunately, however, the year 1878 turned out to be one of lawlessness and disorder in the Panhandle. One press account reported fifty-one stills operating in Sitka, a town of 300 people. There were other stills in the Indian village, and hochinoo, the locally-brewed booze, sold for twenty cents a quart on the streets. There were frequent troubles between whites and Indians, and by the end of 1878 it had become apparent that the Treasury Department was unable to administer Alaska. For example, a miner named Boyd who was wintering at Wrangell shot and killed another man in a quarrel over an Indian woman. Deputy

The Alaska Commercial Company took over many of the assets and trade of the Russian-American Company. Here the old Russian Battery at Unalaska is shown. During the gold rush Unalaska became a fueling and supply stop for ships heading for Nome or Saint Michael, and some of the riverboats that plied the Yukon and Tanana rivers were built on Unalaska. This picture was taken sometime between 1906 and 1908. Courtesy of the Anchorage Historical and Fine Arts Museum

Collector R. D. Crittenden refused to take charge of the murderer, claiming he had no jurisdiction. Disgruntled miners thereupon organized a court, tried Boyd, and hung him the next day.

Finally, in early 1879 there again was fear of an Indian massacre in Sitka, and some residents decided to appeal to the British for protection. The H.M.S. *Osprey,* commanded by H. Holmes A'Court, sailed from Victoria, British Columbia to Sitka on February 18, 1879, on the same day on which the U.S. Government ordered the cutter *Oliver Wolcott* to proceed to Sitka with all practicable dispatch. Whether or not there was an imminent threat of violence, the *Osprey* affair was humiliating, and thereafter, until Alaska gained its Organic Act, the United States Navy had the task of maintaining law and order in the district.

On March 13, 1879, Secretary of the Navy Robert W. Thompson ordered the U.S.S. *Alaska,* a twelve gun steam sloop, to sail to Sitka. Captin George Brown sailed the sloop to Sitka, arriving there on the morning of April 3, 1979. With his arrival, naval rule had begun.

The chief figure in this episode was Commander Lester Anthony Beardslee, U.S. Navy, and his sloop of war, the U.S.S. *Jamestown.* The forty-three-year-old skipper established a quasimilitary government involving thousands of individuals. There were few precedents, but many problems. Beardslee left San Francisco on May 22, 1879, together with a crew of 140 which had been augmented by 26 marine guards. Secretary of the Navy Thompson had instructed Beardslee to restore harmonious relations between settler and Native, and in the admitted absence of law and government to use his "own discretion in all emergencies that might arise."

Both Indians and whites looked upon Beardslee as the man to rectify all deficiencies resulting from the lack of law and government. He was fully aware of the difficulties of his position, and knew that in order to govern he had to secure the support of the governed, for there was no other covenant or mandate. As it turned out, Beardslee had to devote attention mainly to those actions likely to produce trouble with the Indians. Drunkenness, assaults, and other disturbances of the peace the marines handled. But rather than using marines to arrest Indians, Beardslee felt it wiser to have the Indians police themselves as much as possible, using their own laws. To this end he appointed five of the most trustworthy and influential Tlingits in Sitka's Native

town as policemen. Particularly astute was Beardslee's selection of the respected and influential Chief Annahootz of the Kakwatons family as chief of this police force. So successful was the Sitka experiment that Beardslee extended the principle to other trouble spots.

Beardslee served the first fifteen months in this five-year period of naval rule. Thanks to his initiative and resourcefulness, territorial conditions improved markedly. His immediate successor, Commander Henry Glass, admired Beardslee's accomplishment, commenting on the latter's role in establishing a school system for Indian and Creole children. He also mentioned that Beardslee's encouragement had caused missionary activities to flourish. Beardslee left Alaska, and later on returned for a second

tour of duty. He went on to a brilliant naval career, rose to rear admiral (the highest naval rank at the time) and commanded the North Pacific Squadron before retiring in 1898.

Congress Passes Alaska's First Organic Act

In the meantime, twenty-five bills dealing with Alaskan civil government were introduced and died in committee, while visiting naval officers in Alaskan ports administered law and provided intermittent services. A Senate bill in 1882-83 launched a semi-serious discussion about Alaskan affairs. The original measure proposed to

In 1839 the Russians leased their redoubt, Saint Dionysius, to the British, who renamed it Fort Stikine. In 1867 the Americans established Fort Wrangell here but abandoned it in 1877. The post office in the remaining community was called Fort Wrangell and was changed to Wrangell in 1902. It survived as a supply point for fur traders and miners. This view is from 1878. Courtesy of the Alaska Historical Library

vest both the executive and judicial powers in one man. A legislative branch was not to be included. The Senate committee reported out a substitute bill which provided for a governor, a secretary and a host of other appointed federal officials. The legislative authority was to be vested in the governor; the one-man Supreme Court, called the chief justice; the territorial marshal; the surveyor-general; and the collector of customs, all appointed by the president. The only elective territorial office was that of delegate to Congress. Inadequate as the bill was, Congress adjourned without action. Not until the next year, 1884, did Congress enact an Organic Act for Alaska, chiefly sponsored by Indiana's Senator Benjamin Harrison. It made Alaska a "civil and judicial district," with a

governor, one district federal judge, a clerk of court, a marshal, four deputy marshals, and four commissioners who functioned as justices of the peace. All officials were given multiple jobs in an area one-fifth the size of the continental United States. The marshal, for example, was to act as surveyor-general despite the lack of legal provisions for a land system. These officials were to administer the laws of Oregon and those written for Alaska by Congress. Administration of some territorial affairs was to be carried out from Washington. The Secretary of the Interior, for example, was to direct education in the territory. The Organic Act prohibited both a legislative branch and a delegate to Congress. Earl S. Pomeroy, a historian of territorial government, observed that Alaska "stood in an outer political anteroom without the most rudimentary territorial status, governed (when governed at all) more like the Newfoundland fisheries of the Seventeenth-Century British empire than like a territory." Jack E. Eblen, another scholar of territorial government, concluded that the Organic Act "provided a cruelly modified first-stage government and made no provision for eventual representative government."

Senator Harrison, chief sponsor and chairman of the Senate Committee on Territories, recognized the deficiencies of the Organic Act, stating that "indeed, I am willing to confess upon the challenge of almost any Senator that all of the provisions of the bill are inadequate. It is a mere shift; it is a mere expedient; it is a mere beginning in what we believe to be the right direction toward giving a civil government and education to Alaska. I hope more will follow, but the committee in considering this matter adjudged what

In 1872 San Francisco became the headquarters of the Alaska and Aleutian Diocese. This 1879 photo shows the Russian archbishop in Sitka.

The North American Orthodox Church declared its independence from the Moscow Patriarchate in 1924. This was formally recognized in 1970 when the Russian Orthodox Church in North America was granted independent jurisdiction, with a new name, the "Orthodox Church in America." Courtesy of the U.S. Library of Congress

Seldovia, on the west coast of the Kenai peninsula, is pictured here. The 1880 census stated that the seventy-one inhabitants were "sea otter hunters and live here in loghouses and have a small chapel." The influence of Russian Orthodoxy is seen in the neat church rising above the town. Courtesy of the Anchorage Historical and Fine Arts Museum

they believed to be the probable limit of the generosity of the Senate."

In the meantime, the Navy had refurnished the U.S.S. *Pinta* and then ordered it from New York on a lengthy voyage around Cape Horn to San Francisco. On August 17, 1884, the *Pinta* finally arrived at Sitka with its fifty-man crew and three guns to relieve the U.S.S. *Adams*. The Navy's reign in the Panhandle, however, was almost over, for in September of that year Lieutenant Commander Henry E. Nichols relinquished his civil responsibilities to John H. Kinkead, Sitka's first postmaster. Kinkead, a former post trader who had once been governor of Nevada, became Alaska's first civil district governor. The *Pinta* remained in Alaskan waters until 1897 in order to assist the civil government. ■

In 1877 jurisdiction over Alaska was handed to the Revenue Marine Service. Their ships carried out all sorts of functions along the coast from maintaining order to transporting people and goods. The revenue cutter *Bear* was one of the most famous of the ships. Well-known in the Arctic, she is shown here about 1910 in the sea ice. Courtesy of the Historical Photograph Collection, Alaska and Polar Regions Dept., Rasmuson Library, UAF

Chapter 5

Gold and Settlement: 1884-1928

From the start, the civil government was plagued with a lack of money. None of the appropriations reached the ex officio treasurer during the first year, and disbursements had to be made by the customs collector. The marshal even found that when ordered to deliver an insane man to an asylum in California, he had no funds to do so. Inadequate transportation further limited the civil government from the start. Governor John H. Kinkead wrote his annual report two weeks after his arrival in the north. He pointed out that no regular communication line linked southeastern Alaska with the commissioner at Unalaska. For example, for a case to be tried in district court, the accused or litigant from western Alaska had to travel to Sitka by way of San Francisco, a trip of nearly 4,000 miles. And although the governor was supposed to report on the Alaska Commercial Company's fur harvesting activities on the Pribilof Islands, there were no travel funds to do so. The *Pinta,* available for occasional inspection cruises and emergency use, was too small and its range was too limited to serve civil government transportation needs.

Indeed, the lack of transportation severely restricted the effectiveness of the district government. For example, even in southeastern Alaska, warrants for the arrest of accused criminals remained in the marshal's hands for months if the accused could not be reached by the mail steamer. In 1887 Governor Alfred P. Swineford stated that district government was a myth except for the Panhandle. In 1888, he complained that since 1884 several murders had been committed, but that the culprits were still at large because the authorities could not get to them. There were other problems as well. The Organic Act of May 17, 1884 had finally provided a limited civil government for Alaska, and also arbitrarily extended the Oregon statutes to the northern frontier, but without any modifications or changes making such laws adaptable to Alaska. Consequently, the laws of Oregon were largely inapplicable in Alaska because they referred to political subdivisions and local officials which did not exist in Alaska. Oregon law, for example, required that all jurors be taxpayers. Alaska levied no taxes. The attorney general found it impossible to compile and furnish Alaska copies of applicable laws of the United States and Oregon. This left district officials without guidance as to what laws they were supposed to enforce.

Civil government was not very popu-lar with the district's white population, in part because white Alaskans felt slighted in education appropriations. These increased more rapidly for Indians than for whites after the appointment of Sheldon Jackson as General Agent for Education. Dr. Jackson, a Presbyterian, had pioneered missionary work in Alaska, and was to introduce reindeer to the territory in the 1890s. His Christian zeal, near dictatorial manner, and abrasive personality often put him at loggerheads with white residents and many governmental officials as well.

It long had proved impossible to prohibit alcoholic beverages, but missionaries still insisted that Alaska remain dry. This incensed white Alaskans, many of whom liked their booze. Juries refused to indict or convict whites guilty of liquor offenses. District and customs officials ignored schemes of whites to obtain liquor, and saloons and breweries flourished in many Alaskan settlements. Nevertheless, however ineffective and unpopular the district government was, at least it was a legal one, and that had not been the case with the earlier Army, Treasury Department, and Navy administrations.

Prospecting for Gold

While the new administration struggled to carry out its duties, men were searching for gold from Ketchikan to Juneau, and along the Yukon River as well. As early as 1883 the Army had dispatched Lieutenant Frederick Schwatka together with seven soldiers to chart the Yukon River from its source to its mouth. To reach the headwaters of the Yukon, Schwatka's party hired a group of Chilkat Indian packers and scaled the Chilkoot Pass, an ancient trade route between coastal and interior Indians. Schwatka's party met two American prospectors on the upper Yukon on their way back to the coast to replenish their supplies. They also passed the ruins for the Hudson's Bay Company's Fort Selkirk (burned by the Chilkats in 1882), and drifted by the Fortymile River into Alaska. Near where the Tanana River joined the Yukon, Schwatka's party abandoned its raft, which had carried the men 1,300 miles, and continued downriver on a schooner lent them by trader Arthur Harper. At Saint Michael, just upcoast from the Yukon River delta, they took passage back to Fort Vancouver on August 30, 1883. Schwatka's account of the journey was published in 1885, entitled *Along Alaska's Great River.* It increased public interest in the area, and doubtlessly encouraged numerous prospectors to examine the sandbars of the Yukon for gold.

By 1886 about two hundred miners had gradually worked their way down the Yukon to the mouth of the Stewart River. There trader Leroy N. McQuesten and his partners built a trading post. That winter, Arthur Harper, one of the traders, convinced two prospectors to explore the gravels and bars of the Fortymile River which joined the Yukon a hundred miles farther downstream. The two found gold later in the season and a minor stampede followed.

That same year gold was discovered on the bars of the Fortymile River at Franklin Creek, named after Howard Franklin, its discoverer. The following year, in 1887, prospectors found gold placers in Franklin Gulch, and in the spring of 1888 discoveries were made on Davis Creek, a headwater tributary, as well as the main Walker Fork. Further discoveries followed, and mining activities began on Dome Creek in 1893. By 1893 it was estimated that miners took out approximately $100,000 worth of gold. This increased to $400,000 in 1894. Soon thereafter the placers of Wade Creek were located in 1895, and those of Chicken Creek were found in the spring of 1896.

In the summer of 1893, two miners named Pitka and Sorresco, who had previously worked the Fortymile district, discovered gold on Birch Creek. The news of the strike encouraged many men in the Fortymile to seek their fortunes in the new district. By 1895 the center of the footloose mining population had shifted from Fortymile to Circle City on the banks of the Yukon. It quickly became the most important settlement in the interior, with an estimated population of seven hundred.

The Great Klondike Gold Strike

In the late fall of 1896 miners at Circle and Fortymile first heard about a discovery on the Klondike, or Throndiuck, a tributary of the Yukon River in Canada's Yukon Territory. A miner named Robert Henderson had found good prospects there, and passed the word along to George Washington Carmack. Then Carmack and two Indians, Skookum Jim and Tagish Charley, found gold in quantities never before seen on the Yukon. In one pan they scooped up four dollars worth of gold and quickly realized that

they had found a bonanza. Prospectors who realized five cents or ten cents a pan considered themselves lucky, so four dollars was unprecedented. Carmack staked his first claim in the region on August 17, 1896. After a slow start, most miners of the Fortymile district deserted their camp and staked in the Klondike. The news took longer to reach Circle City, but by the end of January most men had deserted the camp and rushed for the Klondike. When news spread to the outside world, it quickly became infected by "Klondikitis." The great rush to the new settlement at Dawson was to change Alaska.

At first it was just a rumor in Seattle that huge new gold fields had been discovered in the Klondike, but the arrival of the *Portland* from Saint Michael, on July 17, 1897, ended all speculation. Banner headlines in the *Seattle Post-Intelligencer* proclaimed: "Gold! Gold! Gold! Gold! Sixty-Eight Rich Men on the Steamer *Portland.* Stack of Yellow Metal Some Have $5,000, Many Have More, And A Few Bring Out $1,000,000 Each. The Steamer Carries $7,000,000 Special Tug Chartered by the *Post-Intelligencer* To Get The News."

From Seattle the news spread quickly and the rush was on. Thousands took off for the Klondike, using principally two routes. The first was by steamer up the inland passage to Skagway and Dyea, and from there over the White and Chilkoot passes. Both passes reached the lakes that form the headwaters of the Yukon River about forty miles inland. From there to Dawson, the new boom town, the distance was more than six hundred miles. The other route led by steamer from Seattle, through the Bering Sea to Saint Michael, then by sternwheeler upriver to Dawson.

In the meantime, the stampede to the Klondike spilled over into Alaska, and disappointed Klondikers were drawn to various Alaskan locations in their search for the yellow metal. In early 1898 a party under the leadership of Daniel B. Libby landed at Golovnin Bay on the Seward Peninsula. Eventually, in March of that year, this party found gold on what they called Mesling Creek, a tributary of the Niukluk River. Some time later the rich deposits on nearby Ophir Creek were found. Mining began in the spring of 1898, and the men recovered gold to the value of $75,000. By midsummer there were several hundred miners in the region.

The discovery did not make a big stir, but one who was attracted was Jafet

Lindeberg, a Norwegian. He made his way to Ophir Creek on the Seward Peninsula and there met two Swedes, John Brynteson and Eric O. Lindblom. These three men formed a prospecting partnership in August of 1898. They traveled to the present site of Nome, and made their way up the Snake River, prospecting as they went and finding some gold. On a stream they named Anvil Creek they found the most promising prospects and there located their discovery claim on September 22, 1898.

In a short period they recovered about $1,800 worth of coarse gold from the gravels on Anvil Creek, the first mined in the Nome district. Miners from Golovnin Bay and Ophir Creek joined them on October 18, 1898, recorded their claims, and organized the Nome mining district. Approximately forty men filed on about seven thousand acres of promising placer ground.

People were skeptical of the reports, but by late June in 1899 several vessels reached Anvil City, later called Nome, from the Puget Sound region. By the fall of 1899, the word had spread and about 3,000 people lived in Nome. By then a regular rush to the new El Dorado was under way. Soon there was claim jumping and disorder, and tensions mounted.

At that point, someone accidentally discovered that the beach sands were rich in gold. Within days, a large part of the population went to work on the beach with shovels and rockers. During the height of the excitement, as many as two thousand men worked in beach mining. The yield of the beach placers gave the settlement great prosperity. By January 1900, approximately 4,500 claims had been staked in the Nome district, but perhaps no more than fifty claims had been developed and not more than one hundred were prospected. However, those fifty claims yielded about $1.5 million in gold.

As the word spread about the new discoveries, many made preparations to leave for Nome. On May 23, 1900 the old steam whaler *Jeannie* dropped anchor at Nome, the forerunner of a large fleet to follow. By July 1, some fifty vessels had already discharged passengers and freight on the Nome beach. The census, taken in June, showed that Nome had a population of 12,488. Estimates by midsummer placed the population at over 18,000 people, in addition to some 2,000 who had wintered at Nome.

Other discoveries followed. Felix Pedro found gold on Pedro Creek near

The Organic Act of 1884 provided the first civil government for Alaska. President Chester Arthur appointed the first governor, John H. Kinkead, a former governor of Nevada. He is shown seated in this May 1885 photograph. Other appointees were, standing, from left to right: Edwin H. Haskett, attorney (from Iowa); Munson C. Hillyer, marshall (from Nevada); Ward McAllister, Junior, judge (from California); and Andrew T. Lewis, clerk (from Illinois). They are in front of the Custom House, Sitka. The photo was taken at the end of Kinkead's short term as governor. Courtesy of the Alaska Historical Library

Lieutenant W. K. Abercrombie of the Second U.S. Infantry attempted to explore the Copper River basin in 1884. He was thwarted by high waters and ice, and also had difficulty in the glaciers of the Valdez area. As a captain he later came back to the area to establish Fort Liscum. Courtesy of the U.S. Army Signal Corps Collection, Alaska Historical Library

Lieutenant Henry T. Allen of the Second U.S. Cavalry (center) with Private Fickett (left) and Sergeant Robertson (right) were able to explore the Copper River basin and continue on to the Tanana and Yukon rivers in 1885. The long arduous journey brought back new information on the Copper and Tanana rivers and news of large deposits of copper in the Chitina area. Courtesy of the Historical Photo Collection, Alaska and Polar Regions Dept., Rasmuson Library, UAF

Congress Pays Renewed Attention to Alaska

The flood of Klondike-bound gold seekers motivated Congress to consider Alaska's form of government, its resources, and their development. Between 1890 and 1900, the great land experienced an influx of more than thirty thousand persons, primarily due to the gold rush. The 1900 census showed a total population of 63,592. In 1897, President William McKinley took note of the gold rush boom, and in his first annual message observed that conditions in the North demanded significant changes in the laws relating to Alaska. In 1899 the president again reminded Congress that Alaska needed immediate legislature relief. He asked for a system of local government and at least two federal judges. Congress responded, and between 1897 and 1899 it passed two major pieces of legislation pertaining to Alaska. One, enacted before the end of 1898, made various provisions for the construction of railroads, and extended the homestead laws to the region. The size of homesteads was restricted to eighty acres, and the applicant had to bear the expenses of the survey. Prospective homesteaders were allowed to use soldier's scrip. The act also provided that Canadian citizens were accorded the same mining right as American citizens were granted in the dominion. Goods were allowed duty-free transportation between Alaskan ports and Canadian ports if Canadians granted reciprocal privileges.

Another piece of legislation in 1899 clarified punishment of crime in Alaska, and also gave the North a code of criminal procedure. It was a lengthy and complicated act, which codified the Oregon laws and modified them for Alaska. It included a rudimentary system of taxation, the first levied in the district. It imposed license fees for forty occupations, varying from $250 annually for banks, to $500 for breweries. Mercantile establishments paid on a sliding scale. Those who grossed $100,000 per year paid $500. The act finally legalized the sale of liquor and imposed a tax on the dealer. There were various other taxes, such as those on railroads and canned salmon. The funds derived from these taxes and license fees were to pay for Alaska's government. The system, with only slight modifications, persisted for almost fifty years.

the present site of Fairbanks in 1902; gold was discovered at Valdez Creek in 1903; Kantishna in 1905; Chandalar in 1906; Iditarod in 1909, Nelshina in 1912; Marshall in 1913; and Livengood in 1914.

As in other mining regions of the frontier West, Alaskan miners' meetings and law (the so-called miners' codes), helped fill the local governmental void. Under the authority of this code the miners not only made their own regulations for their claims, but they also enacted rules and regulations which concerned community affairs. In the larger settlements, local law enforcement officers, rudimentary court systems, and elected mayors, councils, and other officials began to appear in time.

Governor Kinkead was followed by Alfred P. Swineford, whom President Grover Cleveland appointed in 1885. An itinerant printer in Wisconsin and Minnesota, Swineford also studied law and was admitted to the Minnesota bar in 1857. From 1853 to 1867 he was the editor and publisher of the *Mining Journal* in Marquette, Michigan. He served in the Michigan state house of representatives, and as Michigan's commissioner of mineral statistics.

After a stint as Alaska's governor from 1885 to 1889 Swineford returned to Michigan, then served as inspector-general of the U.S. Land Office in Washington, D.C. from 1893 to 1898. He went back to Alaska and became the publisher of the Ketchikan *Mining Journal* from 1901 to 1905 and the Ketchikan *Miner* from 1907-1908, the two papers merging in the meantime. He had mining interests on Prince of Wales Island and died in Juneau on October 26, 1909. Swineford also authored a volume entitled *Alaska, Its History, Climate and Natural Resources.* Courtesy of the Alaska Historical Library

This is a picnic at Sitka in the 1880s. Governor Swineford and his friends dined from china on the fern-covered table. Photo by E. DeGroff; courtesy of the Alaska Historical Library

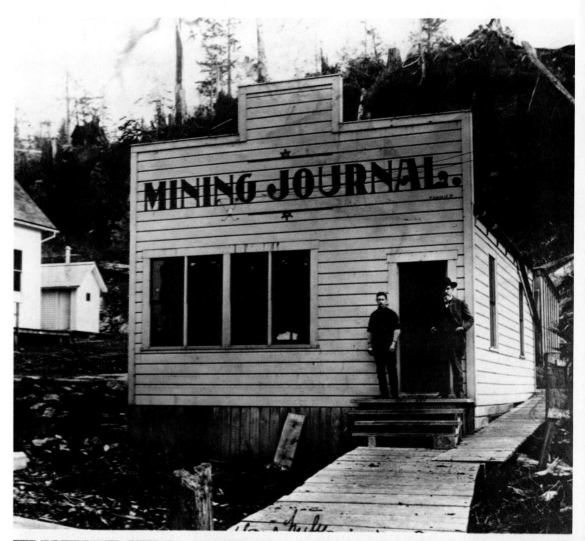

Legislators and citizens both were interested in the economic development of Alaska, and in the wake of the various gold rushes, schemes to exploit the territory's riches and make it self-supporting abounded. Investors were attracted by gold and other minerals, and numerous companies competed for railway franchises. The federal government extended much help, and as early as 1897 the Department of Agriculture sent agents to the territory to assess its agricultural potential. Based on their recommendations, several agricultural experiment stations were established, the first at Sitka in 1898. Others followed at Kenai; Kodiak; Rampart; Copper Center; Fairbanks; and last, at Matanuska in 1917.

Congress again passed numerous Alaskan measures between 1899 to 1901, including bills dealing with Native welfare; education; the judiciary; fisheries; and reindeer (introduced by Sheldon Jackson in the 1890s). In 1900 Congress passed a civil code and a code of civil procedure.

With this latter piece, Congress dealt directly with the problem of providing a general governmental system for Alaska. The district was divided into three regions, and courts were established at Sitka, Nome, and Eagle City on the Yukon, with authority to convene elsewhere when necessary. The president appointed the three judges, and the act also made possible the incorporation of municipalities for the first time. Finally, in 1904, amending and codifying legislation passed. This, together with the act of 1900, was the beginning of statutory self-government in Alaska.

Developing A Transportation System

The development of an adequate transportation system was very important. The Klondike gold rush had greatly increased steamboat traffic on the Yukon, and later, the Tanana River. There were few roads or trails. When the Army returned to Alaska during the gold rushes, it undertook a number of notable explorations, and in 1900 again created the "Department of Alaska." It located garrisons at Fort Davis near Nome, Fort Saint Michael near the mouth of the Yukon River, Fort Gibbon near Tanana, Fort Egbert at Eagle, Fort Liscum near Valdez, and Fort William H. Seward at Haines. It soon became obvious that the

military forts needed to be connected by telegraph and cable lines and then tied into Washington, D.C. Work on constructing the Washington-Alaska Military Cable and Telegraph System, or WAMCATS as it was called, got underway promptly. In just a little over three years the men of the U.S. Army Signal Corps completed the 1,506 miles of overland lines and a few hundred miles of submarine cables, a truly impressive achievement. By 1904 the Alaska system was connected to the contiguous states.

The United States Senate appointed a subcommittee of its Committee on Territories to journey to Alaska in 1903 and make a "thorough investigation of existing conditions, her resources and her needs, with the purpose to ascertain what, if any, legislation is required for that district." The four senators assigned to the subcommittee met in Seattle and sailed for Alaska on June 28, 1903. They traveled widely, and heard much testimony. On their return to Washington, D.C., they summarized their impressions to their colleagues. They had been awed by Alaska's vastness and surprised at the lack of transportation facilities. The senators recommended that the government construct a system of transportation routes, and that the basis for such a system should be a well-built wagon road connecting the Pacific Ocean at Valdez with Eagle on the Yukon River, a distance of about four hundred miles. They made other recommendations, and in early 1904 a deluge of Alaska bills descended on both houses.

Creation of the Board of Road Commissioners for Alaska

Among these many bills was one introduced by Senator Knute Nelson of Minnesota which created a Board of Road Commissioners for Alaska. Placed under the War Department, it was to consist of an engineer officer of the U.S. Army to be appointed by the Secretary of War and two other officers drawn from troops stationed in Alaska. The board was empowered "upon their own motion or petition, to locate, lay out, construct, and maintain wagon roads and pack trails from any point on the navigable waters... to any town, mining or other industrial camp or settlement, between any such town, camps or settlements...,if in their judgment such roads or trails are needed and will be of permanent value for the development of the district." The board also was to construct, repair and maintain tramways, ferries, bridges, aviation fields, and military and post roads. It was a tall order, but in 1926 the Alaska Road Commission, as the Board was now referred to, reported that it had built 1,433.5 miles of wagon roads, 100 miles of tramroads, 1,086 miles of sled roads, 6,671.5 miles of permanent trails, and 712 miles of temporary flagged trails, for a total of 10,003 miles. Between 1905 and 1926, the organization had expanded a total of $10,813,165.11 on its work. It had achieved a great deal. Transferred to the Department of the Interior in 1932, the Alaska Road Commission continued its activities until 1956, when the Bureau of Public Roads absorbed it.

Railroad Plans

Perhaps lured by the prospect of fabulous profits, some eleven companies reportedly petitioned for railroad right-of-ways between September 1897 and March 1898. Several more applied, but the economic panic brought speculation to a halt in 1907. In 1903 the Alaska Central Railroad began construction from Seward toward the interior, but went bankrupt in 1908. It reorganized as the Alaskan Northern Railroad, and finished 71 miles of track before it ceased operation. Several narrow-gauge railroads served local needs, such as one on the Seward Peninsula and another one in the Tanana Valley. Only two railroads made any money: the White Pass and Yukon Railroad, built to connect Skagway with Whitehorse, in Canada's Yukon Territory; and the Copper River and Northwestern Railway, completed by the Alaska Syndicate primarily to carry copper ore from its mines at Kennecott to the port of Cordova.

Land Claims in Alaska

President Theodore Roosevelt (1901-1909) made the conservation of natural resources a major concern of his so-called Square Deal program. Gifford Pinchot, a close friend and adviser of the president as well as the first chief forester of the United States, became the major advocate of a comprehensive national program of conservation. Roosevelt and Pinchot believed that all basic resources, such as forests, farm and range lands, and minerals and water, in either private or public ownership, should be used wisely and with the least possible waste. In case of danger to the public interest, they maintained, the federal government could legally require proper utilization practices.

Many uncertainties and ambiguities surrounded the existing land laws, so in order to clear these President Roosevelt appointed a Public Lands Commission in 1903 to investigate and report upon the whole question. The commission recommended that Congress repeal or modify unsuitable laws and close existing loopholes. And although the commission never officially completed its work, it continued as an informal group of administration leaders who supported a new set of land management principles. Pinchot and his supporters argued that the old practice of disposing of nonagricultural lands to private owners should cease, and be replaced by public ownership and management.

Efficient land management, however, required an exact knowledge and careful classification of resources. Eventually, after 1905, the Roosevelt administration began a more systematic program of classifying all public domain resources, including water power sites; and coal, oil, and phosphate lands. On November 12, 1906, Roosevelt directed Ethan A. Hitchcock, the secretary of the interior, to withdraw from entry all valuable coal lands until they could be examined and properly classified.

The president's 1906 withdrawal order halted all further location of coal claims in Alaska, and also stopped proofs and payments on existing locations. On May 16, 1907, however, the executive modified the order, allowing those claims located before November 12, 1906, and found to be legal, to proceed to patent. He also asked Congress to pass a coal leasing act, and asked that the law be changed to meet Alaska's peculiar needs.

While the 1907 executive order modified the 1906 withdrawal order and granted certain grandfather rights, it also directed the cancellation of claims found to be defective or fraudulent upon investigation by the General Land Office, particularly if evidence showed intention to consolidate claims. Approximately 900 claims in Alaska awaited investigation. Of these, thirty-three were known as the "Cunningham claims," covering about five thousand acres in the Bering River coal field.

Although some people thought the Cunningham claims were fraudulent because of intention to consolidate, on December 26, 1907 Richard A. Ballinger,

Richard Harris and Joseph Juneau were two miners who had been staked by George Pilz and N. A. Fuller of Sitka to prospect along the Gastineau Channel. They found gold-bearing quartz in the area. A rush was soon on and a town founded. It was at first called Harrisburg but renamed Juneau in 1881. Juneau went on to the Klondike and Harris eventually left Alaska. Courtesy of the Alaska Historical Library

In 1896 the city of Juneau was still rough but growing fast. Lumber and firewood lined the narrow dirt streets. Courtesy of the Rose Collection, Alaska and Polar Regions Dept., Rasmuson Library, UAF

The Franklin Hotel in Juneau was a popular establishment in the 1890s. In this picture a group of guests is gathered on the wide boardwalk. Firewood is stacked in the foreground. Courtesy of the Alaska Historical Library

head of the General Land Office, ordered that they be processed for patenting. On January 22, 1908, Louis R. Glavis, chief of the Portland field office then investigating entries for the General Land Office, filed an adverse report on the Cunningham claims, and the following month Ballinger informed the Cunningham claimants that their entries had been suspended. In March Ballinger left the General Land Office and returned to private law practice in Seattle.

The May 28, 1908 Alaska Coal Act,

The G. A. Anderson store on Seward Street in Juneau was in a large and substantial building. It carried ship and mining supplies as well as general hardware. A church reading room was in the back of the building, and notices were posted on the pole at the front corner of the building. Courtesy of the Alaska Historical Library

which did not contain a leasing system, permitted consolidation of claims up to 2,560 acres. The act prevented the monopolization of Alaskan coal and eliminated the use of dummy entrymen, that is, individuals who claimed lands with the intention of conveying them to someone else.

As later investigations revealed, the Cunningham claimants had illegally in-

tended to consolidate their claims before locating them. The story broke in 1909, and a bitter and lengthy controversy ensued about the validity of these claims. The dispute, which became known as the Ballinger-Pinchot Affair, quickly assumed political overtones. Historians and others generally agree that it contributed to the subsequent political eclipse of President William Howard Taft, helped split the

In 1897 sons and daughters of the pioneers posed in Juneau for Winter and Pond, prolific photographers who did much to record the area and the people. These handsome young people had been brought up in a new mining town before the Klondike gold rush made Alaska and the Yukon common words in the rest of the United States. Courtesy of the Alaska Historical Society

92

Across the channel from Juneau another big discovery was made by Peter Errusard. John Treadwell bought Errusard's claims and developed the Treadwell Mine on Douglas Island, which proved to be among the most productive quartz gold mines in the world. The mine grew into a major complex of buildings and facilities and the town of Douglas grew with it. Douglas can be seen on the left with a dock extending into the channel. Juneau is in the distance, across the channel beyond the island. Courtesy of the Harold Fox Collection, Alaska Historical Library

Republican Party, and aided Democrat Woodrow Wilson in gaining the presidency. The General Land Office cancelled the Cunningham claims in 1911.

A Delegate to Congress

In May of 1906, before this scandal broke, Congress passed a measure allowing Alaskans representation in the House of Representatives by electing a delegate to Congress. This delegate would act as a nonvoting member of the House of Representatives, receiving the same salary and allowances as his colleagues. He would serve on committees, speak on the floor, and introduce bills. ·

Soon, territorial Democrats and Republicans held conventions to select their first candidates for the position of delegate. But despite vigorous campaigns, the major party candidates were defeated by the "Independent" nominees of the Seward Peninsula and the Tanana region miners. In accordance with the 1906 act a prosperous young miner, Frank Waskey, was elected to serve for the rest of the current congressional session. Thomas Cale, a middle-aged, popular, but financially unsuccessful pioneer, was victorious for the first full term to start in 1907. The Waskey-Cale platform had included a demand for a territorial form of government. In the 1908 election, Alaskans chose former federal judge James Wickersham, a powerful personality who was to dominate territorial politics for the first three decades of the twentieth century. It was he who succeeded in pushing the second Organic Act through Congress in 1912.

The Second Organic Act

In 1912, Congress passed the Second Organic Act which provided Alaska with an elected legislature. The work of this body was subject to the veto of a federally appointed governor and to approval or disapproval by Congress. The act prescribed the structure of the territorial legislature, the nature of its membership, the method of electing members, and its general internal organization and procedures. Additionally, specific limitations were based on its authority. For example, the management of Alaska's fur, game, and fishery resources remained a federal responsibility. The governor was given

broad responsibilities. But despite all of its apparent defects, the Second Organic Act of 1912 ended Alaska's mysterious legal and constitutional status. It specifically stated that "The Constitution...shall have the same force and effect within the Territory of Alaska as elsewhere in the United States." The distinction between an incorporated territory and a district was a crucial one, because the former was destined for statehood while the latter was not.

The first territorial legislature was to convene "at the capitol at the city of Juneau, Alaska, on the first Monday in March" in 1913, and on the same date every two years thereafter. The first legislature convened in a temporary capitol, the Elks Hall in Juneau, rented for the session. With the first piece of legislation the lawmakers passed they gave the franchise to Alaskan women, long before politically or constitutionally required to do so. The second measure established legal holidays for the territory, including Alaska Day. Other laws enacted during that first session established the Alaska Pioneers' Home; created the office of territorial treasurer; regulated the practice of medicine and dentistry; added to the existing system of taxation, including a poll tax; provided for compulsory education; established juvenile courts; and created a system for registering vital statistics. The lawmakers also passed much labor legislation, including a workman's compensation law, the eight-hour day for work on territorial and municipal projects, and the declaration that mining and associated occupations were of a dangerous nature

and subject to the eight-hour day rule. It also prohibited the dumping of sawdust, planer shavings, and other lumber waste into Alaskan waters. A total of $75,143.75 was appropriated for the biennium (although at least $11,000 of this amount was not expended).

The Federal Government Constructs A Railroad

The federal government finally realized that Alaska presented too many obstacles for private enterprise, and Congress authorized the construction of a railroad in 1914. In April of 1915 it began building the railroad which ran from Seward, on the coast, to Fairbanks in the interior, but the work was not finished until 1923. Railroad construction generated a boom in Alaska, with more than 2,000 men working on the railroad in 1914. Eventually, about 4,500 men worked on the project. Anchorage, now Alaska's largest city, owes its beginnings to the railroads. Starting as a construction site, it eventually became the headquarters for the Alaska Engineering Commission, which supervised construction, and became the center for railroad maintenance as well.

The Jones Act

While the federal government built the railroad, Congress passed the U.S. Mari-

"Ready Bullion" was one section of the Treadwell Mine. At the 1,500-foot level miners worked well below sea level. Courtesy of the J. N. Dexter Collection, Alaska Historical Library

The Treadwell Mine was productive until a major cave-in and resultant flooding closed it in 1917. It was never able to recover, and eventually the buildings were removed or destroyed by fire. Courtesy of the Gibson Collection, Alaska and Polar Regions Dept., Rasmuson Library, UAF

time Act which placed restrictions on Alaskan commerce. Commonly called the Jones Act after Senator Wesley Jones of Washington State, its prime sponsor, the main purpose of the legislation was to build up the American merchant marine. All goods traveling between American ports had to be carried on American-owned and built ships. A clause of the act gave shippers the choice of using either American or Canadian-owned transportation in carrying goods from a point of origin in the United States to any destination on the Atlantic or Pacific. Alaska was the single exception. In effect, this gave Seattle a monopoly on the Alaskan trade.

Alaska's Economy

By the time the United States entered the First World War, Alaska's economy could best be defined as a colonial one—that is, the territory was primarily a supplier of raw materials to the mother country from whom she obtained most of her finished goods. It was Alaska's remoteness and difficult geography which were responsible for this condition, not government decree. Alaska supplied furs, fish, gold, and various other minerals, and after 1911, copper as well. These extractive industries were seasonal, employed men, and were not conducive to settlement and the growth of a permanent population. Indeed, the First World War created employment opportunities in the contiguous states which drained population from Alaska. Census statistics between 1910 and 1920 showed a drop of 9,320 in the population.

President Warren G. Harding Visits Alaska

In 1921 Warren G. Harding of Ohio succeeded Woodrow Wilson as president of the United States. In that same year, Secretary of the Interior Albert B. Fall proposed to centralize all responsibility for the management and development of Alaska's resources under a single, responsible head, and also proposed that Alaska's resources be exploited quickly. This proposal prompted Harding to visit Alaska pesonally. The occasion offered itself after the completion of the Alaska Railroad in 1923. Harding came north and drove the official golden spike near Nenana, and visited other parts of the territory. He made speeches and listened a great deal to what citizens had to say. After his return to the states, the president delivered a major talk at the University of Washington stadium on July 27, 1923. He spoke of the future of the territory and indicated that he opposed radical changes in its administration. He rejected the idea of a sudden exploitation of Alaska's resources such as Secretary Fall had advocated, and, instead, endorsed the conservation policies of his predecessors. The president favored a slow, planned evolution which would protect Alaska's natural resources but yet permit their gradual use. He also declared that Alaska was destined for ultimate statehood. After traveling to San Francisco, the president died. Years later Ernest Gruening, former territorial governor and later U.S. senator from Alaska, once stated that Alaska "lost a great friend at court" with the president's death.

Decline of the Salmon Fishery

It was during the Harding administration that the federal government made a serious attempt to deal with the catastrophic decline of the Alaskan salmon fishery. Overfishing had seriously depleted the runs, but government regulation was largely ineffective. Numerous acts and regulations had addressed the problem before, but by 1921 the salmon fisheries were in a real crisis. Herbert Hoover, serving as secretary of commerce in the Harding administration, held lengthy hearings, but was unable to secure the legislation he felt was necessary to restore the resource. He therefore recommended that the president, by executive order, temporarily establish reserves in which fishing was to be by permit only. After much controversy, Congress finally passed the White Act which President Calvin Coolidge signed into law in 1924. A complex measure, it put salmon conservation on a scientific basis.

Troubles with the Alaska Railroad

Alaskans had welcomed the opening of the Alaska Railroad, but it soon became apparent that the construction had been of poor quality. The costs of operation, as a consequence, were unusually high. Successive railroad managers worried about continuous defects. Maintenance costs were high, the rail belt population remained small, and load factors were low. Still, the railroad was accused of taking business away from steamboats, and therefore causing a decline in river commerce. Worse, there always seemed to be individuals in Congress who talked about abandoning the line. During the administration of President Coolidge, the territory did not fare well. ■

Seattle was the major departure point for those heading north to the Gold Rush. Steamers plied the inland passage to Skagway and Juneau. Others went further to Nome or to Saint Michael where connection could be made with the riverboats going up the Yukon and Tanana rivers to Dawson and Fairbanks. Many small and unreliable vessels were pressed into use during the height of the traffic. There were few women in this well-dressed group on a Seattle dock in the early 1900s. Courtesy of the Norma Hoyt Collection

This shot was taken aboard a ship in Alaskan waters, in 1888. This is obviously a comfortable and well-cared-for vessel. Courtesy of the A. Shattuck Collection, Alaska Historical Library

Fort Egbert, near Eagle on the Yukon River, was close to the Canadian border. Traffic on the Yukon to the Klondike was heavy, and later miners stampeded along the Yukon to the strikes at Nome and Fairbanks. Today some of the buildings of the fort still stand and have been restored. Courtesy of the Anchorage Historical and Fine Arts Museum

July 4, 1886 was celebrated with a thirty-nine-gun salute by the small military detachment at Sitka. The town was called New Archangel by the Russians, but was called Sitka, a Tlingit Indian name, after the transfer. In the background is a blockhouse that once formed part of the fortification around the Russian town. The fenced graves of the cemetery are to the right of the blockhouse. Courtesy of the Historical Photograph Collection, Alaska and Polar Regions Dept., Rasmuson Library, UAF

Tanana, near the confluence of the Tanana and Yukon rivers, was on the route to both the Klondike and the gold camps of the Fairbanks area. It had been the site of Native gatherings for many years and grew in its crossroads position with the army post close by. The sign in front of the restaurant advertises the special of the day: "April 26th, Turkey Dinner, $1.50." Courtesy of the N. Todd Collection, Alaska Historical Library

Tanana was a prosperous community with a variety of services available to the people of the area. It was ideally situated to serve the river trade. A stern-wheel steamer, a barge, and local boats are drawn up at the waterfront. Docks or other waterfront structures were seldom built along the rivers

because of the destructive power of the ice and current at breakup. Courtesy of the Norma Hoyt Collection

Sheldon Jackson, a Presbyterian Missionary, was born in Minaville, New York on May 13, 1834. Assigned to mission work in the Rocky Mountain district in 1865, he went to Alaska in 1877 and founded missions at Wrangell, Sitka, Haines, and Prince of Wales Island. Jackson favored the Harrison Act of 1884, creating a civil government for Alaska. He lobbied and lectured throughout the United States, and wrote magazine articles. Appointed General Agent of Education for Alaska, he persuaded various religious groups to establish missions in the North. He also persuaded the U.S. Congress to support the importation of reindeer from Siberia for starving Eskimos. Jackson retired in 1908 and died in Washington, D.C. in 1909. Courtesy of the Sheldon Jackson College Collection

In 1891 Dr. Sheldon Jackson and Captain M. A. Healy, commander of the U.S. Revenue Cutter *Bear*, used $2,146 collected from private sources to purchase and transfer sixteen live reindeer to the Aleutian Islands to test deer reaction to the voyage. In 1892 the first reindeer arrived on the Seward peninsula at Port Clarence, together with four Siberian natives to instruct Eskimos in animal husbandry and construct the first reindeer station. In 1894 the Siberians returned to their homes and six Lapp herders arrived to instruct Native apprentices. On July 30, 1898 sixty-seven Lapp, Finn, and Norwegian families arrived to care for the herds on the Seward peninsula. By the turn of the century there were a few thousand reindeer on the Seward peninsula and the federal government paid the bill. The Lapp herders in this picture probably were photographed in

Scandinavia. Courtesy of the H. Levy Collection, Alaska and Polar Regions Dept., Rasmuson Library, UAF

The Sitka Training School, founded in 1878, later became the Sheldon Jackson School and then Sheldon Jackson College. Some of the staff and families posed between 1900 and 1910. Those who can be identified are Phoebe Whitmark in the white shirtwaist on the lowest step; Esther Gibson, nurse, with "zigzag" trim on her dress, left center; W. G. Beattie, superintendent, far left on porch; George Beck, assistant superintendent, center-right; and Adeline Carter, assistant matron, seated, bottom-center. Jackson worked hard raising money for this school and other mission activities. Courtesy of the Sheldon Jackson Collection

Sitka looked like this in 1890. The old Russian warehouse is in the foreground. The old Russian "castle" just above it has a rundown and abandoned look. Courtesy of the Bunnell Collection, Alaska and Polar Regions Dept., Rasmuson Library, UAF

Sitka was a small isolated settlement in 1887. The First Organic Act of 1884 had ended naval rule in Alaska and the commercial enthusiasm that followed the purchase had died down. Hope of prosperity had dwindled, although gold had been discovered in the Juneau area. At the far right can be seen the buildings of Sheldon Jackson College, which had been founded in 1878. Courtesy of the Anchorage Historical and Fine Arts Museum

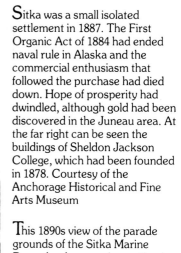

This 1890s view of the parade grounds of the Sitka Marine Barracks shows an inspection in progress. Courtesy of the Alaska Historical Library

To the left of this photograph, taken at Sitka, is the small Russian steamer *Rose*. The Alaska Oil and Guano Company at Killisnoo bought the steamer and used it for whaling. It was the cause of an incident at Angoon which led to a naval bombardment of that community by the U.S.R.C. *Corwin*. The *Jamestown* is in the center of this 1894 scene. Courtesy of the Walter A. Soboleff Collection, Alaska and Polar Regions Dept., Rasmuson Library, UAF

Here, Sitka is shown, about 1898, when a few tourists were beginning to appear. The Sitka Trading Company is at the right in one of the old Russian buildings. Just beyond is a small establishment advertising general merchandise and photographs by E. de Groff. The sign on the roof just to the right of the church also advertises "Alaska Views, Curios." Courtesy of the Historic Photograph Collection, Alaska and Polar Regions Dept., Rasmuson Library, UAF

Major General Adolphus W. Greely, head of the Signal Corps, was in charge of developing telegraphic communication between the widespread military outposts. About 1900 he was photographed at Fort Liscum with an unidentified group. (Greely is the bearded man in the center.) Fort Liscum at Valdez, Fort Davis at Nome, Fort Egbert at Eagle, Fort Gibbon at Tanana, and Fort Seward near Haines were all important to protect the routes to the newly discovered gold fields. The headquarters for "The Department of Alaska" was at Saint Michael. Courtesy of the U.S. Army Signal Corps Collection, Alaska Historical Library

This photo labelled "Co. F 3rd Reg. U.S. Army Fort Liscum, Alaska" shows the men lined up with their bedrolls on a street in Valdez. There seems to be an informality about the way the hats and other parts of the uniform are worn. The sergeant at the left had difficulty suppressing a laugh.

Courtesy of the Whalen Collection, Alaska and Polar Regions Dept., Rasmuson Library, UAF

103

Men assemble in front of the buildings at Fort Gibbon. The buildings were well built and attractive, and were probably constructed from plans used at other Army posts of the period. Courtesy of the N. Todd Collection, Alaska Historical Library

Some of the riverboats used on Alaskan rivers were built in Alaska rather than having them make the difficult voyage across the Gulf of Alaska. This 1898 scene in the Aleutians shows a sternwheeler under construction. Courtesy of the M. Murphy Collection, Alaska and Polar Regions Dept., Rasmuson Library, UAF

The river steamer *Reliance* of Saint Michael was a small sternwheeler of a type commonly found working the rivers of interior Alaska. These steamers relied on wood that was cut, stacked, and ready to be loaded for fuel at the many wood camps and villages along the rivers. The *Reliance* is shown pulled up in Fairbanks below the steel bridge which was built across the Chena River in 1917. Courtesy of the Norma Hoyt Collection

104

Fort Seward (at left) near Haines (at right) was at the end of the Inland Passage. From Haines the Chilkat (or Dalton) Trail led over the mountains to the gold rush town of Dawson. It was close to Skagway and Dyea, where miners used the Chilkoot Pass and the White Pass heading for the Klondike. Courtesy of the Norma Hoyt Collection

This is the Kadeshan house, with totems before it, at Wrangell. The steamer *Queen* is at the dock. Kadeshan was a chief in the early 1900s. Courtesy of the Alaska Historical Library

A sternwheeler pushes two barges up the Yukon, probably to Dawson, about 1900. Several enclosed barges of this kind were refrigerated and carried luxury food items to the booming city. Courtesy of the *Fairbanks Daily News-Miner*

105

With the discovery of gold in the Klondike, fortune hunters headed north. Most had no idea how remote Dawson was or how difficult to reach. Many died along the way. From Skagway, at the northern end of the Inland Passage, the long hike to Dawson began. One of its challenges was the trail over the Chilkoot pass. In 1898 stampeders gathered at the Scales, a small level area, before the final climb to the summit. The Canadian authorities required they bring supplies for one year, a full ton, before they could enter Canadian territory. The stampeders stored their supplies at this point before joining the single ascending line, then returned for other loads till the supplies for a year were at the top. Many quit here when they saw the 30 degree climb. Hegg photo, courtesy of the Anchorage Historical and Fine Arts Museum

This photo of miners and packers climbing the "Golden Stair" trail at Chilkoot Pass was a view for the then popular stereopticon. Over the pass lay Lake Bennett and the Yukon River and one man carries part of a canoe. Today, there is still a pile of abandoned collapsible boats along the trail. Photos by P. E. Larss, courtesy of the Alaska Historical Library

Another route from Skagway to the Klondike was over the White Pass. It was a gentler climb than the Chilkoot, but on the other side was a swampy, badly marked trail to Lake Bennett. At higher elevations these families will probably find snow for their sleds, and terrain to challenge the horse. Courtesy of the Bassoc Collection, Alaska and Polar Regions Dept., Rasmuson Library, UAF

Skagway was wide open, and Jefferson Randolph "Soapy" Smith ruled it for a short time in 1898, until he was killed in July by Frank Reid. He is shown in his saloon with some of his cohorts. Larss and Duclos photo, courtesy of the Alaska Historical Library

The White Pass was chosen as the route for a railroad to the Yukon. By July 6, 1899 the first forty miles of rail were complete to Lake Bennett. The first locomotive in Alaska was looked over in Skagway on July 20, 1898. Courtesy of the Fairbanks Daily News-Miner

This view shows the narrow gauge railroad and a train at the summit of the White Pass. Courtesy of the F. B. Bourne Collection, Alaska Historical Library

172

Another possibility for getting to the Klondike lay over the Chilkat Pass north of Haines. The route was known as the Dalton trail after Jack Dalton who surveyed it. It was an easier route suitable for animals, but all overland and longer. Dalton had earlier been at Juneau and this photo was probably taken there. Courtesy of the Alaska Historical Library

In September 1898 John Brynteson, Jafet Lindeberg, and Erick O. Lindblom discovered gold on Anvil Creek on the Seward peninsula. The news went out to Dawson, where disappointed men were looking for new hope, and to Seattle where more were ready to head for a chance at wealth. By the summer of 1899 the rush was on. Courtesy of the *Fairbanks Daily News-Miner*

DISCOVERERS OF THE NOME GOLD FIELDS.
Jafet Lindeberg.
John Brynteson.   E. O. Lindblom.

There was no harbor at Nome, and the sea was shallow, forcing ships to anchor well out and lighter goods and passengers to shore. The beach ridge was the only dry ground available as the tundra further inland was low and soggy. Materials were stored and construction concentrated on the low ridge. Because there were no trees or building materials of any kind available great quantities of material were shipped in and piled up on the beach. Townsites and claims were in dispute and tents sprang up everywhere. The excitement increased when the beach sands were found to contain gold. Eighteen thousand people were supposed to have arrived in 1900. Courtesy of the Mulligan Album, Alaska and Polar Regions Dept., Rasmuson Library, UAF

In 1900 Nome was growing and the streets were full. Saloons and dancehalls were plentiful. Courtesy of the Bunnel Collection, Alaska and Polar Regions Dept., Rasmuson Library, UAF

The Golden Gate Hotel was one of the more elegant establishments in Nome in the early 1900s. Courtesy of the Norma Hoyt Collection

The John J. Swenson Company's cableway in Nome was one of the systems tried to unload ships and barges. Hay and grain had to be imported in great quantities to feed the horses and mules that served the freighting companies and the mines. Courtesy of the Norma Hoyt Collection

Mining the beach at Nome was popular because it required little equipment—a rocker, shovel, and bucket would do—and it was easy to reach. A lot of the debris in the background is driftwood that had washed up for years along the shore. That resource was also exhausted as the hordes of goldseekers tried to keep warm through the bitter winters of the Seward peninsula. Courtesy of the Bunnell Collection, Alaska and Polar Regions Dept., Rasmuson Library, UAF

While many worked the beach sands with rockers and pans, there were others who looked for bigger and faster methods. This is one of many that were tried and abandoned. Courtesy of the A. G. Simmer Collection, Alaska Historical Library

Abandoned Machine for working the Beach. Nome, Alaska.

The banks of Nome were important and imposing institutions. The polished wood and the shining glass was in marked contrast to the rough shacks of many miners. They handled the more than seven million dollars in gold that was taken out by 1906. An assay office is at the end of the row of teller's windows. Photograph by B. B. Dobbs, courtesy of the Alaska Historical Library

The Rowe Transfer Company in Nome posed its staff and equipment on October 20, 1907. The horses were groomed, the harnesses cleaned, and the wagons loaded. They gave the impression of a well-run, prosperous outfit. Many who provided the equipment and services that the miners needed had more success than the miners. Courtesy of the Skinner Foundation Collection, Alaska Historical Library

Rowe Transfer. Nome Alaska Oct 20 1907

The caption on this photo reads: "'May Day' in the Northland—On the Ice Hummocks of the Bering Sea opposite Nome, Alaska, 1910." By this time Nome was an established and stable town, with large companies doing the mining, and a business community that was growing.

Outdoor pleasures included skiing and sledding. In this group many of the Lomen family appear. The Lomens were involved in many enterprises, but they are most often remembered for developing a reindeer industry. From left to right, the members of the group are: Bottom row, Mr. Hanks, Parker Hilton, Mrs. Treagove, Mrs. McManus, W. D. Fleming, Mrs. Jeffort, Mrs. Hanks, and O. B. Wist. Middle row, on the ice, Carl Lomen, George Lomen, unidentified, L. L. Scott, Helen Lomen, and Hazel Murray. Top row, "Pop" Lomen, Joseph Jourden, Mrs. Jourden, Mrs. Otto Watson, Mrs. George Lomen, E. C. Devine, Mrs. Lomen, Master Andrews, and H. Lomen. The man at the very top of the ice hill is unidentified. Lomen Brothers photo, courtesy of the Anchorage Historical and Fine Arts Museum

The well-built ski jump implies a popular sport. The action in this 1906 photo taken at Nome is remarkable for the time. Courtesy of the Alaska Historical Library

The Chancy Cowden residence in Nome, 1908 was carefully and elaborately decorated. Notice the tube from the ceiling fixture to the gas lamp on the table. Courtesy of the Anchorage Historical and Fine Arts Museum

This scene shows the interior of a Third Avenue home in Seward in the early 1900s. With her fire in the stove, her phonograph, and mementos of the family about, the woman reading in the rocker looks comfortably settled. Courtesy of the Wheatley Album, Anchorage Historical and Fine Arts Museum

Miners came to Fairbanks by many routes. The most difficult at first was the trail from Valdez over the Alaska Range. Just a little way from Valdez was the first challenge, Thompson Pass, which involved a long steep climb to a windblown summit. Courtesy of the Norma Hoyt Collection

Felix Pedro, an Italian immigrant, discovered gold in the Fairbanks district on July 22, 1902. By chance, the trader E. T. Barnette had landed a cache of supplies at the present site of Fairbanks. With the stampede to the area the trading post became a permanent town.

Gold was not easy to recover in the Fairbanks district. The gold lay in gravel under a layer of frozen muck and the gravel had to be brought up from shafts to where it could be run through the sluice boxes. Miners worked through the winter bringing up the gravel to be washed in the warmer weather when water was available. Photo by A. J. Johnson, courtesy of the Alaska Historical Library

Fairbanks in 1904 was a primitive camp. Buildings like the Northern Commercial Company were going up along the Chena River waterfront and small cabins and tents were being erected in the new townsite. Some of the original Northern Commercial Company buildings are now occupied by the Nordstrom store. The men shown here have gathered for the arrival of the steamer from which this photo was taken. Courtesy of the Jones Collection, Alaska and Polar Regions Dept., Rasmuson Library, UAF

E.T. Barnette, the trader who founded Fairbanks, was seldom photographed, This undated photo shows him in the center of the group. Courtesy of the Norma Hoyt Collection

In 1900 President William McKinley appointed James Wickersham judge for the third judicial district in Alaska. This new position was to be at Eagle City, 100 miles down the Yukon from Dawson and the Klondike gold strike. After the discovery of gold in the Fairbanks area, Judge Wickersham moved his court to the rapidly growing community. This picture of the judge feeding a moose dates from the early 1900s. Courtesy of the Lulu Fairbanks Collection

The Tanana Valley Railroad ran from Chena on the Tanana River to the mining camps north of Fairbanks, ending at Chatanika. It was one of several small railroads promoters developed in the territory to profit from the expected mining boom. Mrs. E. T. Barnette, wife of the founder of Fairbanks, drove the golden spike completing the line. She is at the right smiling and holding it to be seen. To her left, without a hat, is Judge James Wickersham, who had moved his court from Eagle to Fairbanks, where he expected the mining district to prosper. He gave an address on this occasion. Courtesy of the *Fairbanks Daily News-Miner*

DRIVING GOLDEN SPIKE, TANANA VALLEY RY. FAIRBANKS, ALASKA

Golden City on Pedro Creek · 1905

Many small mining towns grew on the creeks north of Fairbanks which served as a supply center. The Tanana Valley Railroad connected many of them. Golden City near Felix Pedro's original discovery was one of these short-lived camps. Two hotels and a saloon were its main business establishments. Anchorage Historical and Fine Arts Museum

118

Rika's Roadhouse at the Tanana River crossing was a major stop along the Richardson Highway. This roadhouse, like many others, was practically a self-sufficient homestead, raising animals and vegetables for the dining room and heating the building with local wood. The guylines in the center of the photo helped support the tower from which the cable that guided the ferry ran to the other side of the Tanana River. Courtesy of the Anchorage Historical and Fine Arts Museum

This small building belonged to Meier's Roadhouse on the Richardson highway, a popular stop for early stages and travellers. In 1975 the last remaining buildings of the establishment still stood at the side of the road. Courtesy of Richardson Highway Project, Alaska and Polar Regions Dept., Rasmuson Library, UAF

In the late nineteenth and early twentieth centuries, promoters proposed the construction of numerous railroads in Alaska, but only a few were built. Here the Alaska Home Railroad unloaded one of its engines in Valdez in 1907. H. B. Reynolds, a clever promoter, had sold Valdez citizens on the railroad scheme after they had despaired over failing to get the Copper River and Northwestern Railway terminal. This railroad scheme, with little behind it except Reynold's personality and local excitement, was doomed to early extinction.

Shortly after the Alaska Home Railroad started construction, its workmen entered Keystone Canyon, a part of the Morgan-Guggenheim abandoned right-of-way from Valdez. A fight ensued between employees of the Alaska Home Railroad and Morgan-Guggenheim men, and one of the former eventually died from wounds received. Courtesy of the Whalen Collection, Alaska and Polar Regions Dept., Rasmuson Library, UAF

This tent sheltered the Morgan-Guggenheim marshals in Keystone Canyon. They were guarding the right-of-way here and had erected a stone barricade on the left. From this spot they shot and wounded men of the Alaska Home Railroad who contested their right to the area. Courtesy of the Whalen Collection, Alaska and Polar Regions Dept., Rasmuson Library, UAF

Ambulances with the wounded Alaska Home Railroad men head back to Valdez after the fight in Keystone Canyon. Courtesy of the Whalen Collection, Alaska and Polar Regions Dept., Rasmuson Library, UAF

NEAR VIEW OF NORTHWESTERN RY. CO'S GRADE, MARSHALS TENT AND BARRICADE FROM WHICH THE HOME RY. MEN WERE SHOT, SEPT 25-07.

SNAP SHOT OF FIRST AND SECOND AMBULANCE FROM THE THIRD AMBULANCE HEADED FOR VALDEZ WITH MEN WOUNDED BY NORTHWESTERN RY. MARSHALS IN KEYSTONE CANYON, SEPT. 25-07.

Valdez became a major port for the Fairbanks area as the trail improved eventually into the Richardson Highway. The trail was the only way out in the wintertime, and the stage companies could make the trip in about seven days. About 1918 "auto stages" began to make the run to the ice-free port from the interior. Courtesy of the Bunnell Collection, Alaska and Polar Regions Dept., Rasmuson Library, UAF

At Valdez passengers and freight could travel the Richardson Highway 365 miles north to Fairbanks, a route first used by miners during the new gold stampede in 1902. The historic town was built on an unstable bed of glacial silt and gravel, and the 1964 earthquake destroyed much of the town, including the docks. Citizens rebuilt the new town at a more stable location nearby. This 1940s view was taken from an incoming ship. Courtesy of the Skinner Foundation Collection, Alaska Historical Library

Valdez was a thriving port in the early 1900s. Traffic to Fairbanks grew and an active mining district developed locally. Courtesy of the Norma Hoyt Collection

This early 1900s picture was taken on a Fourth of July in Valdez. The Hotel Phoenix is new and decked with flags. Courtesy of the Norma Hoyt Collection

A large outfit with twenty-one mules and horses and forty-six sleds, carrying twelve tons of whiskey and hardware, left Valdez for Fairbanks in 1905. The whiskey was an important component of the load as there were many saloons in Fairbanks and the camps that had to be supplied. Courtesy of the Anchorage Historical and Fine Arts Museum

While dog teams were an important means of transportation for years in many parts of Alaska, this 1908 expedition by "Caribou Bill" and "Missouri Kid," from Valdez to Seattle, does not look bound for success. They are "loading their photo supplies" at the photo shop of P. S. Hunt, a well-known photographer of the period. The clothes on the men and the small amount of supplies look inadequate. The Valdez Bank and Mercantile Company apparently sponsored the trip. The street scene shows part of the business district of the thriving town. The snow cover is very light. Courtesy of the Whalen Collection, Alaska and Polar Regions Dept., Rasmuson Library, UAF

This picture of the U.S. census taker in Valdez was probably taken about 1909 as there are railway cars in the background and the Alaska Home Railroad was begun there in 1907. Alaska's population, according to the 1910 census, was 64,356. Courtesy of the Norma Hoyt Collection

MAY DAY 1910

The Valdez area is noted for its heavy snows. Fort Liscum, across Port Valdez from the town, is still buried in the remaining drifts of winter on May Day, 1910. Courtesy of the Norma Hoyt Collection

There are always innovative ways to solve transportation problems. This bear-drawn dogsled was apparently being tried for commuting to the office, judging by the rider's attire. This picture may have been taken in Valdez early in the 1900s. Courtesy of the Norma Hoyt Collection

The Fairbanks-Valdez Stage, run by Ed S. Orr and Company, carried passengers and freight along the Richardson Highway. The trip was in many ways easiest in the winter when the mud of the trail and the creeks and rivers had frozen. There were many road-houses along the trail, of varying quality, where meals and lodging were available and the horses could be fed and cared for. In 1913 Robert E. "Bobby" Sheldon made the first trip by automobile between Valdez and Fairbanks, and soon "motor stages" took over. The roadhouses continued in use because it was still a long and arduous journey. Courtesy of the Archie Lewis Collection, Alaska and Polar Regions Dept., Rasmuson Library, UAF

The Sourdough Roadhouse began to serve stampeders on their way to the Fairbanks district and continues to operate in the same building. It became a national historic landmark in 1979. Roadhouses in Alaska, whether along the highways, dog trails, or in isolated communities, provided lodging, food, and shelter for men, dogs, and horses alike. Later on, many added garage facilities and sometimes developed a small air-field nearby. Today many are gone, but the traditional kind of roadhouse can still be found along the highways and in small communities in Alaska. Courtesy of the Norma Hoyt Collection

Circle City 1895

McQuesten's trading post was established in 1887 and grew into the mining supply town of Circle. It was given the name because residents thought the town was on the Arctic Circle. At one time Circle claimed to be the biggest town on the Yukon, but the population was likely to stampede at the least rumor of a new gold strike. In this 1895 photo, McQuesten is second from the left in the front row. Courtesy of the Bunnell Collection, Alaska and Polar Regions Dept., Rasmuson Library, UAF

By 1904 Circle had grown. McQuesten had become an agent for the Northern Commercial Company and his store had two new wings. A loading platform led down toward the Yukon where the rig on a ship's boom may be seen. The large log building in the center of the photo offered furnished rooms. Courtesy of the Anchorage Historical and Fine Arts Museum

The charter members of the Yukon Order of Pioneers, most of whom had come into the Yukon area well before the Klondike gold rush, gathered for a formal portrait (probably in Circle City). Standing, from left to right, are: Gordon Bettles, Pete McDonald, Jim Bender, Frank Buteau, G. Matlock, Al Mayo, Pete Nelson, Tom Lloyd, Bill Stewart and unidentified. Sitting, from left to right are: H. H. Hart, William McPhee, unidentified, Jack McQuesten, G. Harrington, unidentified, and H. Albert. The three men in the center are unidentified.

Some of the men moved on to the new camp at Fairbanks. Before the oldtimers organized the Pioneers of Alaska in 1902, other similar fraternal and social groups had been formed in some Alaskan and Yukon communities. The earliest lodge was the Sons of the Northwest, organized at Sitka in 1887, but no longer in existence today. The oldest active organization is the Yukon Order of Pioneers, started at Fortymile in 1894. The Arctic Brotherhood was formed aboard the steamer *City of Seattle*, enroute to Alaska in 1899. Later groups include the Order of Alaska Moose at Valdez; the Alaska Pioneers at Kodiak; and the '87 Pioneers Association at Juneau, started in 1908. Elk lodges also existed in many Alaskan mining camps in the early days. These lodges seem to have been composed exclusively of Alaskan pioneers, unlike the earlier ones whose membership also included men from Canadian communities. The Pioneers of Alaska organized in Nome, and its chapters are called igloos. Membership once was restricted to those who had come to Alaska prior to 1930. Today, thirty-year residency in Alaska qualifies for membership. Courtesy of Alaska and Polar Regions Dept., Rasmuson Library, UAF

This interior view of the Gulkana Roadhouse in the early 1900s shows well-draped doorways and shelves, elaborate wallpaper, and a dining room table well stocked with condiments. It served a small local community as well as highway travellers. Courtesy of the Norma Hoyt Collection

The Gulkana Roadhouse was the focal point for the small village of Gulkana, founded about 1903 as a telegraph station by the U.S. Army Signal Corps. The local post office is shown here in the section of the building on the left, and the store is just beyond the autos, which were well loaded for the highway trip. Courtesy of the Norma Hoyt Collection

The roadhouse at Paxon was established in 1903, and, in a modern building nearby, continues in business today. During the 1970s it housed pipeline workers and served the heavy construction traffic on the Richardson Highway. Only a small log pile remains of the old building. Courtesy of the Norma Hoyt Collection

Tailings from the Alaska-Juneau gold mine were transported along trestles and dumped into Gastineau Channel. The resulting fill areas created much of the level ground in Juneau and allowed for expansion of the town. Photo by Paul J. Sincic photo

Wilford B. Hoggatt (left front) was the first governor of Alaska to use Juneau as a capital, moving there in September 1906. A former hydrographic officer in the Navy, he stayed in Alaska to become involved in mining. U. G. Myers, (right front) was U.S. Commissioner. In the back row, from left to right, were Lieutenant C. C. Herman; Dr. John M. Mosely; Major Wilds P. Richardson, president of the newly formed Alaska Road Commission; and C. L. Andrews, with the U.S. Customs Service. Courtesy of the Guilbert Thompson Collection, Alaska and Polar Regions Dept., Rasmuson Library, UAF

The Federal courthouse and jail in Juneau was constructed in 1904. It was demolished to make way for the present State Office Building. Courtesy of the L. C. McConnel Collection, Alaska Historical Library

Seward was another base for railroad development. The Alaska Central Railway went bankrupt in 1909 and was later taken over by the Alaska Northern Railway which pushed the right-of-way as far as Turnagain Arm. This company also had financial difficulties and the line eventually became part of the Alaskan Railroad. Seward served as a major terminal for rail shipments north until the 1964 earthquake destroyed much of the port.

John E. Ballaine, a young Seattle newspaper and real estate man, early saw the value of an "All-American" or trans-Alaska route to the Yukon. He selected Resurrection Bay and the town of Seward as the terminus of a railroad to run north along Turnagain Arm of Cook Inlet, along Turnagain's north shore to near the junction of Knik Arm, and north from there through the Matanuska Susitna valleys through Broad Pass of the Alaska Range, reaching the Tanana, the Yukon's largest tributary, near Nenana. In March 1902 Ballaine and others organized the Alaska Central Railway and at the end of 1904 the company had completed 18.3 miles of track. In 1905 Ballaine sold out, and the new group built to mile 47 and graded several miles beyond. In 1909 the company went bankrupt and bondholders reorganized it as the Alaska Northern Railway. The renamed line struggled on to Kern Creek, mile 72 at the head of Turnagain Arm. There it ceased track laying, financially exhausted.

The federal government bought the line and incorporated it into the Alaska Railroad. Courtesy of the Anchorage Historical and Fine Arts Museum

The trestle of the Alaska Central Railway at Mile 49 was a beautiful piece of engineering. The problems of building through such difficult terrain were often more than the railroad promoters planned on. The construction camp is in the foreground of this 1907 photo. Courtesy of the Alaska Historical and Fine Arts Museum

Seward folk were on a picnic at Bear Creek, July 4, 1907. A railroad handcar is at the left. The picnickers were, seated, from left to right: Mr. Nelson, unidentified, Emma Trigg, Mr. Reed, May Trigg, Mr. McNeiley, O. G. Herning, Mr. McAlpine, Alwin Wheatley, Mrs. Cappel, Mrs. Sexton, and Mr. Cappel.

Standing, from left to right were: Mrs. Nelson, George Sexton, Sylvia Sexton, and Mrs. Tillett. Courtesy of the Alaska Historical and Fine Arts Museum

The purpose of this 1907 outing at Mile 34 on the Alaska Central Railway is not known. The lady and the dog seem to be enjoying the trip. Courtesy of the Anchorage Historical and Fine Arts Museum

Red McGee and his camera outfit travelled the line on an Armstrong Speeder after it became the Alaska Northern Railway. The photo was taken about 1910. Courtesy of the Norma Hoyt Collection

Palmer's Store in Knik, is shown about 1900. The boxing lesson doesn't seem of interest to the sidewalk loungers.

Knik was a trading community in the Cook Inlet area before the development of Anchorage. Courtesy of the Wheatley Album, Anchorage Historical and Fine Arts Museum

Iditarod became a small town serving the Innoko-Iditarod mining district about 1910. By the 1920s it had started to fade away. Sometime between 1915 and 1918, Henry Weir's family posed proudly on the porch of their home in the new town. Courtesy of the Norma Hoyt Collection

The steamer *Nenana* was the last of the large sternwheelers to carry freight along the great rivers. Cordwood for fuel is shown stacked on the forward deck. The state eventually placed the *Nenana* in Alaskaland, a theme park constructed with federal funds to celebrate the 1967 centennial of Alaska's becoming an American possession. Courtesy of the Anchorage Historical and Fine Arts Museum

John Goodell, U.S. Commissioner at Knik, was photographed about 1907-08. Courtesy of the Wheatley Album, Anchorage Historical and Fine Arts Museum

Otter or Otter Creek was a little town that sprang up in the Iditerod area about 1910 as a supply point for mines in the area. The ladies at right are probably Mrs. Lange and Mrs. Campbell, standing in the front of their cafe and bakery. Courtesy of the Lewis Collection, Alaska and Polar Regions Dept., Rasmuson Library, UAF

C.J. Meiers was the proprietor of this roadhouse in 1910. Located about two miles south of Paxson Lake along the Richardson Highway, it grew hay for the horses that were an important part of the early transportation system. Housing for travellers, horses, and dogs was available. Courtesy of the Norma Hoyt Collection

The first broad Native organization was the Alaska Native Brotherhood. It formed in Sitka in 1912 with the main goal of gaining citizenship. The founders of the ANB were (left to right) Paul Liberty, James Watson, Ralph Young, Eli Katinook, Peter Simpson, Frank Mercer, James C. Johnson, Chester Worthington, George Field, William Hobson, and Frank Price. Courtesy of the Walter Soboleff Collection, Alaska and Polar Regions Dept., Rasmuson Library, UAF

The Organic Act of 1912 finally gave Alaska the right to elect a legislature consisting of eight senators and sixteen representatives. This photo is labeled "Senators in Session—First Legislature, 1913." The legislature had limited powers, most being retained by the federal government. The first legislation passed extended the franchise to women. Courtesy of Historical Photograph Collection, Alaska and Polar Regions Dept., Rasmuson Library, UAF

Governor John F. Strong gave the dedicatory speech for the Pioneer Home in Sitka in the summer of 1913. He is standing on the porch of the old officers building of the Marine Barracks which became the dwelling of the superintendent of the home. The building at the left, a former barracks, was used to house pioneers. Use of the buildings had been made possible by a congressional bill in 1913.

The first Alaska legislature had proposed a home for aged and indigent prospectors. Courtesy of the Sheldon Jackson College Collection

A small group gathered on the main street of Cordova on Primary Election Day, April 7, 1914. Voting for elected officials had only become possible with the Second Organic Act of 1912. Courtesy of the McKay Collection, Alaska and Polar Regions Dept., Rasmuson Library, UAF

Some land was settled in the Matanuska Valley when the railroad made the area accessible. The inscription on this picture reads: "The R. S. Heckey ranch about 4 miles north of Matanuska Junction. 'Burned,' cleared and planted since April 10th 1916." Courtesy of the U.S. National Archives

Congress created Mount McKinley National Park in 1917. It became part of a larger Denali National Park and Preserve in 1980. Mount McKinley, the major feature of the park, is 20,320 feet high, the tallest in North America. Many feel the mountain should also be called Denali. The gateway in the early 1930s was an impressive log structure. Courtesy of the Norma Hoyt Collection

GATEWAY TO
MT. McKINLEY NATIONAL PARK

Anchorage became the base for the largest railroad project in the territory with the construction of the Alaska Railroad. This view from the railroad yards near the mouth of Ship Creek looks toward the bluff where the new city is beginning to grow. The hospital for the railroad, on the bluff at the left, was built in 1917. Courtesy of the Anchorage Historical and Fine Arts Museum

Camp 83, Turnagain Division, was typical of the small camps from which much of the railroad construction proceeded. Log cabins and tents required a constant supply of wood for fuel. Courtesy of the Anchorage Historical and Fine Arts Museum

These workers are laying steel into Camp 14, Moose Creek, on August 24, 1916. Courtesy of the U.S. National Archives

The small village of Talkeetna became a major construction camp as the Alaska Railroad moved north. It gained a post office in 1916. Its recent fame is as an aerial supply point for expeditions climbing Mount McKinley. Courtesy of the U.S. National Archives

Susitna, or Susitna Station, was still a substantial village when Alaska Engineering Commission Chairman William C. Edes visited it in 1916. It was a supply point on the Susitna River, but much of it has since disappeared. Courtesy of the Anchorage Historical and Fine Arts Museum

In the autumn of 1918, Edes and an "official party" traveled north along the proposed route of the Alaska Railroad. At Talkeetna they loaded pack horses and gear on the commission's riverboat B & B No. 2. Courtesy of the Anchorage Historical and Fine Arts Museum

The *Princess Sophia* was a Canadian Pacific Steamship Company vessel. On October 25, 1918, she was taking passengers from Skagway to Seattle, many of them leaving Dawson for the winter, when she went aground on Vanderbilt Reef north of Juneau. Rescuers offered to take the passengers and crew off, but they all stayed with the ship, assuming it would refloat at the next high tide. The next morning the ship was gone and 343 people on board were lost. Courtesy of the Alaska Historical Library

This photograph, taken March 7, 1919, shows the drafting room at the Alaska Railroad district head-quarters at Dead Horse. This location later was called Curry and was the overnight stop for passenger trains. It was a simple field office for the construction period, with improvised and locally-built equipment. John H. Robinson, special agent, is at the right. Courtesy of the Anchorage Historical and Fine Arts Museum

The Matanuska-Chickaloon train leaves Anchorage in the 1920s. The development of the coal fields in that area was one of the hopes behind the Alaska Railroad. The promise of this area was never ful-filled. Courtesy of the Lulu Fairbanks Collection, Alaska and Polar Regions Dept., Rasmuson Library, UAF

Chitina was the northern terminus of the Copper River and Northwestern Railway built to serve the large copper mine at Kennicott. Kennicott and Chitina were at their heyday about 1920 when this photo of a snow vehicle was made. The bus-like affair was pushed by an airplane engine and travelled on what look like airplane skis. Courtesy of the Norma Hoyt Collection

Nenana, on the Tanana River, became a major river port when the Alaska Railroad connected it with Anchorage and Seward in 1923. Freight was transferred here for river communities. Although tugs and barges eventually replaced the old steamers, many villages today still rely on this supply route for their fuel and

bulk supplies. Yutana Barge Lines carried out this important function for many years. Photo by Eric Muehling, courtesy of the *Fairbanks Daily News-Miner*

The ferry across the Tanana River ran until the 1940s. The small community on the south shore was known as McCarthy and later Big Delta. By this time, in the 1920s, motor vehicles were common on the Richardson Highway.

McCarthy was also the site of one of the telegraph stations that provided Alaska with a modern communication system. Courtesy of the Anchorage Historical and Fine Arts Museum

Chena, incorporated in 1903, was at one time a rival of Fairbanks. It was the southern terminus and

headquarters of the Tanana Valley Railroad, which the federal government eventually purchased and made part of the Alaska Railroad. Only eighteen inhabitants were left when this photo was taken in 1920, and the tracks which ran down the main street appear abandoned here. Much of the site was eventually washed away as the Tanana River cut into the bank on which it was built. Courtesy of the *Fairbanks Daily News-Miner*

President Warren G. Harding's visit to the territory in July 1923 was a sign of hope to Alaskans who felt long neglected by the federal government. Harding was accompanied by three cabinet members; Herbert Hoover, secretary of commerce; Hubert Work, secretary of the interior; and Henry Wallace, secretary of agriculture; as well as several congressmen.

In this scene at Sitka, at the Pioneers Home, Mrs. Harding is seated with the president at her right. Courtesy of the Sheldon Jackson College Collection

145

President Harding spoke in Fairbanks in July 1923. Alaskans hoped that in Washington there would be greater understanding of the problems of Alaska after the presidential visit. These hopes were lost with the death of Harding in August in San Francisco. Courtesy of the Mrs. George L. Keys Collection, Alaska and Polar Regions Dept., Rasmuson Library, UAF

Carl Ben Eielson (in cockpit) flew this De Havilland plane on pioneer mail flights in Alaska in 1924. This is a rare view of the interior of the shop where mechanics apparently assembled the plane. The specially made skis are at the right. Courtesy of the Norma Hoyt Collection

The Wien brothers were pioneers in the aviation business in Alaska. Their early efforts led to the formation of a major Alaskan airline. In the 1920s Noel Wien landed near Circle Hot Springs at this airfield in the bush, which Frank Leach, the proprietor, built using a team of horses. Taking off seemed to offer more of a problem. The team was kept ready to render further assistance. Courtesy of the E. L. Bartlett Collection, Alaska and Polar Regions Dept., Rasmuson Library, UAF

146

Brigadier General William Lendrum "Billy" Mitchell (right) was born in Nice, France, on December 29, 1879 while his parents were temporarily abroad. Raised in Milwaukee, Wisconsin he attended Racine College of Wisconsin, a preparatory school, then entered Columbia (now George Washington) University in Washington, D.C. At age eighteen, when still a student and anxious to play a part in the Spanish-American War, he enlisted as a private in the First Wisconsin, a volunteer regiment. Within a few weeks, Brigadier General Adolphus W. Greely, Chief of the Signal Corps, recommended Billy for a commission. As a young second lieutenant, Mitchell

was assigned to the Second Volunteer Signal Company in the spring of 1898. From there the Army sent him to the occupation of Cuba where he supervised the stringing of 136 miles of telegraph wire in Santiago Province. Posted to the Philippines in July 1899, at the age of twenty he became acting Chief Signal Officer in the division staff of General Arthur MacArthur. He supervised the stringing of many miles of telegraph lines, and while in the islands made the acquaintance of Colonel Frederick Funston who had prospected in Alaska. The far north attracted him. After his Phillipine service Mitchell intended to resign, but General Greely asked him to go to Alaska

where establishing a telegraph system connecting the Army posts went slowly. He went to Alaska in 1901 and reported to Greely that the line could be built more rapidly if the soldiers worked throughout the winter. Greely sent him back to Alaska to carry out the plan in the fall of 1901. Mitchell supervised building a portion of the line, primarily along the route between Fort Egbert (at Eagle City on the upper Yukon) and Fort Liscum (at Valdez). He finished in 1903, and as a reward for his accomplishments the Army promoted him to the rank of captain, the youngest in its ranks. Later on Mitchell became interested in aviation, and became commander of air forces

in the American Expeditionary Force in France in World War I. The war convinced him of the efficacy of air power, and he urged that the Army's Air Service become a separate air arm. In 1920 he organized the Army air-mapping tour of Alaska, commanded by Captain St. Clair Streett, to call attention to aviation's capabilities. He warned of war with Japan, and predicted that she would strike without warning. In 1925, as a result of his continued agitation, the Army reduced him in rank to colonel and assigned him to a minor post in Texas. Eventually, he was court-martialed, and resigned in 1926 after a brilliant career. In 1935 Mitchell testified before Congress, and stated that Japan was America's most dangerous enemy. "They will come right here to Alaska. Alaska is the most central place in the world for aircraft, and that is true either of Europe, Asia, or North America. I believe in the future he who holds Alaska will hold the world, and I think it is the most important strategic place in the world." In this early 1920s picture he stands beside a SE5. Mitchell truly was a visionary. Courtesy of the Historical Photograph Collection, Alaska and Polar Regions Dept., Rasmuson Library, UAF

Originally built as Fort William Henry Seward in 1902, this post was renamed Chilkoot Barracks in 1922. Situated at the upper end of the inside passage, it could observe the traffic bound inland or back over three historic trails, the Chilkoot, Chilkat, and White Passes. The post had a complement of eleven officers and about 300 men equipped with Springfield rifles. It did not even have an antiaircraft gun, but it alone remained the symbol of the army's strength in the territory after World War I. Chilkoot Barracks was not connected with roads to the interior, and the company's only transportation was a fifty-two-year-old tug, the U.S.S. *Fornance*. Returning in 1939 from Juneau with the com-

manding officer on board, the tug encountered a thirty-knot headwind which halted her progress. She had to be rescued by the Coast Guard. Closed on the eve of World War II, the surplus installation was purchased by a group of veterans after the war and they developed various business and cultural activities in the complex of buildings. As part of the town of Haines, the former post today serves as the northern port of the Alaska ferry system to connect to the Alcan Highway north to the interior Yukon and Alaska. The post is shown here in 1939. Courtesy of the Machetanz Collection, Alaska and Polar Regions Dept., Rasmuson Library, UAF

Major General Hines conducted an inspection at Chilkoot Barracks on July 3, 1928. Companies E and F of the Seventh Infantry were stationed here, then with other supporting units. Courtesy of Colonel V. W. Pinkey, USA Retired

In 1924 the U.S. Army sent out an around-the-world expedition. On April 10, 1924 its planes were at Crescent Cove in Sitka in front of Sheldon Jackson School. Courtesy of the Sheldon Jackson College Collection

WORLD FLIERS

NI NORGE

Landing at Tell...

These army fliers posed in Sitka in 1924. From left to right, they were: Sergeants Ogden and Harvey; Lieutenants Nelson, Smith and Arnold; Mr. Gilpatrick, a resident of Sitka; Lieutenants Harding and Wade; Major Martin; and Ealer Hansen, who was in charge of supplies. Courtesy of the Sheldon Jackson College Collection

In May 1926, Roald Amundsen, a Norwegian; Lincoln Ellsworth, an American; and Umberto Nobile, an Italian, took off in the dirigible *Norge* from Spitzbergen. They flew 3,400 miles to Alaska in a successful, but perilous flight. As the *Norge* headed north, ice began to coat its sides; then, torn loose by the airstream from the whirling propellers, the ice was flung against the gasbags, nearly puncturing their thin skins. The weight of the encrusted ice made the airship difficult to maneuver, and the ice and subzero temperatures made many of the navigation instruments useless. The airship's ultimate arrival in Teller, Alaska was plainly the result of courage and luck, not good planning. Courtesy of the Alaska and Polar Regions Dept., Rasmuson Library, UAF

In 1928 Captain Hubert Wilkins (left) and Carl Ben Eielson (right) made the first flight over the North Pole from Point Barrow to Spitzbergen. Here they are shown in Point Barrow before the flight, which they made in a Lockheed Vega. Courtesy of the U.S. National Archives

Alaskans have always taken advantage of the benefits of winter. This hockey game in Fairbanks in 1938 drew a good audience. Photo by Paul J. Sincic

Chapter **6**

In 1928 Herbert Hoover, who had spent so much time with Alaskan problems as secretary of commerce, became president of the United States. It was his misfortune to be in office when the Great Depression struck. On October 24, 1929, stock market prices fell disastrously on the New York Exchange and reached all-time lows in 1932. Nationwide, economic activity slowed down in the wake of the crash, unemployment increased tremendously, and America began to experience its worst depression.

The effects of this economic misfortune were soon felt in Alaska. Governor George A. Parks euphemistically reported in 1930 that "during the early summer a surplus of laborers was reported in a few places...." The 1930 census showed that Alaska had gained 4,242 people over the number reported in 1920, bringing the population up to 59,278. This increase was attributable, in part, to the poor economic conditions on the Pacific Coast which had brought many individuals north, hoping to wrest a living from the land and sea. And with the depression worsening, prices paid for fish and copper, the territory's two chief commodities, declined. This drop, in turn, curtailed production of these commodities, and many more Alaskans joined the ranks of the unemployed. In 1931 economic conditions worsened, and by 1933 unemployment became the major problem in Alaska, as it was elsewhere. The fishing industry work force dropped from 29,283 in 1929 to 12,695 in 1933, accompanied by wage cuts. During the same period, the value of fish products declined from $50,795,819 to $32,126,588. Likewise, imports of goods and supplies from the continental states dwindled from 350,193 tons in 1929 to 240,379 tons in 1933. Exports from Alaska for the same period, consisting mainly of fish products, minerals, and furs, shrank from 449,944 tons to 260,138 tons. Government employment in the territory was cut back proportionately.

1932 Elections

The economy looked bleak in April of 1932 when Alaskans chose their delegates to the national party conventions and elected candidates for the delegateship. The Republican delegation was pledged to the renomination of Herbert Hoover for president. Republican James Wickersham, who had returned from political retirement in 1930 to retain his old seat as delegate, faced no opposition for renomination.

The Democrats chose Anthony J. Dimond, a Valdez lawyer and territorial legislator, out of a field of three candidates for the delegate nomination. In the nationwide Democratic landslide, Dimond also won by a substantial margin, and Alaska Democrats gained large majorities in both houses of the territorial legislature. Dimond's election began the preeminence of the Democratic Party in Alaska—Dimond served from 1933 until 1944, throughout the New Deal and most of the war.

Dimond arrived in Washington at a time of great political change brought about by the election of Roosevelt. He generally followed the example of his predecessors in submitting legislation which was designed to expand the powers of the territorial government, give the territory control over the administration of its fish and game resources, and prevent the appointment of a nonresident as governor. In 1934 he joined forces with Hawaii's delegate and submitted legislation which would have given both territories representation in the Senate comparable to that in the House. Most of these proposals never passed, but the delegate was successful in most of the necessary housekeeping measures for Alaska, such as gaining congressional approval for various cities to issue bonds for civic improvements.

New Deal Measures

Alaska did participate on a modest scale in some of the recovery programs of the New Deal. The president's decision to devalue the dollar by raising the price of gold from $20.67 to $35.00 stimulated activity in the territory's gold mining industry. The National Reforestation Act of 1933 gave employment to several hundred men. Direct relief payments, besides aiding their recipients, helped stimulate the economy. Alaska also benefited from projects undertaken by the Public Works Administration and the Works Progress Administration, as well as the Civilian Conservation Corps. Many projects of enduring value were completed, such as waterworks, schools, playgrounds, fire stations, roads, airfields, and a steel bridge across Gastineau Channel connecting Juneau on the mainland with Douglas on Douglas Island. In addition, trails and shelter cabins were built in the national forests. By 1936, the PWA alone had

Alaska was a challenge to the intrepid fliers of the 1930s. The celebrated Charles Lindbergh flew to Point Barrow in 1931. In this photo, from left to right are: J. R. Trindle, government school teacher; Mrs. Greist; Mrs. Lindbergh; David Greist; Sergeant Stanley Morgan, U.S.S.C., and his daughter Beverly; Colonel Lindbergh; and Dr. Greist. Courtesy of the U.S. National Archives

Wiley Post made a historic round-the-world trip in the *Winnie Mae* in 1933. The plane crashed at Flat but was repaired so it could continue on to Fairbanks for further work, before continuing on to New York. (Flat was a small mining community with few facilities.) Today, the Smithsonian Aerospace Museum houses this historic aircraft. Courtesy of the Norma Hoyt Collection

allocated some $4,463,233 to the territory.

Of all the New Deal activities in Alaska, the Matanuska Valley Colony generated the greatest interest, extending beyond the boundaries of Alaska. Envisioned as an opportunity to take Americans from depressed agricultural areas and give them a chance to start anew and become self-sustaining, it elicited about fifteen thousand letters of application from potential settlers. The settlers were to be sponsored by the Federal Emergency Relief Administration under its Rural Rehabilitation Division. The number of settlers was finally limited to 202, to be chosen from Michigan, Wisconsin, and Minnesota on the assumption that the climatic similarities between these areas and Alaska would best fit the pioneers for life in the Matanuska Valley.

In the spring of 1935, amidst much publicity, the 202 families arrived in the Matanuska Valley, in the rail belt area of south-central Alaska. Palmer, its leading settlement, is about forty miles from Anchorage. Prior to the settlement there had been some homesteading in the valley connected with mining activities in the Willow Creek mining district. Together with four hundred relief workers from the transient camps of California, the settlers cleared land for the projected forty- to eighty-acre tracts each settler was to receive, depending on the quality of the soil. They also built living quarters, a school, a trading post, a cannery, a creamery, and a hospital.

In retrospect, the Matanuska Colony became a qualified success. With the start of the Second World War and the construction of military bases near Anchorage, the colony found a ready market for its products. Many of the settlers, however, left their farms and went to work in the construction industry.

The New Deal did not ignore the Natives. In 1934 Congress enacted the Indian Reorganization Act which was extended to Alaska two years later. It included Alaska's Eskimos and Aleuts as well. The Wheeler-Howard Act, named for its sponsors, enabled several Native communities to incorporate and devise charters for self government. A loan program enabled some villages to construct canneries, and individuals to purchase boats and gear. Perhaps the most controversial aspect of the legislation was that it allowed the secretary of the interior to withdraw lands for the establishment of reservations. Both Natives and whites vehemently opposed these reservations.

They were considered a step backward and an attempt to thwart the territory's economic development. A number of reservations were established, but in the 1940s, following continuous protests, the reservation plan was finally withdrawn.

Although the New Deal quickened Alaska's economic pace, its effect on the territory was hardly profound. It brought no basic changes. In 1937 the National Resources Committee issued a study which found that there was no need to speed the development of the territory. ■

Wiley Post stands before the *Winnie Mae* at Fairbanks in 1933. Courtesy of the Norma Hoyt Collection

Post & Rogers at Fairbanks 1935

In 1935 Wiley Post returned to Fairbanks with the well-known humorist Will Rogers. They flew on to Barrow, where their plane crashed. Both were lost. Photo by J. P. C. Scattowe, courtesy of the Alaska Historical Library

The Alaska Road Commission was responsible for the construction and maintenance of "military and post" roads in Alaska, and of other roads, bridges, and trails. Established by Congress in 1905, it operated under the War Department until 1932, when Congress transferred the organization to the Department of the Interior. In 1956, the Bureau of Public Roads absorbed the venerable Alaska Road Commission. This grader, used on the Gulkana-Chisana road in 1931, is typical of the heavy equipment in use during the time. Courtesy of the Ray Huddleston Collection, Alaska and Polar Regions Dept., Rasmuson Library, UAF

Even after mechanical equipment and autos became common, the need for horses continued in many areas. This load of hay is pulled by a "Five Ton Caterpillar" and headed to feed the horses at a mine in the Chitina area.
Courtesy of the Norma Hoyt Collection

This aerial view shows the Alaska Railroad yards with the city of Anchorage at the upper left. For many years the railroad was the mainstay of the city's economy. Today Anchorage still remains the base for the railroad operations.
Courtesy of the Anchorage Historical and Fine Arts Museum

Because there was little space for airfields, and little chance for emergency landings on land, seaplanes were used throughout southeastern Alaska. This plane is at the Alaskan Southern Airways hanger in Juneau in the 1930s. Courtesy of the C. R. Scothorn Collection, Alaska Historical Library

The community of Douglas is across the Gastineau Channel from Juneau. At one time, during the heyday of the Treadwell Mine,

Douglas was larger than Juneau. The two were connected by ferry until the Douglas Bridge was built in 1934-35. A new span now replaces this bridge. Courtesy of the Bayer Collection, Alaska Historical Library

The S.S. *Aleutian* was one of the steamers of the Alaska Steamship Company which served the ports of southeastern Alaska and the south coast. At Seward it connected with the Alaska Railroad, which carried passengers and freight to Anchorage and the interior. The earthquake of 1964 destroyed many of the port facilities and the railroad terminal. Courtesy of the Anchorage Historical and Fine Arts Museum

159

The "social hall" on one of the passenger vessels did its best not to look nautical. The wicker furniture, fireplace, and flowered curtains created a typical 1930s interior. Courtesy of the Skinner Foundation Collection, Alaska Historical Library

Harriet Pullen, a widow from Wisconsin with four small children to support, and a total capital of seven dollars, built the Pullen House in Skagway during the gold rush. She made and sold pies, freighted, and engaged in various other enterprises allowing her to construct and run a large and comfortable hotel. The guests here in the sunny, spacious lounge might be anywhere, except for the caribou and Dall sheep heads mounted on the wall. Courtesy of the Skinner Foundation Collection, Alaska Historical Library

The Matanuska Colony was one of the great social experiments of the 1930s. The colonists who were brought to Alaska (about 202 families in all) drew for farm plots on a sunny day in 1936. The valley had already been the site of some farming activity, and many of the farms prospered. Courtesy of the Lulu Fairbanks Collection, Alaska and Polar Regions Dept., Rasmuson Library, UAF

This Matanuska Valley farm, with land cleared, cattle grazing, and neat farmstead in a scenic setting seems to be the ideal that the colony was striving for. Courtesy of the Lulu Fairbanks Collection, Alaska and Polar Regions Dept., Rasmuson Library, UAF

With its false fronts, in 1935-36 the main street of Palmer was like some small town in the Old West, except for the cars. Palmer was the center of the Matanuska Colony. The town was first established in 1916 as a railroad station for the Matanuska Branch of the A.K.R.R. Courtesy of the Alaska Historical Library

All the work was not mechanized in the Matanuska Colony. Courtesy of the Alaska Historical Library

Governor John W. Troy is pictured with members of the territorial legislature, 13th session, 1937. The governor stands at the woman legislator's right. Photo by Trevor Davis, courtesy of the Alaska Historical Library

In 1938 Juneau was still a small town. The old federal building dominated the skyline, although the new federal building had been built in 1931. Indian houses on pilings lined the beach area. The beach area later was filled in, which extended the shoreline out into the Gastineau Channel. Courtesy of the Anchorage Historical and Fine Arts Museum

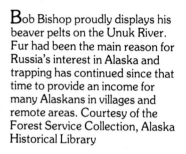

Bob Bishop proudly displays his beaver pelts on the Unuk River. Fur had been the main reason for Russia's interest in Alaska and trapping has continued since that time to provide an income for many Alaskans in villages and remote areas. Courtesy of the Forest Service Collection, Alaska Historical Library

The Circle Roadhouse is shown in 1938. The man on the left cut wood for the steamers that were still on the river, and the man on the right ran the roadhouse. Circle's days as an important town were long gone, but, like other small communities, it continued to be home for a few oldtimers. Photo by Paul J. Sincic

Chapter 7

World War II brought the strategic importance of Alaska to the fore and Anchorage became the center of command for the buildup of bases and military activities in the territory. Anchorage boomed with the construction of Fort Richardson and Elmendorf Air Force Base. The boom continued after the war as the cold war brought further military development and growth of public services. Fourth Avenue was the main business street and was a mixture of buildings from the old railroad townsite days and modern structures like the Federal Building. This shot was taken about 1945. Courtesy of the Lulu Fairbanks Collection, Alaska and Polar Regions Dept., Rasmuson Library, UAF

World War II:
Alaska is Rediscovered

It was the outbreak of the Second World War which caused Alaska to be rediscovered. Delegate Dimond had asked Congress as early as 1933 for appropriations to build military airfields, a highway link to the contiguous United States, and various military garrisons to protect Alaska from a potential Japanese threat from across the Pacific. The outbreak of war in Europe in 1939 intensified the delegate's anxiety. In 1940 Congress finally authorized the construction of Navy and Army bases and forts at locations ranging from Unalaska to Kodiak and from Anchorage to Sitka, appropriating $29,108,285 for these projects. However, it was not until the Nazis invaded Denmark and Norway in 1940 that military construction slowly commenced in the territory. Many congressmen then realized for the first time that Alaska was vulnerable to air attack.

When the Japanese struck Pearl Harbor on December 7, 1941, none of the Alaska bases were ready. Then in the summer of 1942 the Japanese invaded and occupied Attu and Kiska on the Aleutian chain. America's pride was hurt, and the United States quickly armed its northern territory.

In the spring of 1942 construction started on the Alaska-Canadian Military Highway, the Alcan. Exactly nine months and six days after the start of construction, the 1,420-mile pioneer road opened for military traffic on November 20, 1942. On that date, the formal ribbon cutting ceremony took place at Soldier's Summit above Kluane Lake, Yukon Territory. Starting at Dawson Creek, British Columbia, the road went to Whitehorse in the Yukon Territory and then to Big Delta in Alaska. The road cost a total of $135 million or $56,160 per mile to build.

While the Alcan rapidly took shape, thousands of American soldiers came to Alaska to participate in its defense and take part in the recapture of Kiska and Attu. By the fall of 1943, the Japanese had been pushed out of their Alaskan toeholds. After this, ground forces were reduced from a high of 150,000 men in November 1943 to 50,000 in March 1945. Forts closed, bases were dismantled, and airfields were turned over to the Civil Aeronautics Administration.

The military impact irrevocably altered the pace and tenor of Alaskan life, and the residual benefits to the civilian economy and the development of the territory were tremendous. Between 1941 and 1945, the federal government spent

well over one billion dollars in the territory. The modernization of the Alaska Railroad, the expansion of the airfields, and the construction of roads benefitted the civilian population. Between 1940 and 1950, the civilian population increased from 74,000 to 112,000. In short, the war was the biggest boom Alaska had ever experienced, including any of the gold rushes.

At the end of the war the curtailment of defense spending once again confronted Alaskans with the problems of a seasonal economy. At this juncture, however, the development of tensions between the United States and the Soviet Union, resulting in the Cold War, rescued Alaska from the economic doldrums and obscurity. The territory's geographical position astride the northern Great Circle routes gave Alaska a strategic importance in the defense of the Free World. Once again, thousands of troops and millions of defense dollars poured north. Alaska prospered, and with this new prosperity came renewed demands for self government. ■

Ernest Gruening served Alaska both as the first director of the Division of Territories and Island Possessions, Department of the Interior, and as Alaska's governor from 1939 to 1953. He later served as the state's junior U.S. senator from 1959 to 1968.

In this photo, taken during World War II, he visited Barrow wearing a fur parka and mitts. Courtesy of the Klerekoper Collection, Alaska and Polar Regions Dept., Rasmuson Library, UAF

Anthony J. Dimond, a former teacher, gold miner, and lawyer, was Alaska's voteless delegate to Congress. Elected in the Democratic landslide, he took office in 1933 and served until 1944 when he chose not to run again in order to accept an appointment as federal district court judge for the third judicial division. A very effective delegate and highly esteemed judge, Dimond was a strong proponent for Alaskan statehood. Courtesy of the Lulu Fairbanks Collection, Alaska and Polar Regions Dept., Rasmuson Library, UAF

Housing was a problem in the burgeoning community of Anchorage and many military families and workers were forced to live in whatever was available. This technical sargeant and his family occupied a tar paper shack. Courtesy of the U.S. Army Signal Corps Collection, Alaska Historical Library

This motorcycle race was held in Anchorage, in 1940. Photo by Paul J. Sincic

A sound detecting device, part of an air raid warning system, was shown on Fourth Avenue in Anchorage on July 4, 1940. Preparation for the defense of Alaska had begun and soldiers were everywhere. Photo by Paul J. Sincic

Contractors build a naval air station at Dutch Harbor in the Aleutians in the early 1940s. It was capable of servicing submarines as well as providing an airfield. It was one of the first responses to the recognition of the strategic importance of Alaska. Much of the war in the Aleutians was fought in the air and Dutch Harbor was the base for much of the American effort.

On June 3, 1942, the Japanese attacked and bombed Dutch Harbor, hoping to repeat the Pearl Harbor surprise. Although fifty-two Americans were killed or injured, the American troops, were prepared and met the attack. The Japanese returned the next day for another bombing run. The two attacks damaged the base lightly and loss of life fortunately was low. Courtesy of Hanna-Call Collection, Alaska and Polar Regions Dept., Rasmuson Library, UAF

The base at Dutch Harbor was raided on June 3-4, 1942. Here some of the Japanese bombs are shown falling into the bay. Courtesy of Hanna-Call Collection, Alaska and Polar Regions Dept., Rasmuson Library, UAF

The Alaska Highway was a pioneer road cut through previously unbroken wilderness. This scene is in the southern Yukon Territory or northern British Columbia. Ditching and gravel were refinements that came well after the road began to be used. Army photo, courtesy of the Anchorage Historical and Fine Arts Museum

The need for a highway to connect Alaska and the rest of the United States led to the building of the Alaska-Canada Military Highway, in 1942. Completed in a major nine months and six days effort, it connected many of the airfields on the route north through Alberta, British Columbia and the Yukon. It was a difficult construction job and the original road was rough and crude, but army convoys put it to immediate use. With continual improvement, it continues to be Alaska's important land link to the rest of the country. This scene is in Delta Junction where the new road con-

nected to the Richardson Highway. Courtesy of the Matchetanz Collection, Alaska and Polar Regions Dept., Rasmuson Library, UAF

169

The Alcan Highway was officially opened November 20, 1942. E. L. "Bob" Bartlett, Secretary of Alaska, (center), helped cut the ribbon. Courtesy of the E. L. Bartlett Collection, Alaska and Polar Regions Dept., Rasmuson Library, UAF

The ribbon cutting ceremonies officially opening the road were held at Soldier's Summit, above Kluane Lake in the Yukon territory. The temperature at the time was -30° Fahrenheit. Bob Bartlett represented the United States and Ian Mackenzie represented Canada. Photo from the collection of C. Naske

The first truck to make the entire trip from Dawson Creek to Whitehorse made it along the rough road in September 1942. U.S. Army photo, courtesy of the Anchorage Historical and Fine Arts Museum

At Amchitka Island in 1943, U.S. troops wade to shore from a landing craft. The island, only forty miles from Kiska, a major Japanese base, became a forward airbase for the American attack on Kiska. Courtesy of the U.S. Army Signal Corps Collection, Alaska Historical Library

On August 14, 1943, U.S. forces staged a major attack on Kiska, a major Japanese base. But unbeknownst to the Americans the Japanese had successfully evacuated all their forces from the island in late July. They had slipped away under cover of the heavy Aleutian fog, abandoning many supplies and weapons. Courtesy of the J. S. Macinnon Collection, Alaska Historical Library

At Kiska the Japanese abandoned many supplies in their hasty departure. In a shed cluttered with abandoned gear an American soldier samples some rice. Courtesy of the Hanna-Call Collection, Alaska and Polar Regions Dept., Rasmuson Library, UAF

Two American officers sit at their improvised desk at the captured Kiska base. Courtesy of the J. S. MacKinnon Collection, Alaska Historical Library

American Forces landed on Attu, a major Japanese position, on May 11, 1943. It took almost three weeks for the island to be taken. Some Japanese soldiers held out in the hills for three months after the battle. It was one of the costliest battles of the Pacific area. Only twenty-eight prisoners were taken of the original Japanese garrison of 2,600 men. Courtesy of the Hanna-Call Collection, Alaska and Polar Regions Dept., Rasmuson Library, UAF

Brigadier General Simon Bolivar Buckner headed the Alaska Defense Command for the U.S. Army. On June 2, 1943, he was able to view the American flag flying over the former Japanese headquarters on Attu. Courtesy of the U.S. Army Signal Corps Collection, Alaska Historical Library

On recaptured Attu on June 4, 1943, General A. M. Landrum (right), Commanding General, U.S. Forces in Alaska; and Ernest Greuning, governor of Alaska, (left) were able to visit Brigadier General Archibald V. Arnold who was in charge of the garrison at Attu. Courtesy of the U.S. Army Signal Corps Collection, Alaska Historical Library

Private Simeon Plotinkoff, an Aleut fighting with the U.S. Army, is shown aboard the transport which took him and other soldiers to Attu where Japanese occupation forces were wiped out. Private Plotinkoff's home was on Unimak Island. Most Aleuts were evacuated from the islands to southeastern Alaska where conditions were difficult and many died. Courtesy of the U.S. National Archives

The Yukon River was used to move supplies during the war. At Tozi Cache drums were rafted and moved to Galena. Courtesy of the U.S. National Archives

During the war Russian airmen helped fly planes and war materials from Alaska across the Bering Strait to Siberia and Russia. A series of airfields was built across Canada and Alaska for the ferrying operation. In Nome a dance at the officers' club brought together the cooperating servicemen. The Russian officer at the right is Lieutenant Boris Brodkin. The American to the left is Lieutenant Frank L. Woodward. Courtesy of the U.S. National Archives

Marvin R. Marston, widely know as "Muktuk" Marston, was an Anchorage business man and real estate developer. During the war he was a lieutenant colonel stationed at Elmendorf Air Force Base. As part of the war effort he organized the Eskimo Scouts for the Territorial Guard. The National Guard in Alaska developed from the Eskimo Scout unit and continues to play an important role in many small villages in the state. Courtesy of the Anchorage Historical and Fine Arts Museum

This shows the Seward waterfront in 1946. Today, with new cargo handling facilities, the prosperous little town of the past is regaining its importance as a port. Its spectacular setting has made it a favorite recreation spot for fishermen and vacationers. Photo by Paul J. Sincic

Chapter 8

Statehood

In 1916, Delegate James Wickersham introduced the first statehood bill. It was merely a trial balloon and quietly died in Congress. The arrival of the military during the Second World War revived the lagging economy and pushed the population over 100,000. However, the War, Navy, Justice, and Interior departments all resisted statehood for the duration, despite two measures introduced in 1943 and 1944. With peace, the statehood movement revived, pushed along in Congress by Delegate E. L. "Bob" Bartlett, who had been elected in 1944. Territorial Governor Ernest Gruening aided the cause in Alaska, and as a former newspaperman, enlisted his erstwhile colleagues in the contiguous United States. In 1946, Alaskan citizens approved a statehood referendum by a margin of three to one, and hearings on an Alaskan measure were held for the first time in 1947. In 1949, at the urging of Governor Gruening, the territorial legislature modernized the tax system, a prerequisite for self government, and created an official Alaska Statehood Committee. In 1950 the House, for the first time, passed an Alaskan statehood measure. The territory's vested interests, the salmon canning and mining industries, opposed statehood, as did a coalition of southern Democrats and conservative Republicans in Congress.

The outbreak of the Korean War in 1950 shifted national priorities, and as American forces became more deeply involved, Alaska statehood took a back seat. Not until 1952 did the statehood movement once again gather momentum, and early in 1953 half a dozen measures were submitted in the new Congress. Statehood hearings by a Senate committee in the fall of 1953 brought out large numbers of Alaskans who organized as "Little Men for Statehood," and out of this group evolved a more formal one called "Operation Statehood." In 1954 opponents suggested partitioning Alaska, with only the populated areas to be included within the boundaries of the new state. Others proposed that Alaska be made a commonwealth on the Puerto Rican model.

In 1955 the territorial legislature voted to force the statehood issue by calling a constitutional convention. The delegates elected William A. Egan, veteran territorial legislator and Valdez storekeeper, as president of the convention. The delegates deliberated on the campus of the University of Alaska near Fairbanks from November 1955 until February 1956, when they signed the document. The new

constitution, a brief document of 14,400 words, was quickly ratified by the Alaskan electorate in the April 1956 primary. The new document spoke well of Alaska's political maturity, and the delegates and citizens alike showed political savvy by opting for the "Tennessee Plan" to help with statehood. Under this strategy, first used by Tennessee and then six other would-be states, a congressional delegation of two U.S. senators and a U.S. representative were sent to Washington to lobby for statehood. Alaska's choice of an all-Democratic Tennessee Plan delegation, including Ernest Gruening and William A. Egan as the "senators," and former territorial Attorney General Ralph Rivers as the "representative," rekindled Republican fears about the prospective state's politics. At that point, however, Secretary of the Interior Fred Seaton persuaded President Dwight D. Eisenhower to back statehood.

Later, in 1958, devoted supporters rounded up the necessary votes in Congress. On May 28 the House passed the measure by a vote of 210 to 166 and the Senate followed on June 30 with a vote of 64 to 20. Then on July 7, the president signed the statehood bill. In August, Alaskans went to the polls and approved the statehood referendum by a five-to-one margin. (Twenty thousand Alaskans voted, more than had turned out for any previous election.) Finally, on January 3, 1959, Alaska formally entered the Union as the forty-ninth state.

Basically, the same arguments against Alaskan statehood appeared in every discussion and at every hearing between 1915 and 1958. Prior to the Second World War, the lack of action was mostly due to Alaska's small population and physical remoteness, as well as to the opposition and lobbying activities of the special interests. The Second World War revolutionized the territory and drastically changed the composition of its citizenry. With the population influx came a new awareness, and many of the new arrivals were unwilling to acquiesce to the status quo. They desired to push Alaska into the mainstream of American life. But despite this new involvement of Alaskans, the attitude of Congress had not changed enough. The old guard viewed both Alaska and Hawaii as potential dangers, because representatives from these two new states, they feared, would threaten the tradition of filibuster.

Furthermore, since both areas contained large minorities there were fears that admission would integrate the hal-

Longshoremen load cars of the Alaska Railroad at Seward in 1946. The ice-free port on Resurrection Bay was named for William Henry Seward, American Secretary of State, who negotiated the purchase of Alaska in 1867. As the terminus of the Alaska Railroad, Seward served as the port from which goods where shipped to the interior and the north, until the 1964 earthquake destroyed most of the port facilities. Photo by Paul J. Sincic

Streamliner service on the Alaska Railroad began with the train *AuRoRa* on October 18, 1947. It was expected to inaugurate a new period of improved passenger service for the railroad. An old engine was brought out for the ceremony marking the new service. Courtesy of the Anchorage Historical and Fine Arts Museum

lowed congressional chambers. In 1957 Congress passed a new civil rights act after prolonged debate. Although at first it was far too weak to overcome the various devices used to circumvent it, the new act was indicative of what the future held. As a result, many members of Congress began to reassess their positions, and led by such modern political leaders as Senator Lyndon B. Johnson, these politicians reluctantly admitted Alaska in 1958 and Hawaii a year later.

The 1958 Elections

Democrats swept the first state and congressional elections in November 1958. In the races for the two U.S. Senate seats, the contest between two former governors, Ernest Gruening, a Democrat, and Mike Stepovich, a Republican, dominated the campaign. Gruening defeated Stepovich by 26,045 to 23,464 votes. The septuagenarian put boundless energy and determination into his campaign. He made known his great abilities and acomplishments and contrasted these with Stepovich's conservative voting record when a member of the territorial legislature. Democrat Bob Bartlett, who had served as Alaska's delegate to Congress since 1945, easily outpolled Republican Ralph Robertson with 40,939 votes to 7,299, and former territorial Attorney General Ralph Rivers, a Democrat, prevailed over Henry Benson by a margin of 27,948 to 20,699 votes. In the gubernatorial race, Democrat William A. Egan, former territorial legislator and president of the constitutional convention, defeated Republican John Butrovich, with 29,189 to 19,299 votes. In short, Alaskan voters handed all top four offices to the Democrats. The latter also swept the state legislative races, gaining a majority of seventeen in the twenty-member senate, and winning thirty-three seats in the forty-member house. Republicans won five seats and independents gained two. It had been a Democratic landslide.

How could this Republican debacle be explained? First of all, there was the matter of party affiliation and timing. Most party-affiliated Alaskans were Democrats, and the election took place during a year of Republican defeats nationwide. Secondly, Democratic politicians were better known and politically more experienced than their Republican counterparts. Thirdly, Democrats were better organized and campaigned enthusi-

INAUGURAL TELEPHONE CONFERENCE CALL
OPENING OF ALCAN CIRCUITS
APRIL 2, 1947
ALASKA COMMUNICATION SYSTEM

astically for their entire slate, while the Republicans concentrated their efforts on Stepovich and Butrovich. And an *Anchorage Daily Times* editorial neatly summed up the fourth reason, namely that for better than two decades competing factions of the Republican party had fought each other as much as the Democrats.

Transition to Statehood

The next step was to affect a smooth transition from territoriality to statehood. Here the Alaska Statehood Committee was very effective. The 1957 legislature had appropriated $53,000 to the committee to enable it to obtain "information and suggestions" on how to bridge the gap between territorial and state government. The committee turned to the Public Administration Service of Chicago (PAS) which had already done excellent work for the constitutional convention. Eventually, in 1958, the committee entered into contracts with PAS to prepare detailed reports and drafts of proposed legislation, and executive orders on the organization of the executive judiciary, local government, and personnel administration. When the first of the reports were completed at the end of 1958, Alaskans eagerly anticipated President Eisenhower's proclamation of admission.

On January 3, 1959, six invited Alaskans gathered at the White House to witness the president signing the proclamation admitting the territory as the

For many years the military supplied Alaska's communication needs. The Alcan circuits of the Alaska Communication System were officially opened in April 1947 with symbolic calls linking Alaskan and "outside" cities. Courtesy of the Signal Corps, U.S. Army

While still chief of staff, General Dwight D. Eisenhower visited Alaska in 1947. He was given an opportunity to play golf at the Fairbanks Golf and Country Club course. A rather thin line separated the course from the neighboring farm field. Courtesy of the *Fairbanks Daily News-Miner*

Pan American Clipper Service linking Alaska with the other states was important in reducing the geographic isolation that affected everyone's perception of the territory.

The airport at Annette Island was built during World War II and served as the airport for Ketchikan for many years. This photo was taken in 1948. Photo by Paul J. Sincic

forty-ninth state into the Union. At noon, Eisenhower began signing the first of the three copies of the document of admission. In the meantime, in Juneau, where it was three hours earlier, United States District Court Judge Raymond Kelly administered the oath of office to Governor-Elect Egan and Secretary of State-elect Hugh Wade.

The length of Bartlett's and Gruening's first terms in the Senate had yet to be decided. There also was the question of who would be designated as senior senator. Both matters were decided by the toss of a silver dollar. Gruening drew a four-year term and Bartlett received a two-year term, and the latter became Alaska's first senior senator.

The Omnibus Bill

Alaska's congressional delegation soon found occasion to flex its newly-acquired political muscle when it pushed for the passage of the omnibus bill for the new state, a measure designed to put Alaska on an equal footing with the other states. Among other items, the apportionment and matching formulas of various federal grant-in-aid programs had to be revised. Equal treatment also required that the federal government cease developing policies for Alaska, and conducting governmental functions in Alaska carried out by state and local governments else-

In the 1940s the Public Health Service provided clinics to the isolated communities of south-eastern Alaska by using the motor vessel *Hygiene* which travelled with doctors, nurses, and medical equipment. Courtesy of the Health and Social Services Collection, Alaska Historical Library

The postal service in Alaska was negligible until the gold rush at the turn of the century. Until 1885 the only civilian post office in the area was at Sitka. Mail that once had to travel by ship or dog team now generally is transported by air. The post office at Fort Yukon was in this log cabin in the late 1940s. Courtesy of the U.S. Forest Service Collection, Alaska Historical Library

where. Equality, everyone realized, would be expensive. The Bureau of the Budget had recommended that the new state receive $27,500,000 in the form of transitional grants over a five-year period, after which time Alaska would receive enough revenues from oil and gas leases, monies from the Pribilof fur seal operations, and the sale of state lands to be on its own. In the final form, the omnibus bill granted the new state $28.5 million, and also recognized that the state legislature had passed a measure creating the Alaska Board of Fish and Game. A provision in the Admission Act temporarily retained federal jurisdiction over Alaska's fish and wildlife resources until the secretary of the interior certified that Alaska was able to meet its management responsibilities. Soon thereafter on January 1, 1960, Secretary of the Interior Fred A. Seaton reported to Congress that Alaska had met the requirements of the Admission Act, thereby transferring to the state effective control over its fish and wildlife resources.

The First State Legislature Meets

In the meantime, the first session of the first state legislature met in Juneau between January 26 and April 16, 1959. Its most important piece of work was the drafting and passage of the "State Organization Act of 1959." The original bill considered intended to concentrate authority and responsibility in the governor in a simple organization. There were to be nine principal departments, each headed by a single appointed executive. The departments were to be: Administration; Law; Revenue; Health, Education and Welfare; Labor and Commerce; Military Affairs; Natural Resources; Public Safety; and Public Works. During debates on the measure, however, lawmakers modified the organization law. They split the proposed Department of Labor and Commerce in two, and created additional departments of Education, and Fish and Game, from the original combinations. This brought the total number of departments to twelve. The executives heading Education, and Fish and Game, were to be appointed by the governor from nominations made by boards affiliated with these departments. Advocates of curbs on gubernatorial powers, however, pointed out that the powers and duties of the two boards were so limited that they were boards in name only.

Governor Egan Ill

Governor Egan became very ill and was hospitalized in Seattle for most of the time the first session of the first state legislature met. Hugh Wade, the secretary of Alaska, became acting governor. Wade recalled that "I hadn't talked with him (Egan) for twenty minutes before or during the campaign and I didn't know which way he would go on this subject or that subject...so it was very difficult....I was more or less on my own." Wade appointed one cabinet officer, Commissioner of Administration Floyd Guertin. Egan came back in the spring and Wade recalled that Egan "came down to the office on the last night of the session and he named some of his cabinet officers."

Statehood Benefits

Statehood advocates had known that the achievement of their goal would bring full self-government with improved efficiency and responsiveness of local government, increasing control over natural resources, and an Alaskan orientation of management policies. It also would enable Alaskans to break the economic bonds of colonialism. Most immediately, Alaskans were granted the status of a sovereign people with full self-determination. Some parts of this sovereignty were delegated to the federal government in return for representation in the United States Congress and a voice in the choice of a president. The congressional statehood land grant of 103,300,000 acres and the transfer of natural resource management functions enabled Alaskans to correct what had appeared to them to be federal mismanagement in this area. Article VIII of the state constitution, the natural resources article, clearly ended the federal ambivalence in that field, which had hovered between unrestrained exploitation or sustained yield harvesting, and between development for the benefit of nonresident or resident interest. The resource article clearly stated that state policy would be to "encourage the settlement of its land and the development of its resources...for maximum use consistent with the public interests...the utilization, development, and conservation of all natural resources belonging to the state...for the maximum benefit of its people. Wherever occurring in their

183

natural state, fish, wildlife, and waters are reserved to the people for common use... replenishable resources belonging to the state shall be utilized, developed, and maintained on the sustained yield principle, subject to preferences among beneficial uses." There were provisions for covering the development of facilities and improvements by the state, the management of the state public domain, and the definition and manner of establishing and limiting a whole host of private rights to various natural resources uses.

Statehood Cost Money

Alaskan political leaders and citizens alike soon discovered that statehood cost money. In presenting the first complete state budget to the second session of the first Alaska state legislature, Governor Egan drew attention to these costs. He compared territorial and state government functions, and stated that "during the last half of the current fiscal year, we will have assumed full responsibility for the management of our fish and game resources, an excellent start will have been made on a State Land Management Program, the judicial and other purely state and local functions will have been fully assumed. How will we fare beyond June 30, 1961? Most immediately, we are faced with a progressive reduction of the transitional grants...with those grants ending by June 30, 1964. At that time we will have to make up several millions of dollars if we are not to curtail services."

Economic Development

Alaskans had desired statehood in part because they believed that it would result in fairly rapid and diverse economic development. In order to survive as a political entity capable of fulfilling the role of a self-supporting state, Alaska desperately needed basic economic development. It possessed a few small lumber operations, a couple of pulp mills, a mining industry consisting of one underground and several relatively minor placer operations, and an ailing and seasonal salmon fishery and fish-processing industry. The only bright prospects were the potential for tourism to expand and oil and gas production to increase. Both were slow to grow. In the meantime, the state slowly selected

Granite Creek basin above Juneau is enjoyed by hikers on a warm day in 1948. Photo by Paul J. Sincic

resource-rich lands, a difficult task because no adequate inventories of Alaskan lands existed, and the Bureau of Land Management moved at a snail's pace in approving, surveying and patenting state selections. The state moved slowly because it did not have the necessary monies to properly manage its selections.

Federal Government Continues To Play Important Role

Alaskans also quickly discovered that the federal government continued to play an important role in the state's government and economy. The Department of Defense, for example, continued to spend hundreds of millions of dollars annually on manning, maintaining, and improving its defense installations in Alaska. It also continued to operate the state's telephone and telegraph communication system until it was sold to private enterprise in 1971. The Department of the Interior continued to loom large in state affairs; the Bureau of Land Management continued to manage the extensive public domain; and the Bureau of Indian Affairs provided a broad range of social, educational, and economic services for Alaska's Native population. The Department of Transportation managed the Alaska Railroad, and the U.S. Forest Service of the Department of Agriculture managed the extensive Tongass and Chugach national forests. In

Within the store image, hand-lettered signs read:

Libby's
DR-Lux
PLUMS
22¢

ELBO
MACARONI
40¢

YELO
Split
PEA

OLIVE
OIL

GERBERS
Baby
Food
8¢

FREE
DELIVERY
ON-ALL
$10.00
ORDERS
OR-OVER

HUNT'S
HOMESTYLE
PEACHES
40¢

Libby's
CORNED
BEEF
52¢

Prices at Gus George's Atomic Grocery Store in Juneau in 1949 look pleasantly low today, but were higher than those on comparable items in the Seattle area. The cost of living differential is always a surprise to those who have not experienced it. Photo by Paul J. Sincic

The Coliseum was the movie theater in Skagway in 1952, and as in many small towns the Saturday matinee was popular with kids. This day was special because it was sponsored by Jimmy Patterson, the soda fountain proprietor. Photo by Paul J. Sincic

In 1950 Native houses on pilings still occupied the present site of the Coast Guard Building in Juneau. The neat house on the left has a woodpile beside it and more wood is available on the beach. Photo by Paul J. Sincic

fact, the list of federal agencies involved in Alaskan affairs seemed endless. A few figures will illustrate the pervasive federal influence. Of a total employed work force of 62,900 in 1959, 16,890 were federal employees. And although federal employment slowed in subsequent years, federal workers still numbered 17,300 in 1971, of a total employed work force of 110,600. By 1971 all government employees constituted more than one-third of the total employed work force. This growth was attributable to the expanding needs of local and state government. In 1959 the former employed a modest 3,000, and the latter 2,600. These figures had risen to 9,000 and 11,700, respectively, by 1971.

Economic Prospects

Although numerous citizens worried about their state's economic future, others were cautiously optimistic. Statehood had put Alaska in the national limelight. Increased numbers of new settlers, investors, and tourists had arrived in the state in 1959. And since Richfield Oil Corporation's 1957 discovery of oil in the Swanson River field on the Kenai Peninsula, more oil had been found. Alaska now possessed four modestly producing wells, and oil companies planned to continue exploratory work. This was reflected in the state's first competitive oil and gas lease sale in December 1959, when several companies paid approximately $4 million for a total of 77,000 acres. Japanese investment groups which, together with American capital assistance, had built the second pulp mill at Sitka, had also interested other Japanese companies in examining Alaska's coal, iron, and oil potential as a possible source of raw materials for the Orient.

But there were many uncertainties as well. Federal defense spending was tapering off, and the long-ailing salmon industry recorded a record low pack in 1959. Japanese fleets in the Bering Sea and the mid-Aleutians continued to fish Alaska-spawned salmon stocks. For the first time, big Russian trawlers and factory ships appeared in the Bering Sea, utilizing fish species such as sole, haddock, flounder, rockfish, and cod. Americans did not use these species but feared that the Russians would soon be dragging the halibut grounds.

Revenue Requirements

When the legislature met in 1961, it considered Alaska's revenue requirements and raised tax rates where they would do the least harm to future economic development. Luck was with the new state—for while defense spending, Alaska's major industry since the 1940s, steadily dropped during the 1960s, the value of the major natural resources rose. Crude petroleum worth $1,230,000 was extracted in 1960; by 1967 the value had risen to $88,187,000. The value of gas rose from $30,000 in 1960 to $7,268,000 in 1967. While the state treasury had received a modest $3,372,000 in oil taxes in 1960, by 1967 this had risen to $35,613,000.

There were significant gains in the fishing and timber industries as well. By 1967, a vigorous king crab fishery worth in excess of $10 million per year had been created. And while the wholesale value of the fish catch had amounted to $96,689,000 in 1960, it had risen to $166,572,000 by 1965. It declined to $126,696,000 in 1967, primarily because of a drastic decline in the salmon runs. The timber industry grew more modestly. In 1960 it had an estimated annual payroll of $18.3 million and turned out wood products with an estimated end product value of $47.3 million. By 1967 these figures had risen to $25 million and $77.7 million, respectively.

Alaskans Vote for a President for the First Time

With many worried about the state's economic future, Alaskan voters went to the polls on November 8, 1960, to participate for the first time in a presidential election. Many were surprised when Vice President Richard M. Nixon narrowly defeated Senator John F. Kennedy at the Alaska polls. Within the state, the Republican party reduced the Democratic lead in the statehouse from thirty-four to twenty-one seats. In the senate the Republicans gained five seats. Alaska's congressional delegation was still Democratic, and the state legislature still had a

Democratic majority, but the 1960 election clearly ended the overwhelming Democratic predominance and made Alaska a two-party state.

Republican Drift

Statewide elections between 1958 and 1972 showed a significant drift toward Republican voting, although the Democrats were dominant for most of the period. Perhaps reflecting this Republican drift, Alaskan voters in 1966 ousted veteran Democrat William A. Egan, who was seeking a third gubernatorial term, and narrowly elected colorful and ambitious Republican Walter J. Hickel, Anchorage real estate developer and hotel owner. The state constitution limited the chief executive to two consecutive terms, and Egan was not eligible to hold that office again until a full term had intervened. He argued that he had not served two full terms since he had been sick for a few months at the beginning of his first term. Many Alaskan voters, however, did not accept his arguments and elected Hickel instead. The new governor abandoned the governor's chair two years later when President-elect Richard M. Nixon nominated him as secretary of the interior. Also, in 1968, Democrat Mike Gravel defeated veteran Ernest Gruening in the primaries and general election. Gravel, an aggressive and somewhat erratic individual, had come to Alaska in 1956. The son of French-Canadian immigrants to New England, he made some money in real estate. In time Barney Gottstein, an Anchorage millionaire and substantial contributor to Democratic causes, became Gravel's patron. Gravel had served in the statehouse and defeated the eighty-one-year-old Gruening with a very clever media campaign.

Senator Bartlett Dies

On December 11, 1968, Senator Bartlett died after undergoing major arterial heart surgery in a Cleveland hospital. Before Hickel's successor as governor, Keith H. Miller, took over, Hickel appointed Republican Theodore F. Stevens to fill Bartlett's position. Stevens had recently lost his bid in the primary for the U.S. Senate when he was defeated by Elmer Rasmuson, president of the National Bank of Alaska. Stevens thus gained the coveted Senate seat by appointment after he had failed to win it by election, and won election in his

own right in 1970. In 1970, the GOP suffered reverses, with the House seat reverting to the Democrats with the election of Nick Begich, a school administrator and state senator. The legislature also shifted in a Democratic direction.

Disasters

The first decade of Alaskan statehood was an exciting and trying time for its citizens and leaders. Statehood had been no panacea, and the state government struggled to provide for an ever-growing demand of badly needed services. Then, on March 27, 1964, one of the greatest recorded earthquakes of all times, measuring 8.4 to 8.7 on the Richter scale, struck southcentral Alaska and caused property damages amounting to hundreds of millions of dollars. Prodded by Alaska's congressional delegation, the federal government generously aided the state in reconstruction. When a flood severely damaged Fairbanks in 1967, the performance was repeated.

The Economic Outlook

Despite the generous help, however, the state's economic picture looked anything but promising. There had been various minor oil discoveries in the twentieth century, but it was not until 1957 that Richfield Oil Corporation discovered the Swanson River field on the Kenai Peninsula, the first really commercially viable field. There had been some production in the Katalla field. Between 1902 and 1931, the Chilkat Oil Company drilled thirty-six wells in the Katalla district, eighteen of which produced oil. Production, however, was small, ranging from just a few to twenty barrels per day. In 1911 the Chilkat Oil Company built a small topping plant which began operating in 1912 and for twenty-one years supplied local demands for gasoline and heating oils. Late in 1933 a fire destroyed the boiler house at the topping plant, and the company abandoned the entire operation. That had been in the past, and the Swanson River field returned but modest revenues to the state.

In order to maintain governmental services at a minimum, the state taxed its citizens at one of the highest rates in the country. It spent more money, per capita, than any other state on education and highways. In health care it ranked sixteenth among the states, and in welfare twenty-third. Despite the high taxes, the yield was less than the federal government sent in grant-in-aid funds. Alaska's inflated prices, the far-flung territory, and the high cost of operating the government only bought the minimum of services with the money available. The administrations of Bill Egan, Wally Hickel, and Keith Miller had barely limped from one oil lease sale to another.

Then, on January 16, 1968, the Atlantic-Richfield Company discovered the ten billion barrel Prudhoe Bay oilfield on Alaska's North Slope, a find of truly Middle Eastern proportions. On September 10, 1969, the state held its twenty-third competitive oil and gas lease sale. At the end of the day, the state had received a 20 percent down payment on the $900,220,590 in bonus monies. A jet stood ready at the airport to rush the checks to outside banks so that not a day's interest would be lost. Many Alaskans were euphoric. Oil revenues, at long last, would help stabilize Alaska's economy and enable the state to provide sorely needed services. The problem now facing the petroleum industry was how to get the oil to market.

Alaska Native Claims

How that was accomplished is a long and complicated story, going far back into Alaska's history. When Congress passed the Alaska Statehood Act back in 1958, it was determined to make certain that the new state would be an economically viable one. This, most realized, could only happen through heavy reliance on the development of the land and its resources.

Earlier states admitted to the Union had been granted certain sections in surveyed townships. Alaska was largely unsurveyed. Congress therefore decided to grant the new state in excess of 103 million acres, to be selected from the vacant, unappropriated public lands within a twenty-five-year period after admission. Perhaps most importantly, the state was to own the subsurface mineral rights to these lands as well, a major departure from precedent. Some forty million acres of unsurveyed tidelands and submerged lands were also automatically transferred to the state.

Many officials were aware of Native rights, but the issue generally was not well understood. In the Organic Act of 1884,

Forrest Bates was the agent at U.S. Customs in Skagway in 1952. The Alaska Communication System, run by the U.S. Army Signal Corps, continued to handle long distance communications in Alaska. Photo by Paul J. Sincic

The Brown Derby in Skagway was a soda fountain and cafe operated by Jimmy Patterson. The photographer included himself in this 1952 photo. Photo by Paul J. Sincic

for example, Congress declared that the determination of Indian Claims was reserved for future legislation. Congress reaffirmed this stand from time to time. For example, in the Alaska Statehood Act of 1958, it declared that Alaska and its citizens disclaimed all right and title to any lands which were claimed by Indians, Eskimos, or Aleuts, or were held in trust for them by the federal government. The final determination of what to do with

The supply ship *North Star* brought supplies to many of the Bureau of Indian Affairs (BIA) schools along the coast of Alaska. The BIA schools were run as a separate system from those under the territorial and state education departments. The one visit of the ship each year had to provide all the needs of the school for the year. Here the ship is anchored in the ice off Barrow in August 1964. Photo by C. Naske

Those on board the *North Star* watched a small boat from the ship make its way toward the village of Little Diomede at the point of the long slope in 1955. Courtesy of the *Fairbanks Daily News-Miner*

these claims Congress reserved for itself. In effect, Congress postponed action on the issue.

After statehood, the chief executive had to implement the state constitution. William A. Egan, the state's first chief executive, put together a bureaucracy designed to staff the initial twelve departments. Among these was the Department of Natural Resources, which, through its Divisions of Lands, had the responsibility to select, manage, and dispose of the state's 103 million acres. In 1961, the Native claims began to come into conflict with state selections. Four Native villages claimed about 5.8 million acres of land near Fairbanks, although the state had

already filed for patents on nearly thirty percent of the land. Thereupon, the Bureau of Indian Affairs, as guardian of the villages, filed a protest on their behalf. The state director of the Bureau of Land Management, however, had been ordered to dismiss all claims unless they involved lands actually occupied by Natives. He had been directed to implement this policy since the Department of the Interior's regional solicitor had ruled that the determination of Indian title was not within the department's jurisdiction. A dispute ensued when neither the state nor the Natives yielded their respective land claims.

The *Tundra Times*, a Native weekly

paper, publicized the dispute. The paper had been established in October 1962, with a grant from the Association on American Indian Affairs, Alaska Policy Committee. The publicity generated by this paper aided in the establishment of other Native groups across the state.

At the same time threats to Native-claimed lands multiplied between 1962 and 1966. The most spectacular involved the proposal for building a dam 530 feet high and 4,700 feet long at the Rampart Canyon on the Yukon River. A gigantic project which would have cost billions of dollars, it would have put the entire Yukon Flats under several feet of water. The Yukon Flats is a vast network of sloughs, marshes, and lakes that represents one of the great wildfowl breeding areas in North America, and the project would have caused major adverse environmental impacts. While the project eventually died because of adverse ecological and economic reports, the opposition of Alaska's Natives, and the opposition of an increasingly well-informed public, it demonstrated the continuing threat to lands claimed by Natives.

As early as 1963 the Department of the Interior's Alaska Task Force on Native Affairs issued a report that stated that a resolution of Native land rights was long overdue. Numerous proposals for resolving the problem were made by various groups over the years. In 1967, numerous Natives founded the Alaska Federation of Natives, a statewide organization. Before that occurred, however, Secretary of the Interior Stewart Udall stopped the transfer of lands until such time as Congress had resolved the issue.

While the controversies continued, the state continued to claim its statehood allotment. By 1968 it had selected 19.6 million acres, of which only over 6 million acres had been patented. As state selections continued, Natives filed protests. Between 1961 and 1968, protest filings covered 296 million acres, and by the middle of 1968 they covered 337 million acres.

When the Trans Alaska Pipeline System (TAPS), the incorporated joint venture of Atlantic-Richfield, British Petroleum, and Humble Oil, applied to the Department of the Interior to construct a pipeline from Prudhoe Bay to Valdez, it soon became apparent that no pipeline would be built until the Native claims had been settled. In early December, Congress approved the Alaska Native Claims Settlement Act, a measure which President Nixon signed into law on December

18, 1971. Under its provisions, Alaska's Natives were to receive forty-four million acres of land, with compensation amounting to $962 million, of which $462.5 million was to come from the federal treasury and the rest from mineral revenue sharing. Twelve regional corporations would administer the settlement.

It was an incomplete measure, one hastily drawn. Implementation was to prove difficult because of the many ambiguities of the act. The act also authorized the secretary of the interior to withdraw up to eighty million acres of land in Alaska for study and possible inclusion in existing national parks or forests, wildlife refuges, or wild and scenic river systems. On January 23, 1974, the secretary signed the primary federal right-of-way permit for construction of the Trans Alaska

The Bureau of Land Management has been responsible for fighting fires in the extensive forests of Alaska. In this late 1950s scene the "Antique Five," a B25 retardant plane flies over a 29,000-acre fire near Chalkitsik. Two hundred and thirty fire fighters were involved in fighting this blaze, many of them recruited in Native villages of the interior. Courtesy of the *Fairbanks Daily News-Miner*

One of the biggest military construction jobs surveyed, administered, and supervised by the Alaska District of the Corps of Engineers was the Ballistic Missile Early Warning System (BMEWS) station at Clear, Alaska. The three large detection antennas, capable of "seeing" an object in space 3,000 miles away, are 165 feet high and 400 feet long, installed like three football fields standing on edge, but in such fashion as to resist 180-mph winds and earthquakes. Enormous amounts of steel and concrete went into the construction of the installation. A mile of passageways gives access to all technical buildings and protects employees from possible radiation. Begun in 1959, construction was under the supervision of the Alaska District of the Corps of Engineers, which announced in 1960 that the total value of the project was $60 million. Courtesy of the U.S. Army Corps of Engineers

The Distant Early Warning System (The DEW Line) stretches across the top of Alaska and Canada. It is a 3,600-mile net of radar and communications stations reaching from Cape Lisburne in northwestern Alaska to Kulusak Island on the east coast of Greenland. Conceived by scientists at MIT's Lincoln Laboratory in 1952 as a "warning fence" protecting the United States and Canada on the northern frontier, construction began under Air Force supervision in 1954. In 1957 the Air Force, through competitive bidding, turned the system over to the Federal Electric Corporation, a subsidiary of IT&T, for maintenance and operation. The closeup view is a 1965 photograph showing the DEW Line station just outside of Barrow, Alaska. Today, most of the stations have been closed down. Photo at left by C. Naske. Photo below courtesy of the Balchen Collection, Alaska and Polar Regions Dept., Rasmuson Library, UAF

Pipeline. By late summer of 1974 construction had begun creating a substantial boom in Alaska. The line was completed by the summer of 1977 and the boom dropped off as suddenly as it had begun. At 10:05 a.m. on June 20 of that year, the first oil flowed into the pipeline, nine years after the initial discovery of oil at Prudhoe Bay.

The Election of Jay Hammond

In the meantime, in the 1974 gubernatorial election, Alaskans had elected Jay S. Hammond, a Republican outside the mainstream of his party. Hammond brought a varied background to his job, having been a U.S. Marine Corps fighter pilot in the South Pacific between 1942 and 1946, and an apprentice-guide, fisherman, hunter, and trapper in Rainy Pass in the Alaska Range between 1946 and 1949. He then served with the U.S. Fish and Wildlife Service from 1949 to 1956 as pilot-agent. Hammond established his own air taxi service, became a registered guide, and built a sportsmen's lodge on Lake Clark and a fishing lodge on Wood River Lakes. First elected to the statehouse in 1959 as an Independent, he switched to the Republican Party two years later. Hammond served six years in the house, becoming minority and majority whip. He became mayor of the Bristol Bay Borough in 1965, and was elected to the state senate in 1966, finally becoming senate president. Because his district was reapportioned in 1972, he chose not to run again.

Hammond teamed with Lowell Thomas, Junior, son of the famous broadcaster and himself a member of the Alaska legislature. Together they defeated Walter J. Hickel and Keith H. Miller in the primary, and then barely defeated incumbent Democrat William A. Egan.

Hammond was a conservationist, considered a political liability in Alaska. The new governor believed that each particular development project should be weighed individually and the question asked: "Will the people of Alaska really profit from this?" He also believed that the state's general fund monies should be derived from taxes and revenues from renewable resources. Hammond advocated that much of the money derived from oil and gas should be put into a permanent fund. It was no surprise that Hammond announced his desire to run for a second term. After a bitterly fought campaign, he retained the governorship for a second term in 1978.

Increasing Complexity of State Government

Hammond readily admitted that Alaska's government had become very complex in the 1970s, in part reflected by the budget growth rate. Between 1960 and 1965, it grew at a rate of 2 percent; between 1975 at a rate of 26 percent; and between 1975 and 1979 at 18 percent. This made for an average growth of 20.4 percent between 1960 and 1979. A summary of state expenditures shows that in 1970 they amounted to approximately $225,000,000, and had risen to about $1,250,000,000 by 1981. Realizing that the bulk of the wealth came from non-renewable oil and gas resources, Alaskan voters in 1976 approved a constitutional amendment creating a permanent fund. The amendment stipulated that at least 25 percent of "all mineral lease rentals, royalties, royalty sale proceeds, federal mineral revenue sharing payments and bonuses received by the state shall be placed in a permanent fund, the principal of which shall be used only for those income-producing investments specifically designated by law as eligible for permanent fund investments." The hope, of course, is that when the oil bonanza dries up, the income from the permanent fund will sustain the costs of state government. In December 1982 the permanent fund reported investment holdings totaling about $3.5 billion.

The future of the state is uncertain. What is certain is that oil and gas revenues will decline sharply by the end of the 1980s, and Alaskans must find ways to diversify the state's economy before it enters the decade of the 1990s.■

In 1944 Alaskan voters elected E. L. "Bob" Bartlett to succeed Dimond as Alaska's delegate to Congress. He was senior U.S. senator from 1959 till his death in 1968. During his years of public service he worked closely with Gruening to promote statehood for Alaska and then to further the new state's interests in Congress. This photo is from the late 1950s. Photo from the collection of C. Naske

To prepare for statehood and demonstrate the sincerity and ability of the population to govern itself, Alaskan voters elected delegates to a constitutional convention which met at the University of Alaska, Fairbanks, from November 8, 1955 to February 6, 1956. They drafted a constitution for the state that has proved to be a solid and enduring framework for government. The delegates posed informally in Constitution Hall, a new building on campus that had been turned over to them for the meetings. Courtesy of the R. Griffin Collection, Alaska and Polar Regions Dept., Rasmuson Library, UAF

Delegates to the constitutional convention held public hearings in December 1955 to explain the work they had done so far and to solicit public comment. Courtesy of the *Fairbanks Daily News-Miner*

The Alaska Constitutional Convention opened in 1955. William Egan was at the podium. Courtesy of the University Relations Collection, Alaska and Polar Regions Dept., Rasmuson Library, UAF

Some of the leaders gathered at the end of the convention in February 1956. Seated, from left to right are Frank Peratrovich, William A. Egan, and Ralph Rivers. Standing, from left to right are Mildred Hermann, Doris Ann Bartlett, Thomas B. Stewart, and Katherine Alexander.

Delegates elected Egan their president on the third ballot. Forty-one years old in 1955, a territorial senator, he had also been a former speaker of the house and had twice been mayor of Valdez. Delegates elected Peratrovich first vice president on the third ballot. A long-time legislator and president of the senate, he was a leader of the Tlingit Indians of southeastern Alaska, the only Alaska Native serving as a convention delegate. On the first ballot Rivers became the second vice president. A member of the senate, he was a lawyer who had been district attorney from 1933 to 1944 and Alaska's attorney general from 1945 to 1949. He also had been the mayor of Fairbanks from 1952 to 1954. Stewart served as convention secretary. A lawyer, he had been the chief clerk of the territorial house of representatives in the 1946 special session, and assistant attorney general from 1951 to 1954. He served in the state senate from 1959 to 1961 and subsequently was appointed superior court judge for the first judicial division. Hermann, a lawyer and Alaska resident since 1919, had served as the Alaska Director of the Office of Price Administration. As delegate to the convention, she was a member of the Committee on Rules and the Committee on Style and Drafting. Alexander, the secretary of the territorial senate, was appointed chief clerk of the convention. Doris Ann Bartlett, the daughter of Alaska's voteless Delegate to Congress, E. L. "Bob" Bartlett, served in the convention secretary's office. Courtesy of the *Fairbanks Daily News-Miner*

Constitution of the State of Alaska

PREAMBLE

We the people of Alaska, grateful to God and to those who founded our nation and pioneered this great land, in order to secure and transmit to succeeding generations our heritage of political, civil, and religious liberty within the Union of States, do ordain and establish this constitution for the State of Alaska.

13

The completed constitution is shown with the ivory gavel used by the presiding officers. Courtesy of the Historical Photograph Collection, Alaska and Polar Regions Dept., Rasmuson Library, UAF

In 1956 delegates to the Alaska Constitutional Convention decided, at the urging of George H. Lehleitner, a moderately wealthy businessman from New Orleans, to adopt the Alaska Tennessee Plan. Lehleitner had served in the navy in Hawaii during World War II and become interested in that territory's statehood aspirations. He devoted much energy to the Hawaii cause, but eventually was rebuffed by the island's political leaders. Lehleitner had discovered that when Tennessee was denied statehood, it elected its congressional delegation and sent these men to Washington asking to be seated. The delegation made a strong plea for admission, and finally, on June 1, 1796, Tennessee became the sixteenth state of the Union. Other territories followed the example, including Alaska. Alaskan voters elected Ernest Gruening and William A. Egan as their U.S. senators and Ralph Rivers as representative. This picture shows Richard (Dick) Gruel (left), a candidate for the Territorial House of Representatives, and Ralph Rivers. They are in the Democratic headquarters in Fairbanks where Helen Kehn shows them campaign materials. Courtesy of the *Fairbanks Daily News-Miner*

President Eisenhower signed the Alaska Statehood Bill on January 3, 1959. Vice President Nixon is at his right and Speaker of the House Sam Rayburn is at his left. In the back row, from left to right, are territorial leaders Ralph Rivers, Ernest Gruening, and Bob Bartlett; Secretary of the Interior Fred A. Seaton; Waino Hendrickson; unidentified; Mike Stepovich, Alaska's governor; and Robert Atwood, editor and publisher of the *Anchorage Daily Times*. Courtesy of the Bartlett Collection, Alaska and Polar Regions Dept., Rasmuson Library, UAF

President Eisenhower points to the new United States flag with forty-nine stars, following ceremonies at the White House during which Alaska was officially proclaimed the Forty-ninth State. From left to right are: E. L. Bartlett, senator-elect from Alaska; a White House aide holding the flag; the president; Waino Hendrickson; and Sam Rayburn, Speaker of the House of Representatives. From the collection of C. Naske

The *Fairbanks Daily News-Miner* and most Alaskan papers brought out special editions to commemorate Senate passage of the Alaska Statehood Bill on June 30, 1958 at 8:02 p.m. eastern standard time. Word reached George Sundborg, the editor of the *Fairbanks Daily News-Miner* at the moment the Senate had taken the last vote on the statehood measure. It was a little past three o'clock in the afternoon in Alaska's interior city, and the staff of publisher C. Willis "Bill" Snedden worked tirelessly throughout the rest of that day and part of the night in order to make a token air shipment of the special statehood issue to Washington. The special issue was on the desks of members of Congress on July 1, 1958. Courtesy of the Machetanz Collection, Alaska and Polar Regions Dept., Rasmuson Library, UAF

Alaska continued to be thought of in terms of exploration and adventure. Some of those who had been involved in exploits of exploration came together to film an episode of *High Adventure* in the Arctic. They gathered at Ladd AFB on September 11, 1957. From left to right are Sir Hubert Wilkins; Brigadier General Conrad Necrason, 11th Air Division commander; Lowell Thomas, Senior, news commentator and film maker; Colonel Bernt Balchen; and Donald B. MacMillan. Courtesy of the *Fairbanks Daily News-Miner*

Since statehood in 1959, the Alaska Department of Highways has had the difficult task of maintaining roads that are subject to severe weather and ground conditions. This snowplow-equipped truck is working on the Richardson Highway in the Alaska Range. The highway was not kept open all year round until 1955. At that time the Alaska Road Commission built several emergency shelters along the road for motorists who might become stranded in the mountain area. Photo by Richard C. Powers, courtesy of the *Fairbanks Daily News-Miner*

A new pulp mill for Alaska Lumber and Pulp Company was under construction when this picture was taken on August 20, 1958 at Silver Bay on Baranof Island. Japan became a prime market for pulp and lumber products. Courtesy of the U.S. Forest Service Collection, Alaska Historical Library

The University of Alaska campus is shown in 1959. The Bunnell Building is under construction and the old Main Building, the first building for the Alaska Agricultural College and School of Mines (extreme right) is being demolished. Courtesy of the University Relations Collection, Alaska and Polar Regions Dept., Rasmuson Library, UAF

Otto William Geist started ethnographic and archeological collecting for the University of Alaska in 1927. He went on to excavate archeological sites on Saint Lawrence Island, Pleistocene fossils in the interior, and natural history materials on the North Slope. He had broad interests, unquenchable curiosity, and brought back to the university materials of all kinds, from all over Alaska. The collections he made became the base for the University of Alaska Museum, and the museum's new building is named for him.

Geist spent much of 1959 and 1960 in the arctic collecting fossils, birds, and mammals while using the Naval Arctic Research Lab as a base. This photo was taken at that time. He died in 1963. Photo by C. Naske

201

This is a commencement procession on the university campus about 1958. Courtesy of the University Relations Collection, Alaska and Polar Regions Dept., Rasmuson Library, UAF

Otto William Geist, Ivar Skarland, Olaus Murie, and Adolf Murie, (left to right) are shown at the university in the late 1950s. The four were distinguished for carrying out early studies in cultural and natural history in Alaska. Courtesy of the University Relations Collection, Alaska and Polar Regions Dept., Rasmuson Library, UAF

Students of a 1958 workshop on Alaska pan for gold in the Chatanika River. The workshops give students background information on Alaska during the university's summer session. Courtesy of the University Relations Collection, Alaska and Polar Regions Dept., Rasmuson Library, UAF

This is Fort Yukon about 1960. The old Hudson's Bay Company post has become an Athapascan Indian town. The buildings near the river at the left formed the Northern Commercial Company complex. The company once had stores and trading posts throughout Alaska. The three-story white building is now the Sourdough Inn. Courtesy of the U.S. Forest Service Collection, Alaska Historical Library

Hoonah is a small coastal Tlingit Indian village that relies on fishing for both commercial and subsistence reasons. Development of the timber resource of the area is anticipated. Communities such as this were once hard to reach but now the state ferry system ties it to Juneau and Sitka. This photograph was taken in 1959. Photo by C. Naske

A field camp of the Naval Arctic Research Laboratory at Walker Lake in the Brooks Range is shown in May 1960. Courtesy of the University Relations Collection, Alaska and Polar Regions Dept., Rasmuson Library, UAF

For many years Clem Tillion was an influential member of the Alaska legislature, both as a representative and a senator. Once known for the derby he sported on most occasions, he is shown on his forty-three-foot boat, the *Ram* in 1960.

Fisherman, charter boat operator, and state legislator, Tillion was born in Brooklyn, New York on July 3, 1925. He served in the Navy from 1940 to 1945 and worked in a variety of jobs in Anchorage and Fairbanks, and for the Alaska Railroad at Cantwell and McKinley National Park between 1945 and 1948. He lived on his own fifty-eight-acre island in Halibut Cove, Kachemak Bay, from 1948 on. He fished commercially in Kachemak Bay and Cook Inlet and served in the state house of representatives from 1963 to 1975, and in the state senate from 1975 to 1977. A colorful individual, he was retired from politics in 1983 by a change in administrations. Photo by C. Naske

In 1962 Governor William A. Egan and Senator Ernest Gruening looked at a model of the state's first ferry, the motor vessel *Malespina,* in the Alaska State Exhibit at the Seattle World's Fair. The ferry system was planned to provide connection between the isolated communities of southeastern Alaska which could not be connected by road. Courtesy of the *Fairbanks Daily News-Miner*

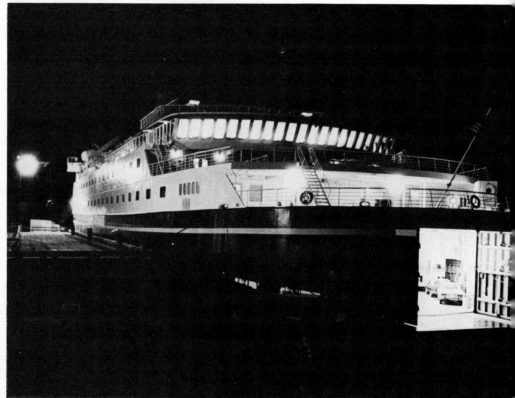

The motor vessel *Columbia,* the state's largest ferry, docked in Juneau, June 14, 1979. Courtesy of the *Fairbanks Daily News-Miner*

In 1784, Gregori Shelikhov, the so-called "Russian Columbus," together with 185 men on three galiots, established Three Saints Harbor on the southwestern coast of Kodiak Island. It remained his company's chief settlement until 1791 when Aleksandr Baranov, the new colonial manager, founded Saint Paul's Harbor at the present site of Kodiak. In 1792 he transferred the headquarters there because of the shortage of timber at the earlier settlement. It soon became one of the largest settlements in Russian America. Built on a steep, rocky beach, it consisted of barracks, shops, smithies, a school within a wooden semi-circular stockade, houses, an infirmary, and a church outside the walls. It remained the headquarters of the Russian-American Company until about 1800 when activities moved to New Archangel. (Baranov had founded New Archangel on Baranov Island in the "straits" or tidal channels of the Alexander or King George archipelago off the Alaska Panhandle). Kodiak, however, continued to be an important outpost of the company. In 1912 the Katmai explosion buried the town under eighteen inches of volcanic ash. During World War II Fort Abercrombie was an important Army base and radar station, and the Navy also developed a base of its own. In 1964 the earthquake and resulting tsunami destroyed much of the downtown area shown in this photo as well as canneries, processing plants and the fishing fleet. Courtesy of the *Fairbanks Daily News-Miner*

Before the 1964 earthquake the main street of Valdez still had many buildings from its boom period at the turn of the century. Courtesy of the *Fairbanks Daily News-Miner*

The 1964 earthquake and huge tidal waves, called tsunamis, destroyed most of old Valdez, but fortunately few lives were lost. One report stated that the waterfront looked as "though it was sawed off." Docks had been shattered and homes "snapped from foundations and shredded into kindling." McKinley Street looking northwest from Keystone Avenue shows some of the destruction. The townsite was eventually abandoned and Valdez relocated to safer ground. Photo courtesy of the U.S. Army

This view shows Seward on March 29, 1964 after the tsunami had destroyed the waterfront. One observer stated that the shoreline looked as if it had been bombed. The Alaska Railroad port facilities, which had served as the southern terminus for shipping activities, were destroyed, and Anchorage took over many of the activities of this port. Courtesy of the *Fairbanks Daily News-Miner*

In Anchorage the 1964 earthquake destroyed many of the businesses along Fourth Avenue. The Army and the National Guard played a major role in the rescue and salvage operations. Courtesy of the U.S. Army Signal Corps Collection, Alaska Historical Library

Elmer Rasmuson, president of the National Bank of Alaska, was a candidate for the U.S. Senate in 1968. While on the campaign trail in Chalkitsik he stopped to repair a plane tire. Pilot Les Risley mans the pump. Simon Francis, Junior is the observer on the left. Courtesy of the *Fairbanks Daily News-Miner*

The need for access seems ever present. To carry supplies to the developing North Slope, in 1969 Governor Walter Hickel authorized the construction of a winter road from Livengood to Sagwon. State workers carried out the construction of the "Hickel Highway" with minimal planning and little consideration of its effect on the areas through which they bulldozed. The following summer the road became a permanent muddy quagmire in many areas, but was opened for one more winter's use before being abandoned. Courtesy of the Alaska Department of Highways Collection, Alaska Historical Library

Many students from rural Native villages had to leave home to attend school. Boarding schools at Sitka and in Oregon tried to provide the education beyond grade school that was not available at home. Now the state has built high schools in many villages and is developing other educational opportunities. These students are returning home for the summer in 1965. Courtesy of the *Fairbanks Daily News-Miner*

Many of the people in Alaska still depend on local natural resources for economic or cultural reasons. The men of many coastal Arctic villages still hunt the migrating whales. In this 1965 photo hunters of Barrow cut the blubber from a Bowhead whale. The skin boat used in the chase is just beyond the piece of blubber. Photo by C. Naske

The Alaska Native Claims Settlement Act of 1971 (ANCSA) was a complex piece of legislation that would affect many aspects of life for Alaska residents. Congress passed it under pressure so that work on the Trans-Alaska Pipeline could proceed.

The legislation was based on the dedicated work of many Native leaders. Here at a 1970 meeting on the issue are, from left to right, Joe Upickson of Barrow, Al Ketzler of Nenana, and Tim Wallace of Fairbanks. Courtesy of the *Fairbanks Daily News-Miner*

The ANCSA also authorized the secretary of the interior to withdraw up to eighty million acres of land in Alaska for study and possible inclusion in existing national parks or forests, wildlife refuges, or wild and scenic river systems. Congress was to decide what areas to include. Soon a bitter fight developed between conservationists and developers in and out of Congress. In this photograph Secretary of the Interior Cecil Andrus (left) and U.S. Senator Ted Stevens are deeply involved in one of the many committee hearings on the so-called d-2 issue, named after section 17(d)(2) of the ANCSA. In December 1980 at the end of the Carter administration Congress finally settled the whole issue when it passed the Alaska National Interest Lands Conservation Act. President Jimmy Carter signed it into law (94Stat.2371). Courtesy of the *Fairbanks Daily News-Miner*

Lieutenant Governor H. A. "Red" Boucher presented the Governor's Cup, for supreme achievement in sled dog racing, to George Attla of Huslia after he had won his third North American Sled Dog Open Championship in March 1972. Attla has gone on to win numerous other NA championships.

One of the regional Native corporations, Doyon, Incorporated underwrote the production of a movie called "Spirit of the Wind," based on Attla's life. It depicted the many obstacles, including tuberculosis of the bones, which Attla had to overcome to become a champion racer. The movie has received critical acclaim. Courtesy of the *Fairbanks Daily News-Miner*

Governor William Egan and Lieutenant Governor Boucher are shown at a Democratic Party picnic in Juneau in 1972. A poster for Nick Begich, Alaska's U.S. representative, is on the cabin behind Egan. Begich was later lost in an air crash. Photo by Paul J. Sincic

215

This photo was taken at the swearing in of new representatives at the 1975 Alaska state legislature. The presiding officer was Lowell Thomas, Junior. Those being sworn in were from left to right, Philip Guy of Kwethluk, Charles Parr, Glenn Hackney, unidentified, Mike Bradner, "Red" Swanson of Nenana, Steve Cowper, Fred Brown, and Brenda Itta of Barrow. Parr, Hackney, Bradner, Cowper, and Brown were all from Fairbanks. Courtesy of the *Fairbanks Daily News-Miner*

The U.S. Army has held military exercises regularly to test arctic equipment and provide training in winter warfare. In an operation in January 1976 the soldiers practice first aid in the field. Courtesy of the *Fairbanks Daily News-Miner*

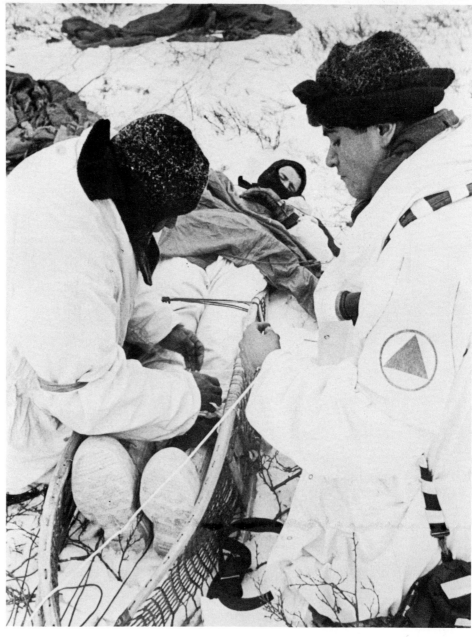

On an exercise in the Alaska Range, Sergeant Cook of the Twenty-third Infantry rappells down a 200-foot cliff. The camp for the group is in the valley. Courtesy of the U.S. Army Signal Corps Collection, Alaska Historical Library

For many years the Naval Arctic Research Laboratory at Barrow functioned as a center for scientific research in the Arctic. The large complex offered laboratory and logistic support to many scientists.

In this July 1976 photo of the research center the shore ice hugs the coast while the open water of the Arctic Ocean is visible at the top of the picture. The recent closing of the laboratory has prompted discussions concerning the need for the development of a national policy for research in the Arctic. Courtesy of the *Fairbanks Daily News-Miner*

In 1980 an act of the Alaska legislature, and the passage of a referendum by Alaskan voters, established the Alaska Statehood Commission to examine various aspects of the relationship between Alaska and the federal government. Governor Jay S. Hammond appointed ten Alaskans to serve on the commission.

Lieutenant Governor Terry Miller is shown addressing a 1980 meeting. Jack Coghill of Nenana (left, foreground) was chairman.

In January 1981 the commission issued its preliminary report

entitled *More Perfect Union: A Preliminary Report,* and on January 11, 1983 it brought out its final report entitled *More Perfect Union: A Plan for Action.* Courtesy of the *Fairbanks Daily News-Miner*

In 1978, after the failure of a compromise d-2 bill in Congress, Secretary of the Interior Cecil Andrus acted swiftly. On November 16 of that year he withdrew 110 million acres under section 204-E of the Bureau of Land Management Organic Act. On December 1, under the provisions of the Antiquities Act of 1906 President Jimmy Carter signed an executive order creating seventeen national monuments containing fifty-six million acres. Here demonstrators protest the actions of Andrus and Carter. Courtesy of the *Fairbanks Daily News-Miner*

The legislature created the Permanent Fund to save and invest 25 percent of the income from the oil-related taxes and leases flowing into state coffers. The fund is designed as a cushion against the time when oil revenues are expected to drop. A board oversees the investment of this fund. Elmer Rasmuson (center), an Anchorage banker, functioned as the appointed chairman for a couple of years. To his left is George W. Rogers, an Alaskan economist. Courtesy of the *Fairbanks Daily News-Miner*

Management of state funds has become a major responsibility of the legislature. The Senate Finance Committee met in Juneau in January 1982 to discuss the declining state revenues caused by the decline in world oil prices. At the head of the table is Senator Don Bennett, co-chairman of the committee, and to the right is Senator Ed Dankworth, chairman of the committee. Courtesy of the *Fairbanks Daily News-Miner*

The Department of the Interior plays a major role in Alaska, as it manages most of Alaska's land. James Watt, secretary of the interior, is at the podium at the Captain Cook Hotel in Anchorage, on August 11, 1981.

Governor Jay S. Hammond and the Alaska congressional delegation are at the table to his left. Courtesy of the *Fairbanks Daily News-Miner*

Flood waters swept Fort Yukon in May, 1982. Alexander H. Murray established the settlement on the Yukon River as a Hudson's Bay Company trading post in 1847. Originally located further upstream, residents moved it to its present site in 1864.

Flooding is an ever-present danger to many of the river villages in the interior with low banks along meandering shallow rivers. In the spring high water from ice jams, heavy rains, and glacial melting create hazardous situations. Courtesy of the *Fairbanks Daily News-Miner*

In this May 1982 photo, a riverboat carries villagers past their flooded homes in Fort Yukon. Courtesy of the *Fairbanks Daily News-Miner*

In 1898, miners, disappointed in their search for gold in the Yukon Territory's Klondike, flocked to the Eagle area. Eagle City emerged that year to cater to and house this new population. Coinciding with these activities, in 1899 the U.S. Army established the Fort Egbert military reservation at Eagle. It had a customs station during its heyday, and still has one today. As mining waned, the military abandoned Fort Egbert in 1911, and a small Native and white population occupied the area in two communities separated by three miles, Eagle City and Eagle Village. Today, as in earlier times, people continue to make a living from the land by hunting, fishing, and trapping, and some hold state jobs. Courtesy of the U.S. Forest Service Collection, Alaska Historical Library

In many parts of Alaska spring is symbolized by the ice "going out." In Nenana, a statewide pool is held to guess when the Tanana River will break up in the spring. The large tripod is set up on the river ice and connected to a wire that stops a clock at the exact moment it moves. Here Nenana residents raise the tripod on the river on March 1, 1982. Courtesy of the *Fairbanks Daily News-Miner*

Native leaders created the Eskimo-Indian Olympics to bring their people from across the state together and to perpetuate, through competition and demonstration, traditional games from many areas. Many spectators attended this session at the Patty Center at the University of Alaska, Fairbanks, on August 2, 1982. Courtesy of the *Fairbanks Daily News-Miner*

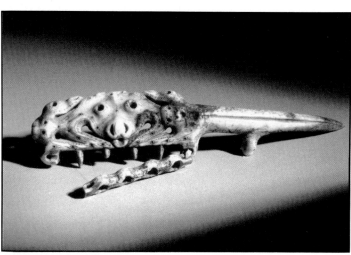

Some of the most dramatic prehistoric materials in Alaska come from Saint Lawrence Island and the Punuk Islands close-by. One of the best known of these is the "Okvik Madonna," the head and torso in ivory of a woman with an enigmatic smile and holding what may be a bear to her breast. The carving is estimated to date from 500 B.C. Courtesy of the University of Alaska Museum

This small mask of ivory, probably from Panuck Island, has a surface that is weathered and cracked from long burial. It is approximately three inches long. Courtesy of the University of Alaska Museum

The Ipiutak (350 A.D.) archeological site at Point Hope is unique in many ways, among these the art style which includes openwork carvings. The purpose of many of these elaborate works is not understood. This ornamental comb of walrus ivory has a bear head between its paws as the main feature. It is 10⅜ inches long. Courtesy of the University of Alaska Museum

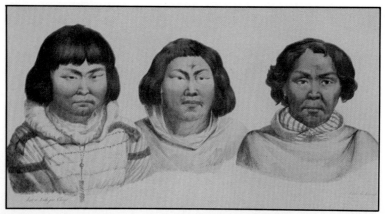

Three inhabitants of the Aleutian Islands were drawn by M. Louis Choris when he was on an 1816 expedition. The man at the left wears a gut parka. The center parka may also be a gut parka. From Choris, *Voyage Pittoresque Autour du Monde*, Paris, 1822, Alaska and Polar Regions Dept., Rasmuson Library, UAF

These two inhabitants of Unalaska have very elaborate parkas. The man at the right wears a bentwood hat decorated with sea lion whiskers.

Unalaska is one of the larger Aleutian Islands. It has a good harbor and once had several villages. Many early explorers stopped here and recorded their visits with sketches and comments. From Gawrila Sarytschew's *Account of a Voyage of Discovery to the North-east of Siberia, the Frozen Ocean and the North-east Sea*. London, 1806, Alaska and Polar Regions Dept., Rasmuson Library, UAF

This interior of a Saint Lawrence Island summer house of walrus skin was done by M. Louis Choris on a 1816 expedition. The two men wear gut parkas, and the seated man is playing the traditional flat Eskimo drum. Coils of seal gut can be seen hanging at the left while other furs and foodstuffs are stored about the interior. The large metal pot was probably secured in trade with Siberia. From Choris, *Voyage Pittoresque Autour du Monde*, Paris, 1822, Alaska and Polar Regions Dept., Rasmuson Library, UAF

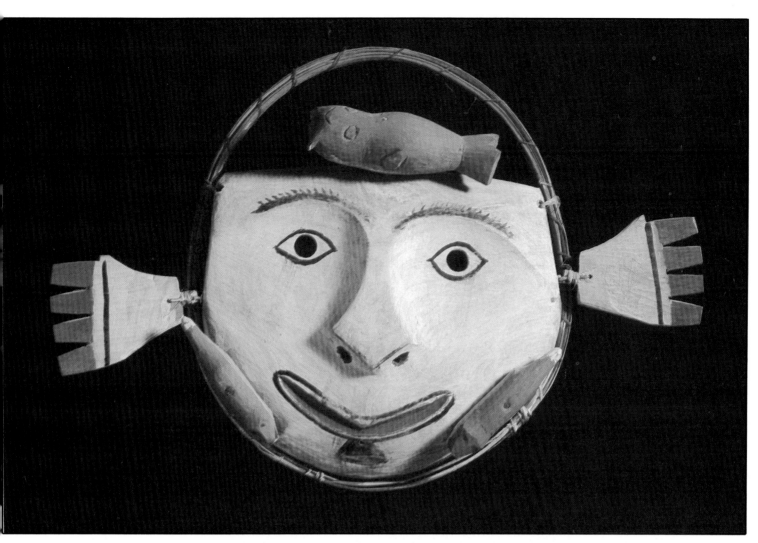

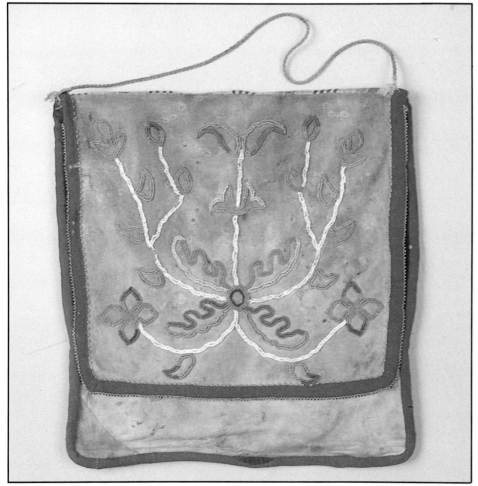

A Yupik Eskimo mask from Hooper Bay presents a smiling face. Although it was made in 1950, it is very much like older masks, since natural local materials, hematite, charcoal, and a clay wash, were used to color it. Large elaborate masks were used in the lower Yukon and Kuskokwim delta areas in dances and ceremonies. Courtesy of the University of Alaska Museum

The Athapascans are noted for their beadwork. Styles will vary from place to place and with the particular artist. This moosehide sled bag shows the open floral design favored in the Koyukuk area about 1895. The bag was designed to be hung between the handles of a dogsled for easy access to small items. Courtesy of the University of Alaska Museum

"Eskimo drummers and singers and one man dancing. All wear the Siberian haircut. The loincloth of the man is merely a discarded white man's undershirt originally obtained from a trader, with the sleeves tied around the waist, and the tail brought up between the legs to the back where it is rolled tight. It happens quite frequently that these get freed during the dance and have to be continually put back and fastened. The drummers are wearing sealskin pants." From the Archives, Alaska and Polar Regions Dept., Rasmuson Library, UAF

"Hanging pieces of walrus meat on rack near house. Much of the meat is cut in strips and hung to dry. This work is generally done by the women although sometimes men and boys may help. The heavy slabs of meat to which blubber and skin are still attached are hauled from the beach to the boat rack or meat cache on long wooden sledges shod with whalebone or, as in recent years, with steel runners. Little if any of the walrus is lost. Even the stomach and intestines are brought in and used." From the Archives, Alaska and Polar Regions Dept., Rasmuson Library, UAF

In 1927-28 a nineteen-year-old married Eskimo women named Nupok drew life as she saw it at the winter camp at North East Cape. She was encouraged by Otto Geist, who was on the island collecting archeological and ethnographic material for the University of Alaska. These five drawings are by Nupok, as described by Otto Geist. *Courtesy of the Archives, Alaska and Polar Regions Dept., Rasmuson Library, University of Alaska, Fairbanks.*

"Eskimo woman splitting a walrus skin. After being stretched on an enormous driftwood frame, the skin, which is nearly an inch thick is split. The split portion is left attached at one end of the skin. It is then removed from the splitting frame of driftwood and restretched on a second frame which is narrow and twice as long to provide for the length of the split skin spread out and joined in the middle where it has been left unsplit. It is left on this frame for several weeks to dry. The dried skin is used to cover oomiaks as well as to cover the siberian type of house. The splitting process requires such skill that only a few women of the Island are able to do this." From the Archives, Alaska and Polar Regions Dept., Rasmuson Library, UAF

"Family group in the agra. The two women, one at each end of the large meat platter, are cutting meat for the male members of the family and the children. Each man will reach into the platter and withdraw such food as may be served. If dry meat happens to be cut, fresh seal blubber is also cut into small strips, and seal blubber and meat are eaten together. For the small children and old people with badly worn teeth, the morsels are cut very small. The frame for drying clothes may be seen suspended from the ceiling; the drum is hanging from the wall; the suspension ties terminating in a large hook to hold a kettle or other food pot over the seal oil lamp are shown. The walrus stomach hanging from the drying frame may contain various articles, in this case probably sinew, raw, stripped, or braided ready for use; needle cases; and patches of reindeer or sealskin for mending skin cloths. At any rate this bag belongs to one of the women of the house. Very likely the two families live under the same roof in the same single room." From the Archives, Alaska and Polar Regions Dept., Rasmuson Library, UAF

"Eskimo man and woman, Ungottingowan and his wife, sitting in their agra. (Nupok) shows a pattern of tattoo marks on the woman; both wear belly strings, arm bands, necklaces, and ear pendants." From the Archives, Alaska and Polar Regions Dept., Rasmuson Library, UAF

Two grass baskets from the Aleutians represent one art form of the Aleuts. The finely twined baskets are decorated with embroidery thread and date from the 1940s. In the treeless Aleutian Islands grass was an important resource and was used for mats, bags, and other needed objects. The fine work of baskets such as these is unequalled. Courtesy of the University of Alaska Museum

The bear-head dagger from the 1800s shows the craftsmanship that makes Northwest Coast art outstanding. The Dall sheep or musk-ox horn carving is decorated with copper and inlaid abalone shell. The hair is gone from the bear skin that covered the back of the head. The copper blade of the dagger was about twenty inches long. Courtesy of the University of Alaska Museum

This small Chilkat blanket was woven in Klukwan in 1934. It shows the traditional colors used in the blankets. It is simpler in form than many larger and older blankets but contains many of the same design elements. It was probably made for sale rather than use.

Klukwan was noted for its fine weaving. Blankets from this area were traded along the entire Northwest Coast where travel and trade were made possible by extensive waterways and large seaworthy canoes. Courtesy of the University of Alaska Museum

Juneau in the late 1950s still had many of the features of the old mining and fishing town. Narrow streets and small false-fronted frame buildings were still common. The Alaska-Juneau gold mine, though closed in 1944, still dominated the town. In the foreground construction was beginning on a future state office building. Photo by L. Rowinski

The village of Minto was located on the Tanana River before it moved in the summer of 1969. The low-lying area had frequently flooded, and the village moved to higher ground near the Tolovana River, where it was connected by road to Fairbanks. While on the Tanana it depended on river freighting, like the tug and barge in the background, for supplies. Photo by L. Rowinski

The Steese Highway runs north from Fairbanks to Circle on the Yukon. The Alaska Road Commission constructed the 162-mile road in the 1920s to connect the mining camps that had once been joined by the stampeder's trail from Circle to Fairbanks. It was named for Colonel James G. Steese who was president of the Alaska Road Commission from 1920 to 1927. This view along the road in the late 1950s was typical of much of the scenery along the route. Since then the section near Fairbanks has been improved and paved and other stretches reconstructed. Photo by L. Rowinski

Kenai has a small chapel built in 1906 to commemorate the burial place of church workers. A small handsome church in Kenai still serves a congregation. (The photo was taken in 1968). Photo by L. Rowinski

When this picture was taken, in 1958, Kotzebue was a small Eskimo town that had grown from the reindeer station that was established there about 1897. Rotman's Store was the hotel and restaurant available to visitors. It has continued to grow as a supply center for a large area and as headquarters for the NANA Native corporation. Photo by L. Rowinski

Lumber for local use or for a bigger commercial market has always been an easily exploitable Alaskan product. Here is an aerial view of log rafts stored in a cove in southeastern Alaska, on their way to a mill. Courtesy of the Alaska Historical Library

Anaktuvuk Pass is a small Nunamint Eskimo village deriving its name from the pass in the Brooks Range in which it is located. Now permanent residents, the people not too long ago were seminomadic, periodically moving the settlement about the valleys near the heads of the John and Anaktuvuk rivers. They called themselves the "Tulugagmint," or "raven people," or "the people living in the vicinity of Tulugak Lake." The present village, comprised of Eskimos from the Killik and Chandler rivers, became permanent in 1951 when the federal government established a post office there. The pass always has been a favorite route of the caribou on which the Nunamiut have relied for food and clothing for centuries. Since this 1969 photograph the village has grown and changed, with new homes, a school, and other buildings. Photo by L. Rowinski

In 1898 boomers established Valdez as a port from which to reach the gold fields of the Klondike and the Fairbanks area. It also became the center of its own mining area. Valdez was built on the delta of the twenty-two-mile-long Valdez Glacier, which came to within four miles of the town. The Richardson Highway connected it to Fairbanks. This 1960 photo shows the town with its dramatic background of the Chugach Range.

In 1898 Valdez was established as a post from which to reach the gold fields of the Klondike. When gold was discovered in the Fairbanks area it became the main route to interior Alaska. The trail to the interior became the Richardson Highway. Valdez also became the center of its own mining area. Photo by L. Rowinski

U.S. interest in arctic research was for many years shown by the Naval Arctic Research Laboratory at Barrow. Among their projects were studies of the Arctic Ocean and the northern atmosphere from field stations set up on the Arctic ice pack. One of these "ice island" laboratories is shown in the 1960s. Photo by L. Rowinski

The first school in Kobuk is shown in the fall of 1952. R. Simonds, the teacher, stands in front of the small log school with his pupils. The wood supply for heating and building is stacked inside the door.

Teachers in such small schools often had to live in the building or find quarters in the village. The population of Kobuk in 1950 was thirty-eight. Courtesy of the Department of Education Collection, Alaska Historical Library

In Alaska the sport of sled dog racing has been gaining in popularity. The races range from informally organized events in towns and villages to the grueling 1,049-mile Iditarod Race from Anchorage to Nome. This scene in the 1960s is in Fairbanks. Photo by L. Rowinski

While air service has become important to many of the isolated villages in Alaska, nowhere is it more vital than in communities such as Anaktuvuk Pass that cannot be reached by road or boat. The arrival of the plane in such places brings out the community to see who has arrived, what the mail has brought, and what supplies are finally being delivered. These villagers greet the Wien Airlines plane in August 1969. Photo by L. Rowinski

The people of Saint Lawrence Island demonstrate the "blanket toss," a sort of human-propelled trampoline of walrus hide from which a person can be bounced many feet into the air. The game may have once served the function of giving an observer an extended view out over the sea when watching for sea mammals to hunt. The two men at the left are wearing white duck parka

covers which help them blend into the snow and ice when hunting. This photo was taken in 1966. Photo by L. Rowinski

Klawock is a fishing and lumbering village on the west coast of Prince of Wales Island. Here, as in many other villages, old and reconstructed totem poles have been gathered together in a "park" in an effort to preserve them. This picture was taken in 1967. Photo by L. Rowinski

Appendix: Alaska's Important Resources

From time immemorial, Alaskan Natives relied for sustenance on the natural resources of the land and the sea. Fish were particularly important for all Native cultures, and efficiently harvested, constituted a major part of the diet in all regions.

The five Pacific salmon species were especially important and remain so today. Originating in the coastal streams, they migrate to the north Pacific Ocean where they mature before returning to the inland waters to spawn and die. The coastal seas also contain large populations of halibut, herring, and a variety of bottomfish, such as pollock, cod, and sablefish. There also are sheefish, whitefish, smelt, tomcod, and candlefish, to name but a few. Shellfish are abundant as well, including king, tanner, and dungeness crab, butter and razor clams, scallops, and various species of shrimp. In addition, Alaskan rivers contain such fish as trout, pike, grayling and char.

The Eskimos, who longitudinally stretch around a large sector of the circumpolar world, also latitudinally occupy areas from the subarctic to the high arctic. For thousands of years they have been masters of marine hunting, using methods successful in bagging a large variety of sea mammals, from the small ringed, harbor, and bearded seals; walrus; and beluga; to the large bowhead whale. They also hunt the polar bear, caribou, and a variety of waterfowl.

In the interior of Alaska, the Athapascans hunt moose, bear, caribou, and small game such as the porcupine, snowshoe hare, and squirrel. They also fish, and the river runs of the salmon in the summer and early fall probably constituted the single most important resource during the aboriginal past.

Forests were important in providing shelter for animals and furnishing fuel and building materials. Natives utilized fur-bearing animals for food and clothing, and although they did not practice agriculture, they harvested berries and wild plants. The Natives used copper from the Copper River, slate from the Aleutians, and jade from the Seward Peninsula for weapon heads.

When the Russians arrived in the 1740s they began to commercially exploit Alaska's natural resources. They came to obtain sea otter and fur seal pelts for the Chinese and Russian markets and for more than a century the fur trade dominated Alaska's natural resource development.

In the beginning the Russians limited their activities to trading voyages. They built small trading posts and forced the Aleuts to hunt the sea otter throughout the island chain. However, by the end of the seventeenth century, Russian fur trading and hunting activities began to move into Prince William Sound, the Kenai Peninsula, and southeastern Alaska. With diminishing returns from sea otter and seal hunting, the Russians put more emphasis on land fur-bearers. They established trading posts along the rivers of interior Alaska.

Together with the fur hunting and trading and settlement activities, the Russians also used other resources. The goal was to become more self sufficient and less dependent on supplies from Russia. The Russians, therefore, harvested salmon for consumption and limited export, used whales for their meat and blubber, and planted gardens and introduced livestock to the Aleutians, Kodiak, Sitka, and the coast of south-central Alaska. They established the first sawmills and used the timber to build forts, homes, and ships, and also used the wood for fuel. They mined a little coal, worked some copper deposits, and even discovered some gold on the Kenai Peninsula. The Russians planned that by 1861 they would use minerals and other resources previously secondary to furs. But the furs were not gone, because the conservation policies inaugurated by Governor Ferdinand von Wrangell were restoring the sea otter and had increased the Pribilof fur seal herd. The Russians even shipped ice to San Francisco in the 1850s, but all of these activities were not enough to reverse the declining fortunes of the Russian-American Company.

Even before Russia sold its colony to the United States in 1867, the commercial whaling era began in the 1830s off Alaska's coast. Beginning in 1835, whalers pursued the sperm, right, gray, and bowhead whales. In 1848, Yankee whalers passed through the Bering Strait and discovered abundant bowhead whales in these northern waters. Within a few years, better than half of the north Pacific whaling fleet, mostly American, worked in the Chukchi and Beaufort seas. However, by the end of the Civil War, whaling slowly declined as crude oil replaced whale oil.

Natural resource development increased after Americans arrived in Alaska in 1867. There was some expansion in the fur industry after an American company bought out the Russian-American Company. Marine and land fur exports increased, trading efforts in the interior expanded, and sea otters and fur seals were overhunted.

Gold and Oil

In 1974 the dollar and other currencies were set free from the gold standard. With increasing inflation, gold prices increased rapidly and Arab nations boosted gold prices still further when they purchased large quantities of the metal with their petroleum dollars. The rising gold prices revived the Alaskan industry. By 1976 gold production was worth $2.8 million, up from just $500,000 in 1971. Gold prices continued to rise, finally climbing to over $800 an ounce, only to decline again. In recent years the price of the metal has responded to free market forces and economic conditions, and in 1983 the price per ounce has been about $400. While hardrock mineral production has been low, the potential for a prosperous mineral-product-based economy is verified by the increased exploratory activity over the last few years.

The main basis for the state's economy has been oil, and probably no single event in Alaska's history has had the impact on the region comparable to that of Atlantic Richfield's discovery of the gigantic 9.6 billion barrel Prudhoe Bay oilfield in 1968. That number represents the recoverable barrels of oil, making Prudhoe Bay the twelfth largest field ever discovered in the world.

The initial discoveries of oil deposits, however, were made long ago, many decades before phrases like "energy crisis" and "environmental degradation" became household words. It was Thomas Simpson, an employee of the Hudson's Bay Company, who first observed oil deposits along the Canadian Arctic shore while engaged in his coastal survey of 1836-37. Somewhat later in the century, Lieutenant George M. Stoney headed the United States Navy's 1886 exploration expedition, which extensively explored the North Slope of Alaska. One of Stoney's men, Ensign W. L. Howard, found oil near the upper Colville River and brought back a specimen.

Subsequent travelers and Natives reported oil seepages at various locations

At Katalla the operation was successful enough for the building of trestles and tracks for work trains to service the shipping docks. This photograph of the construction was taken July 12, 1907. Courtesy of the Moss Collection, Alaska Historical Library

Natives of the area secured jobs clearing the forest and producing timbers for rails and buildings. Courtesy of the Moss Collection, Alaska Historical Library

R.W. Moss called this shot the "Corner in my boudoir." He was in the Katalla area about 1907. Pinups and a photo col-

lection adorned the walls. His fine Indian-made snowshoes and beaded moccasins were probably new and useful acquisitions. Courtesy of the Moss Collection, Alaska Historical Library

Oil continued to be sought in Alaska. This Alaska Gulf and Oil Company drilling rig was testing its luck near Knik in 1955. Courtesy of the Anchorage Historical and Fine Arts Museum

With the discovery of the Swanson River oil field on the Kenai peninsula in 1957, development in that area really began, and soon moved offshore into Cook Inlet. Alaska's role as an oil-producing state and her dependence on oil revenue had begun. Courtesy of the Alaska Historical Library

In 1969 the tanker *Manhattan*, with specially reinforced hull and bow, fought its way through the ice of the Northwest Passage to determine the feasibility of moving oil from the North Slope to the East Coast. Although the voyage was completed successfully, the idea was not feasible enough to be pursued.

The trip followed by a year the announcement of the Prudhoe Bay oil field, the largest in North America. Courtesy of the *Fairbanks Daily News-Miner*

on the North Slope. In 1921, representatives of Standard Oil Company of California and General Petroleum Company examined seepages near Barrow.

Favorable conditions also existed elsewhere in Alaska. In 1856 oil seepages were found on the west side of Cook Inlet, and were noted in the Katalla-Yakataga area in 1896. In 1902 the Alaska Oil Company drilled a wildcat well near the mouth of Cook Inlet. At about the same time the Chilkat Oil Company

drilled another well in the Katalla district on the coast, east of the mouth of the Copper River. Although both were unsuccessful, the operators found enough encouragement to continue testing. Between 1902 and 1931 the Chilkat Oil Company drilled thirty-six wells in the Katalla area, eighteen of which produced oil. It was a small operation, however, ranging from just a few to twenty barrels a day. In 1911, the company built a small topping plant which began production in 1912 and for twenty-one years supplied local demands for oil products. Late in 1933 a fire destroyed the boiler house at the topping plant, and the company abandoned the entire operation. During its thirty-one years of history, the Katalla field produced only a modest 154,000 barrels of oil—not even enough to supply local needs.

Geologist Alfred H. Brooks, head of the Alaska branch of the United States Geological Service, retained his optimism regarding territorial oil deposits despite repeated failures to find commercial quantities. Brooks often voiced his opinion, and perhaps influenced President Warren G. Harding when he created Naval Petroleum Reserve No. 4 by executive order on February 27, 1923. The reserved area on the North Slope comprised approximately 37,000 square miles. The Geological Survey subsequently investigated the area over a period of five years, but not until World War II was the Navy instructed to develop additional oil reserves. In 1944 it started an extensive exploration program on Naval Petroleum Reserve No. 4, which lasted until 1953. Eventually, it found an oil field at Umiat containing approximately 100 million barrels of recoverable oil. At the end of the exploration period, two minor oil and three natural gas fields had been found—but nothing of commercial value.

As previously stated, Richfield Oil Corporation found oil on the Kenai peninsula. By 1965 the industry had developed five oil and eleven gas fields, and between 1958 and 1966, the state had received a total of $122,223,000 in direct cash payments from the oil industry. Most of the money came from bonuses on competitive leases, which provided more than $66,000,000.

While geologists and seismic crews roamed Alaska, annual crude oil production rose from 187,000 barrels in 1959 to 74 million barrels in 1969; and natural gas production went from 310 million cubic feet to 149 billion cubic feet. Wellhead value of this production, on which the state levied its taxes, had risen from 1.5 million in 1960 to $219 million 1969—at which point the oil industry had become the state's foremost natural resource extractive industry.

Finally, on January 16, 1968, the Atlantic Richfield Company struck the Prudhoe Bay field. The discovery proved to be a benchmark in Alaskan economic history. On September 10, 1969, the state held its twenty-third competitive lease sale, this one for North Slope lands. The previous twenty-two leases had netted the state less than $100 million. The twenty-third sale, covering leases on less than .001 percent of the state's land mass, raised more than $900 million.

The oil had to be shipped out of the arctic. Therefore, the Trans-Alaska Pipeline System (TAPS), an unincorporated joint venture of Atlantic-Richfield, British Petroleum, and Humble Oil, applied to the United States Department of the Interior in June 1969 for a permit to construct a hot-oil pipeline across 800 miles of public domain from Prudhoe Bay to tidewater at Valdez on Prince William Sound. There were many difficulties to overcome, and by late 1970 TAPS became the tightly organized Alyeska Pipeline Service Company, Incorporated, headed by Edward Patton, formerly of Humble Oil. After many more delays, the company obtained the necessary permits and started preliminary construction. By the summer of 1974 construction had begun in earnest on the biggest privately financed construction project ever undertaken in the United States.

Three years later, on July 28, 1977, the oil finally arrived at the Valdez tanker terminal. By 1978, oil flowed through the line at 1.16 million barrels per day. During the first year of operation 278 million barrels of oil reached Valdez and by 1982, that figure had jumped to 547 million barrels. In 1978 there had been 9,356 billion barrels of oil in the ground at Prudhoe, and in 1982 this had declined to 7,554 billion barrels.

Clearly, by 1990 the state can look forward to significantly reduced revenues from Prudhoe Bay. Even worse, falling oil prices have further reduced the state's revenues, while at the same time it has become ever more dependent on oil revenues. In 1982, for example, petroleum provided 86.5 percent of state revenues. In the meantime, stimulated by the euphoria of oil wealth, the state legislature abolished the state income tax system. State leaders will face some tough choices in the years ahead to deal with

the declining revenues from Prudhoe Bay. That is not to say that no other oil will be discovered. There indeed will be other finds, but many of these will be offshore on federally-owned submerged lands where the state does not share in the revenues. It also is unlikely that there will be another Prudhoe Bay. In short, the state might once again experience the historical pattern of boom and bust economic cycles. And there is no other natural resource which even comes close to generating the kind of revenues Prudhoe Bay has provided. Alaskans, however, approved a constitutional amendment on November 2, 1976, creating a "Permanent Fund." Under its provisions, one-fourth of the mineral revenues flow into this fund. By 1983, it will contain approximately four billion dollars. The hope is that, with proper management, the earnings from the "Permanent Fund" will sustain state government operations after Prudhoe Bay has run dry.■

The Richardson Highway paralleled much of the southern half of the pipeline route. Traffic, some of it trucks with eighty-foot lengths of pipe, filled the road and pounded the surface to pieces. From the Richardson Highway Project, Alaska and Polar Regions Dept., Rasmuson Library, UAF

During the pipeline boom housing in Valdez was tight and newcomers made do along the roadways in trailers, campers, and vans. From the Richardson Highway Collection, Alaska and Polar Regions Dept., Rasmuson Library, UAF

Here a Sikorsky Skycrane helicopter ferries part of a bulldozer into the Keystone Canyon area, where the Trans-Alaska pipeline crosses atop the ridges and avoids the scenic canyon area. The helicopter was part of an airlift which placed equipment on the ridges to build a pioneer trail for pipeline construction crews. Courtesy of the Alyeska Pipeline Service Company

Sideboom tractors lower a
section of forty-eight-inch pipe
into a ditch in the Brooks
Mountain Range, about 175 miles
south of Prudhoe Bay. Almost half
of the 800-mile-long pipe is buried.
Courtesy of the Alyeska Pipeline
Service Company

The ditch in which the pipe will be
buried and the pipe sections
stretch across a valley in interior
Alaska. Courtesy of the *Fairbanks Daily News-Miner*

The road north of the Yukon River was named the Dalton Highway after James W. Dalton, an engineer who helped call attention to the oil potential of the North Slope. Travel on the road is by permit and a checkpoint is maintained at Dietrich Pass. These are supply trucks to the North Slope in 1981. Courtesy of the *Fairbanks Daily News-Miner*

Dietrich Camp, an Alyeska pipeline camp, was preparing for construction in June 1974. Towers for microwave communication are located at the camps and pump stations. Courtesy of the *Fairbanks Daily News-Miner*

The Yukon River was only one of the obstacles to be crossed by the pipeline. The bridge, which spans 2,290 feet, accommodates vehicles as well as the pipeline. Before it was built, barges, hovercraft, and winter ice bridges were used to cross the river. Courtesy of the *Fairbanks Daily News-Miner*

A sealift to Prudhoe Bay arrived in August 1976 with materials from the West Coast. Large sections of prefabricated buildings and plant units were barged across the north Pacific, through the Bering Strait, and then along the north coast of Alaska during the short period when the arctic ice pack moved away from the shore. Courtesy of the *Fairbanks Daily News-Miner*

At Valdez construction progressed on the oil storage yard and shipping terminal in May 1976. The first oil reached the terminal August 1, 1977. Courtesy of the *Fairbanks Daily News-Miner*

Recently Valdez celebrated the city's founding, and its prosperity, with a Valdez Day parade. Courtesy of the Alaska Historical Library

Valdez continues to bask in its prosperity. It has a new civic center, and a grain terminal and floating dock have just been completed. Across Port Valdez the tanks and buildings of the marine terminal handle a steady stream of tankers carrying the oil to American ports. Photo by L. Rowinski

The Copper River and Northwestern Railway was built to haul copper ore from the great Kennecott Mine. Its terminus was the town of Cordova, which also served as the shipping port for the ore. On April 8, 1911, the first trainload of 1,200 tons arrived and was loaded on a ship bound for a smelter at Tacoma. The mine and the railroad were important to Cordova, but when the mine closed in 1938 and the railroad shut down, Cordova became more dependent on fishing.
Courtesy of the Norma Hoyt Collection

Several attempts and proposals were made to get a railroad to the Kennecott copper mine. The route from Cordova was finally put through successfully. It involved bridges over the delta of the Copper River and over the Copper River at Miles Glacier as well. The man at the left reading an address formalized the opening of this small bridge, as did the Indian girl with a small bouquet, and the photographer who recorded the event for posterity.
Courtesy of the Norma Hoyt Collection

Minerals

There is no question that timber utilization will increase substantially over the next few decades. The fate of the mineral industry is much more cloudy. Mining is an old industry, and as early as the late 1840s Peter Doroshin, a Russian engineer mining coal, found gold on the Kenai Peninsula. Although miners worked Alaska's gold deposits in the latter part of the nineteenth century, it was the large discovery in the Klondike in Canada's Yukon Territory which brought Alaskan gold to the attention of the general public. The gold discoveries on the Seward peninsula in 1898 resulted in a rush to Cape Nome from Pacific coast ports. By mid-May 1899, a tent town contained 250 souls; by early summer the population numbered 1,000, and by late summer a thriving community of 2,000 lined the beach of the Bering Sea. A year later the population reached 20,000. Soon prospectors discovered gold deposits in various regions of Alaska. In 1899 they also found large amounts of copper at Kennicott, and in 1900 placer tin on the Seward Peninsula.

Felix Pedro found gold in the Tanana Valley in 1902, near a site on which the town of Fairbanks grew, and there were discoveries at Kantishna in 1905, the Chandalar and Willow Creek districts in 1906, and in the Iditarod district in 1909. Miners found several mercury deposits in the Kuskokwim region between 1910 and 1920. In 1914 there was a gold discovery in the Tolovana region, and in 1915 large-scale gold quartz mining began at Juneau.

In 1906 all of this activity led to an all-time peak in gold production of 1,034,000 fine ounces, valued at $21,365,000. Thereafter, gold production declined into the 1920s; rose again in the 1930s, until the beginning of World War II; and then declined. In 1964 Alaskan miners produced 63,000 fine ounces worth $2,188,000. Alaska's mineral industry declined substantially from the high levels of activity achieved in earlier times, and during the 1950s it achieved a plateau at a fraction of its previous importance. There were 673 operating units in 1909. By 1956, there were only 156. Over the same period of time the total number of people employed dropped from 3,807 to 976. Like commercial fishing, the mining industry has been highly specialized, mostly producing gold, which has ranged from between 40 to 70 percent of the total value of minerals extracted.

249

After the initial spurt in production at the turn of the century, the level of gold production remained fairly constant between 1918 to 1942, until the War Production Board issued the "Gold Mining Limitation Order L-208" on October 8, 1942. This order made the industry nonessential to the war effort. In 1943 gold production dropped 20 percent over the previous year's level.

Following the war, the mining industry recovered slowly. After a minor resurgence, hindered by high labor and supply costs, gold mining declined in importance. Coal, sand, and gravel production increased to support the postwar building boom and the construction of military facilities. During the decade of the 1950s, the gold, coal, and sand and gravel industries annually alternated in high production values for Alaskan minerals.

In 1957, Richfield Oil Corporation found oil in what became the Swanson River field on the Kenai Peninsula, establishing Alaska's first truly commercial oil production. A new era had begun, and by the 1960s, petroleum had become Alaska's most valuable mineral. Sand and gravel production increased to become the second most important segment of the mineral industry.■

The "Million Dollar Bridge" at the Miles Glacier was an engineering marvel of its time. It stood after the railroad closed, in 1938, until 1964, when one of its spans was destroyed by the earthquake that year. A group of dignitaries viewed it in 1911. From left to right they were Messrs. Lenoir, DeLong, Whittlesey, Romig, Hazlett, Donohoe, Boryer, Dennison, and Kahn. Courtesy of the Anchorage Historical and Fine Arts Museum

These are Kennecott Mine Company buildings. The office is the white building in the center of the photo; below it is the club and then the tram terminal. Courtesy of the Historical Photograph Collection, Alaska and Polar Regions Dept., Rasmuson Library, UAF

The Kennecott Mine in Kennicott is shown. From 1911 to 1938 the mine successfully produced copper, and profits, for the Guggenheim/Morgan interests. The mine was modern and efficient. The town dwindled when the mine closed, but many of the buildings still remain.
Here ore is loaded on the railway cars for transportation to Cordova. Courtesy of the Norma Hoyt Collection

From 1904 to 1930 an isolated copper producing center was on Latouche Island in Prince William Sound. Production increased when the Kennecott Copper Company built a concentrator there in 1914. The photos show an engine room in 1921 and a radio room the same year. Courtesy of the Anchorage Historical and Fine Arts Museum

A marble quarry at Tokeen, in southeastern Alaska, operated from about 1902 to the 1930s. It provided marble for West Coast projects, and in Juneau was used for the columns and lobby of the present State Capitol Building. World War II and changes in style made the quarries unprofitable. Another quarry was operated at Calder. Courtesy of the Alaska Historical Library

Mining development in the Yukon Territory moved ahead in several areas. The old White Pass Railroad was used to bring ore to Skagway where it could be shipped to smelters outside. These longshoremen were photographed in 1952 stacking lead and zinc ore in the hold of a ship. Photo by Paul J. Sincic

In 1912, Congress authorized the Secretary of the Navy to spend $75,000 out of a $500,000 appropriation for investigating, mining, and testing some Alaskan coal for possible naval use. In August 1912 the Navy dispatched an investigating expedition to the easily accessible Bering River coal field. In the late fall, the miners started their work on Trout Creek. Eventually, the workers mined 855 tons of coal from four locations and sacked it for shipment. This picture shows the sacking process. Courtesy of the U.S. National Archives

Coal was long recognized as an important Alaskan resource, but attempts to develop it were never particularly successful. Plans for development were brought to a complete halt in 1906 by President Theodore Roosevelt's withdrawal of coal lands from entry. Later, the route chosen for the Alaska Railroad was near several exploitable fields, and because of the Navy's interest, a mine was developed near Chickaloon, the terminus for the Matanuska Branch of the railroad. The Chickaloon project was a major effort, and its buildings implied permanence, but the operation was short-lived. Courtesy of the U.S. National Archives

The Evan Jones Coal Company mine at Jonesville in the Matanuska Valley operated in the 1920s and continued on to 1968, when the Anchorage military bases switched from coal to gas power generation. In this 1920s shot miners coming off shift were photographed at the mouth of the tunnel. They were obviously met by two local children who were able to ride the horses. Courtesy of the U.S. National Archives

Another area with coal reserves which the Alaska Railroad made accessible to markets was near Healy on the Nenana River. At Healy the coal lay in thick beds and was not far from the market in Fairbanks. (That town's dependence on wood was becoming a critical problem.) The market grew with military buildup in Fairbanks and Anchorage during World War II. This panorama from 1922 shows the dramatic veins of coal exposed in the bluff. Courtesy of the U.S. National Archives

The Nabesna Mining Company led to the formation of a small town in the Wrangell Mountains. Although the company mined for gold, there were many other minerals in the area as well. Courtesy of Norma Hoyt Collection

August 8, 1911, a group gathered at the Wible property on Canyon Creek, south of Sunrise on the Kenai Peninsula. Springer and Reibel were the operators of the gold mine on the property. The creek was the site of an unsuccessful dam project which was to control water flow and provide water for hydraulic operations. Courtesy of the U.S. Library of Congress

Another community sprang up at Gulkana to serve miners, trappers, and even a local fox farm. The matrons of the area gathered in the general store for this picture, taken about 1918. Courtesy of the Norma Hoyt Collection

Although Fairbanks was the last big gold strike in Alaska, prospectors continued their search for gold and other minerals. Courtesy of the Norma Hoyt Collection

TOP RIGHT

This photo from the early 1930s shows a group at Kantishna, a small mining camp at the western end of Denali National Park. Fannie Quigley (second from right) and her husband, Joe, (second from the left) mined in the area for many years. Thelma Hunt is in the center. John Bushea is at the left, and George Lingo is at the right. Courtesy of the Norma Hoyt Collection

Large companies consolidated many of the small claims and brought in large equipment such as dredges. These dredges could handle the difficult ground efficiently, and combined excavating and concentrating the gold ore in one floating plant. The Fairbanks Exploration Company became one of the major employers in the area. Courtesy of the Bunnell Collection, Alaska and Polar Regions Dept., Rasmuson Library, UAF

Agriculture

The Russian promyshlenniki started rudimentary agriculture in Russian America in the late eighteenth century. It was not an important activity, and only served to supplement the Russian diet, primarily with root vegetables. The Russians remained dependent on food imports. For thirty years after the American purchase, travelers and government officials mostly reported that conditions were unfavorable for farming, yet from time to time, observers remarked on the surprising discovery that vegetables and some other crops actually grew in the north.

The gold rushes at the end of the nineteenth century brought thousands of fortune hunters to Canada's Yukon Territory and to Alaska. With this population influx, interest in agriculture revived. In 1897 three special agents supported by a congressional grant of $5,000 traveled through and reported on southeastern Alaska, the southcentral region, Kodiak, the Alaska peninsula, and the Yukon valley. The investigators found that a variety of crops could be grown, that vegetable gardens were a possibility, and that cattle could be raised. They also mentioned numerous difficulties which would hinder agricultural development, such as a lack of land laws, difficult terrain, excessive moisture in the southeast, short growing seasons, bogs and peaty soils, uncertain markets, and transportation problems. The agents recommended the establishment of experiment stations.

Following their recommendations, Congress authorized experiment stations, and the first opened in Sitka in the summer of 1898. Another one followed at Kenai in 1899; and then others at Rampart on the Yukon; Copper Center; Kodiak; Fairbanks; and finally, Matanuska in 1917. Only the last two survived; the others were closed after a few years of operation. In 1916 Congress extended the 160-acre homestead size to Alaska, but agricultural development progressed very slowly.

Finally, during the Great Depression of the 1930s, the administration of President Franklin D. Roosevelt decided to establish one hundred agricultural colonies through the Division of Subsistence Homesteads and other government agencies. One resettlement effort took place in the Matanuska Valley northeast of Anchorage. A total of 202 families, chosen from Wisconsin, Minnesota, and Michigan and one from Oklahoma arrived in Alaska in May 1935. The citizens of Seward and Anchorage greeted the arrivals enthusiastically. They went on to the Matanuska Valley and started the farming experiment, determined, one imagines, to finally refute the myth of Alaska as a land of snow and ice.

Was the experiment a success? Actually, the question has never been resolved. Most authorities in the 1930s predicted that it would be, but conditions deteriorated through 1938. There was much dissatisfaction with subsistence farming—the Anchorage market was not large enough to allow for commercial-scale farming, and production and shipping costs were too high to permit exportation to other population centers. It was America's involvement in World War II which revitalized Alaskan agriculture by expanding the local market. Employment opportunities at high wages in military construction, however, induced many settlers to give up farming.

In the postwar years there was renewed interest in homesteading and farming in the Matanuska and Tanana valleys, and the western portion of the Kenai peninsula. Settlers took out many homesteads, and some even received final patent to their lands. Still, in 1964, the value of farm products sold amounted to only $3,771,000—only a slight improvement over the 1959 total of $3,512,000. At no time did Alaska produce more than 8 percent of the food products consumed by its population.

In 1976, the total value of Alaska's agricultural production amounted to $8.7 million. The value of all crops produced came to $4.4 million—livestock products exceeded $4.2 million; milk, $2.9 million; and hay, $2.3 million. Potatoes had a value of $1.0 million. The 1976 agricultural production value was 6 percent less than 1975's value of $9.2 million. Still, state officials were optimistic, stating that although Alaska's agriculture had not been outstanding in 1977, rising farm prices were expected to push the year's total value of agricultural products slightly above that recorded in 1976.

Alaska's agricultural industry is very small. For example, in 1977 it only had thirteen grade A dairies, 2,300 beef cows, 300 steers, 1,000 bulls, and 1,600 calves. State farmers produced limited quantities of potatoes, oats, barley, mixed grains, and grasses. Poultry farmers delivered eggs to some local markets, many individuals raised vegetables, and some farmers raised hogs. Still, state officials and in-

In 1897, supported by a congressional grant of $5,000, three special agents traveled through and reported on the agricultural possibilities in southeastern Alaska, the southcentral region, Kodiak, the Alaska peninsula, and the Yukon valley. In their cautiously optimistic report they stated that a variety of crops could be grown and urged the establishment of experiment stations. Following the recommendations of the report, Congress authorized experiment stations for Alaska. A station opened in Sitka in 1898, at Kenai in 1899, at Rampart in 1900, another at Copper Center in 1903, in Kodiak and Fairbanks in 1907; and at Matanuska in 1917. All experiment stations soon closed their doors, except those at Fairbanks and Matanuska, which still exist today.

This farm in Fairbanks continues today as part of the University of Alaska. In this early 1920s picture the men in the wheat are apparently a group of visiting dignitaries.

Hope for agricultural development was high in the early 1900s, and when Fairbanks was still an isolated mining town, farms developed nearby to produce hay and grain for the many horses as well as the growing local population. Courtesy of the Lewis Collection, Alaska and Polar Regions Dept., Rasmuson Library, UAF

The barley harvest was photographed at Delta Junction in September 1979. Courtesy of the *Fairbanks Daily News-Miner*

dividuals connected with the experimental farms continued to be impressed by the state's "awesome" agricultural potential. They pointed out that the U.S. Department of Agriculture's Soil Conservation Service has identified nearly 20 million acres of tillable land climatically suitable for growing crops. Of these, less than 20,000 acres were under cultivation in 1977. There are an additional 200 million acres of range for cattle and reindeer. With 20 million acres of cropland in production, Alaska would rank fifth in the United States behind Kansas, North Dakota, Texas and Illinois. If Alaska had only 5 million acres in production, it would be on the same level as Pennsylvania, Idaho, North Carolina, or New York.

As part of a program to diversify the state's economy, the legislature and the governor launched a program to clear and prepare about sixty thousand acres of state land near Delta Junction on the Tanana River, one hundred miles south of Fairbanks, and make it available to private farmers to raise grain, principally barley, both for export and local consumption. The state subsequently spent millions of dollars on this demonstration project and the development of grain export facilities at Seward. However, unfavorable weather conditions resulted in several poor harvests.

What is clear is that farming and ranching are indeed possible in Alaska. There is no single obstacle which time and money cannot overcome, and Alaskan agricultural products could become competitive if farmers engaged in large-scale production. This would reduce costs and make northern farms competitive.

Timber Resources

While agricultural development is slow, the utilization of the timber resources of the Tongass National Forest did not begin in earnest until the opening of the Ketchikan pulp mill in 1954. The Natives of southeastern Alaska had used the timber for thousands of years to build their homes and canoes; construct utensils, armor, and weapons; and heat their homes and cook their food. After 1867, American citizens settled the region and soon discovered gold and other metals. These new residents harvested the trees for home construction, boat building, and for timbers to support mine shafts.

As previously stated, the large volume utilization of timber resources did not begin until 1954. From 1954 until 1965, the harvest expanded from 84 million to 420 million board feet, an increase of 400 percent. American Viscose Corporation, the largest manufacturer of rayon in the United States, formed a combination with the Bellingham, Washington firm of Puget Sound Pulp and Timber to form the Ketchikan Pulp Company. By 1954 its operation at Ward Cove near Ketchikan produced pulp. In the early 1950s the Japanese also became interested in Alaskan timber. After extensive negotiations, a Japanese Company, Toshitsugu Matusi, formed the Alaska Pulp Development Company, incorporated in the United States, and by 1960 the Alaska Lumber and Pulp Company near Sitka had become a reality. The Japanese followed their Sitka venture with the creation of the Wrangell Lumber Company. In 1965, wood products exports to Japan exceeded $26,500,000, nearly one-half of total production value. Of this figure, pulp exports accounted for $21 million. Japanese interests also marketed much of the lumber produced in southeastern Alaska.

The 1970s and early 1980s have been difficult for Alaska's timber industry. There were some legal cases and controversies dealing with types of sales and operational methods in the state. New federal and state regulations related logging to environmental values. A shift in public and political attitudes also occurred. From the early part of the twentieth century until 1968, the Forest Service in Alaska had emphasized large sales and long-term contracts to create a stable economy and the orderly replacement of old forests with new growth. After 1970 there was considerable opposition to long-term sales and a desire to perpetuate, rather than harvest, old-growth forests. Land available for timber harvest in the national forests shrank sharply because of the designation of special management units and because of state and Alaska Native land claims selections. Finally, the recession in the late 1970s and early 1980s severely impacted southeastern Alaska's lumber and pulp industry as Japanese markets shrank.

Besides southeastern Alaska's great forests, there are other wooded regions in the state. In fact, the United States Forest Service has estimated that there are approximately 180 billion board feet of timber on 22.5 million acres of commercial forest land. Of these, about 31 billion board feet consist of saw timber. The estimated net yearly growth amounts to about 2.5 billion board feet, making possible an annual cut of saw timber of approximately 900 million board feet. For years small sawmills in widely scattered communities in Alaska have harvested some of this timber and sold the wood products locally. In addition, the energy crisis has motivated many residents to cut increasing amounts of wood for home heating purposes.

The Fishing Industry

In the 1870s, after steam engines replaced sails in the whaling ships, entrepreneurs made renewed efforts to hunt the bowhead whale, particularly valuable for its baleen. Baleen is a horny and flexible substance growing in independent plates, from two to twelve feet long, attached in two rows along the whale's upper jaw. Manufacturers used the baleen to stiffen stays, corsets, and hoop skirts.

In addition to whaling activities, American fishing fleets soon fished for cod, salmon, herring, and halibut off Alaska's coast. The establishment of the salmon fishery, however, dominated the first few decades. In the 1860s a technique for preserving salmon in tin cans was developed, and with that entrepreneurs quickly realized the potential of the industry. In 1864 the Hopgood Hume Company built the first salmon cannery on the Pacific coast. Although initial canning processes were crude, the venture proved successful, and within a few years salmon canneries dotted the coast from California to Puget Sound in Washington. As the canning process improved and markets for the product expanded, the industry expanded northward into British Columbia and Alaska. In 1878 the industry built the first two canneries at Klawock and Sitka, and within a few years other plants operated from as far north as Chilkat Inlet on Lynn Canal to Ketchikan at the southern extremity of the Panhandle. In the early 1880s the industry also established itself in western and central Alaska.

In the early years the isolation of many of the fishing areas and the primitive nature of Alaska with its small population made necessary the yearly importation of fishermen, cannery laborers, and supplies, primarily from San Francisco and Seattle. These cities also became the storage and marketing centers for the product.

Soon, however, severe competition developed among the growing number of cannery operators. Increased fishing pressures began to reduce annual catches and profits. It was not long before ownership and control of canneries became concentrated in the hands of a few large corporations which attempted to rationalize product and marketing.

In 1893 San Francisco interests took the first steps in the direction which led to the creation of the Alaska Packers Association. In 1894 the association owned or controlled about 90 percent of all Alaskan canneries with a pack equalling about 72 percent of the total output. By the turn of the century the corporation monopolized practically the entire production of Alaskan canned salmon. But because of continued growth of the industry during the next few decades the association was unable to retain its dominant position. New mergers and consolidations took place, and there were struggles between companies for specific fishing regions and salmon species. No single firm, however, has been able to control the production and marketing of salmon as the Alaskan Packers Assocation did during the early period. What emerged was an industrial structure consisting of a few large corporations controlling the greater part of the Alaska salmon pack, and a large but fluctuating number of small, independent firms. Many of these, in fact, were marginal producers.

Canning companies also controlled fishing operations to a large extent. Elsewhere the fishermen generally are independent entrepreneurs, but in Alaska a different pattern developed. During the early years of the fishing industry, the territory's population was small and few fishermen lived in the north. The seasonal characteristic of the fishing industry made it uneconomical for fishermen to settle permanently in the remote fishing areas, and the long distances made it impossible to travel back and forth each year in their own boats. As a result, from the beginning cannery operators organized and financed fishing operations on a large scale to assure adequate supplies of fish. Each spring, they recruited fishermen in San Francisco, Seattle, and elsewhere and transported them north on company vessels. Just like cannery workers, they were paid off at their home ports at the end of the season. Since it was expensive to provide transportation, boats, gear, supplies, housing, and other necessities to maintain this pattern, only the larger companies were able to undertake these annual expeditions. By so doing, they gained much control over Alaska's fishing grounds, especially such remote areas as Bristol Bay. Soon conflicts developed between resident and nonresident fishermen. For example, in Bristol Bay, the greatest red salmon fishery in the world, it was not until the 1930s that a few residents were able to fish in the area even though they were willing to become company employees. Until 1951 private ownership of fishing boats by either residents or nonresidents was practically unheard of.

The canning operators also directly influenced fishing operations through ownership and operation of most of the traps, the most efficient gear for catching salmon. Between 1925 and 1934 traps accounted for 70 percent of all the salmon taken in southeastern Alaska, 62 percent in the decade from 1935 to 1944, 54 percent between 1945 and 1954, and 39 percent during the 1956 season when conservation regulations reduced the number of traps by half. During 1957, 215 traps were operated in all Alaskan waters, and of these, 123 were located within southeast Alaska.

Because the traps were so effective and productive, and because the absentee canning operations owned most of them, the device became a symbol of absentee control of Alaska's fishing industry. Alaskan fishermen used competing forms of gear such as purse and beach seines, gill nets, and trollers. Highly mobile, they used boats of various sizes in their operations and employed many fishermen. Alaskans hated the traps, and upon achieving statehood, abolished the device.

The traps were so effective because of the behavior of the salmon. The several salmon species are hatched in the lakes and headwaters of many Alaskan rivers which empty into the sea. From there they migrate to the open sea, returning upon maturity to the place of their birth to spawn and die. Fishermen harvest the salmon during the few months each summer when the mature salmon return to their home streams and rivers. Typical traps consisted of a rectangle of large logs floating on the surface of the water as an anchored raft, or supported on fixed piles, under which was hung a large netting. The trap connected to the shoreline by netting extending from the surface of the water to the bottom which acted as a barrier to the passage of salmon and directed them through two large V-shaped throats into the "pot" and "spiller" of the trap. Through the converging sides of the throats and tunnels of the trap, the salmon were unable to escape and were held captive until "brailed" or removed by the raising of the net floor, which dumped the fish into the cannery scow.

Requiring few workers and easily supervised, the stationary traps were extremely efficient. Furthermore, trap-caught salmon were of a better quality than those caught by mobile gear because they always were fresh when packed.

The Alaska salmon fishery was very profitable and productive. From its inception in 1878 until the turn of the century, production grew slowly. In the early part of the twentieth century the industry grew rapidly with the opening of new markets and improvements in fishing and canning techniques. The first major peak and decline resulted from the tremendous demand for the canned salmon created during World War I and the subsequent decline in the market. In 1918, the total pack reached a high of 6.5 million cases (there are forty-eight one-pound cans in each case). Thereafter, a brief decline occurred until 1921 when the pack amounted to only a little over 2.5 million cases.

During the 1920s the salmon pack increased again, but it fluctuated widely from year to year. A peak was reached in 1936 with a production of 8.5 million cases. Following this peak, however, the annual pack declined continuously and rapidly except for a short period during World War II. In 1959, the last year of federal management and control, the total pack amounted to only 1.6 million cases.

Addressing a joint assembly of the first Alaska state legislature in January 1960, Governor Walter Egan stated that "On January 1 of this year, Alaska's Department of Fish and Game was handed the depleted remnants of what was once a rich and prolific fishery. From a peak of three-quarters of a billion pounds in 1936, production dropped in 1959 to its lowest in sixty years. On these ruins of a once great resource, the department must rebuild. Our gain is that we can profit by studying the destructive practices, mistakes, and omissions of the past." The new state did rebuild the salmon resource, and harvests once again reached record levels from the 1970s onward—this time on a sustainable yield basis.

The first big fishery in Alaskan waters was for whales. In 1835 New England whalers began fishing the north Pacific and soon moved into the Bering Sea and the Arctic Ocean. In 1897, the *Jeannie, Newport,* and *Fearless,* shown here, were off the north coast. They were equipped with steam engines as well as sails.

In 1897 eight whalers were caught in the ice near Point Barrow and required a rescue operation that involved driving reindeer from Cape Prince of Wales to the starving crews. Courtesy of the Call Collection, Alaska and Polar Regions Dept., Rasmuson Library, UAF

These men were cutting blubber from a whale at sea. The blubber would be rendered into oil, which at one time was used for lighting, and later for industrial uses. Life on the vessels was hard, and the voyages long. The photo is dated 1917, which was at the very end of this kind of whaling from sailing vessels. Courtesy of the Willoughby Collection, Alaska and Polar Regions Dept., Rasmuson Library, UAF

This finback whale is on the dock at a U.S. Whaling Company station on the southern coast of Alaska. Shore stations were set up at a number of places on the Alaskan shore where processing could be handled more efficiently than at sea. The men in the photo give a good idea of the size of the whale. Courtesy of the Grainger Collection, Alaska Historical Library

Charles D. Brower had gone to Barrow in 1884 as a trader and provided supplies for whalers who ventured that far north. His house was a large, substantial building. It must have been difficult to heat in the cold arctic winters. Courtesy of the Anchorage Historical and Fine Arts Museum

This early photo of Kodiak, a major fishing port, was probably taken before 1900. The small community had neatly fenced, well-spaced houses. Courtesy of the Anchorage Historical and Fine Arts Museum

The bark *Paramita* sails the Bering Sea loaded with canned salmon, about 1906-08. This is the end of the sailing ship era. Courtesy of the Wheatley Album, Anchorage Historical and Fine Arts Museum

Charles William Gompertz was in charge of building canneries for the Pacific Steam Whaling Company, which later became Alaska Packers. As superintendent he stayed at the Kenai cannery until 1903, the year the cannery was destroyed by an arsonist. In this 1896 photo Gompertz is dressed in arctic clothing that was probably not needed in Kenai. Courtesy of the K. R. Gompertz Collection, Alaska Historical Library

Cannery communities were often self-sufficient little company towns. This company store was probably photographed in the early 1930s at the Alaska Packers Association cannery at Kvichak. Courtesy of the Angren Collection, Alaska Historical Library

A seine boat makes a haul of salmon. Courtesy of the U.S. Forest Service Collection, Alaska Historical Library

This shows a processing room at a cannery in the 1930s. Courtesy of the Anchorage Historical and Fine Arts Museum

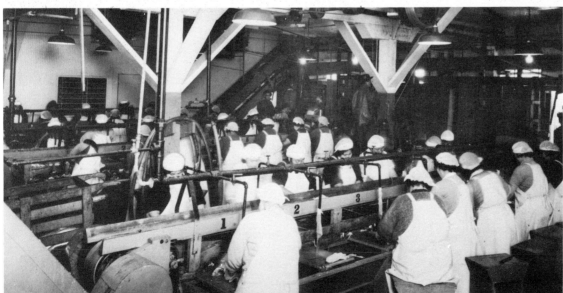

After the Kennecott copper mine and the railroad closed in 1938, Cordova turned to fishing. Here boats are seining for herring off Cordova in 1977. Courtesy of the *Fairbanks Daily News-Miner*

New resources in Alaskan waters remain to be tapped. The king crab fishery, centered near Kodiak, has only developed since the 1950s. Courtesy of the Alaska Department of Fish and Game Collection, Alaska Historical Library

Halibut are important commercial fish, and Ketchikan was for many years the center of the halibut fishery. These halibut are being unloaded in Juneau in 1965. The new Federal building is in the background. C. Naske photo

A Coast Guard cutter is shown in the pack ice off the Alaskan coast on August 10, 1976.

The Coast Guard, with a major base at Kodiak, patrols the Alaskan coast policing international fishing treaties as well as performing vital rescue operations. Courtesy of the *Fairbanks Daily News-Miner*

Bibliography

Books

Berry, Mary Clay. *The Alaska Pipeline: The Politics of Oil and Native Land Claims.* Bloomington and London: Indiana University Press, 1975.

Berton, Pierre. *The Klondike Fever: The Life and Death of the Last Great Gold Rush.* New York: Alfred A. Knopf, 1958.

Chevigny, Hector. *Russian America: The Great Alaskan Venture, 1741-1867.* New York: The Viking Press, 1965.

Congressional Quarterly Service. *Congress and the Nation, 1945-1964: A Review of Government and Politics in the Postwar Years.* Washington, D.C., 1735 K Street, N.W.: Congressional Quarterly Service, 1965.

Cooley, Richard A. *Politics and Conservation: The Decline of the Alaska Salmon.* New York: Harper and Row, Publishers, 1963.

Fisher, Raymond H. *Bering's Voyages: Whither and Why.* Seattle and London: University of Washington Press, 1977.

Fischer, Victor. *Alaska's Constitutional Convention.* Fairbanks, Alaska: University of Alaska Press, 1975.

Garfield, Brian. *The Thousand-Mile War: World War II in Alaska and the Aleutians.* Garden City, New York: Doubleday and Company, Inc., 1969.

Gruening, Ernest. *The State of Alaska.* New York: Random House, Inc., 1968.

Harrison, Gordon. *A Citizen's Guide to the Constitution of the State of Alaska.* Anchorage, Alaska: Institute of Social and Economic Research, University of Alaska.

Harrison, Gordon Scott, Editor. *Alaska Public Policy: Current Problems and Issues.* Fairbanks, Alaska: Institute of Social, Economic and Government Research, University of Alaska, 1973.

Gibson, James R. *Imperial Russia in Frontier America: The Changing Geography of Supply of Russian America, 1784-1867:* New York: Oxford University Press, 1976.

Hanrahan, John, and Gruenstein, Peter. *Lost Frontier: The Marketing of Alaska.* New York: W.W. Norton and Company, Inc., 1977.

Hinckley, Ted C. *The Americanization of Alaska, 1867-1897.* Palo Alto, California: Pacific Books, Publishers, 1972.

Hunt, William R. *North of 53°: The Wild Days of the Alaska-Yukon Mining Frontier, 1870-1914.* New York: MacMillan Publishing Co., Inc., 1974.

Lantis, Margaret, editor. *Ethnohistory in Southwestern Alaska and the Southern Yukon: Method and Content:* Lexington, Kentucky: The University Press of Kentucky, 1970.

This is an exhibit of local produce from the Arctic Greenhouse, at the Tanana Valley Fair sometime before 1920. There were several large greenhouses in Fairbanks, as well as truck farms and hay fields. Courtesy of the Hess Collection, Alaska and Polar Regions Dept., Rasmuson Library, UAF

Morehouse, Thomas A., and Harrison, Gordon S. *An Electoral Profile of Alaska.* Fairbanks, Alaska: Institute of Social, Economic, and Government Research, University of Alaska, 1973.

Naske, Claus-M. *An Interpretative History of Alaskan Statehood.* Anchorage, Alaska: Alaska Northwest Publishing Company, 1973.

Naske, Claus-M. *Edward Lewis Bob Bartlett of Alaska: A Life in Politics.* Fairbanks, Alaska: University of Alaska Press, 1979.

Naske, Claus-M. and Slotnick, Herman E. *Alaska: A History of the 49th State.* Grand Rapids, Michigan: William B. Eerdmans Publishing Company, 1979.

Nichols, Jeannette Paddock. *Alaska: A History of its Administration, Exploitation, and Industrial Development During its First Half Century under the Rule of the United States.* New York: Russell and Russell, Inc., 1963.

Potter, Jean. *Alaska Under Arms.* New York: The MacMillan Company, 1943.

Rogers, George W. *The Future of Alaska: Economic Consequence of Statehood.* Baltimore: The Johns Hopkins Press, 1962.

Sherwood, Morgan B. *Exploration of Alaska, 1865-1900.* New Haven and London: Yale University press, 1965.

Van Stone, James W. *Athapaskan Adaptations; Hunters and Fishermen of the Subarctic Forests.* Chicago: Aldine Publishing Company, 1974.

Vernadsky, George. *A History of Russia.* New Haven and London: Yale University Press, 1966.

Waxell, Sven. *The Russian Expedition to America.* New York: Collier Books, 1967.

Wilson, William H. *Railroad in the Clouds: The Alaska Railraod in the Age of Steam, 1914-1945.* Boulder, Colorado: Pruett Publishing Company, 1977.

Government Publications

Alaska Growth Policy Council. "Wealth Management, 1981." Juneau, Alaska: Alaska Growth Policy Council, 1981.

Division of Budget and Management, Office of the Governor. Alaska Economy Year-End.

Mitchell, Elaine, Editor. Department of Education, Division of State Libraries. Alaska Blue Book, 1973. Juneau, Alaska: Department of Education, 1973.

Orth, Donald J. *Dictionary of Alaska Place Names.* Geological Survey Professional Paper 567. Washington, D.C.: United States Government Printing Office, 1967.

Performance Report, 1981. Juneau, Alaska: Division of Budget and Management, 1982.

Public Administration Service. Functional and Staffing Charts for the Proposed Organization of the Executive Branch, State of Alaska. Chicago: Public Administration Service, 1959.

Public Administration Service. Local Government Under the Alaska Constitution: A Survey Report, Chicago: Public Administration Service, 1959.

Public Administration Service. Proposed Organization of the Executive Branch, State of Alaska: A Summary Report. Chicago: Public Administration Service, 1958.

Public Administration Service. Proposed Organization of the Executive Branch, State of Alaska: A Survey Report. Chicago: Public Administration Service, 1958.

Public Administration Service. Proposed Organization of the Judicial Branch, State of Alaska. Chicago: Public Administration Service, 1958.

State of Alaska. Alaska Session Laws, 1959.

State of Alaska, Budget Document 1960-1961. Message of Governor William A. Egan to the Second Session, First Alaska State Legislature, Recommending Appropriations for Fiscal Year 1961. Juneau, Alaska: Office of the Governor, 1960.

Territory of Alaska. Alaska Session Laws, 1957.

Manuscript Collections

Abilene, Kansas. Dwight D. Eisenhower Library. Papers of Dwight D. Eisenhower.

Fairbanks, Alaska. University of Alaska Archives. E. L. Bartlett Papers.

Fairbanks, Alaska. University of Alaska Archives. Ernest Gruening Papers.

Fairbanks, Alaska. University of Alaska Archives. Papers of Anthony J. Dimond.

Independence, Missouri. Harry S. Truman Library. Papers of Harry S. Truman.

Seattle, Washington. Federal Records Center.

Washington, D.C. The Library of Congress.

Washington, D.C. The Smithsonian Institution.

Washington, D.C. National Archives and Records Service.

Newspapers

Alaska Advocate (Anchorage). 1978.

Anchorage Daily Times. 1958-1959.

Fairbanks Daily News-Miner, 1958-1959.

The Daily Alaska Empire (Juneau). 1959-1962.

Articles

Stone, David B. *Geophysical Surveys 3,* (1977, 3-37) "Plate Tectonics, Paleo-magnetism and the Tectonic History of the N.E. Pacific,"

Index

In 1954, Claus-M. Naske, a native of Germany, immigrated to Alaska's Matanuska Valley as a farm laborer. He eventually finished high school there, and attended the University of Alaska at Fairbanks where he received a baccalaureate degree in history and political science in 1961. Naske received a master's degree in European history from the University of Michigan in 1964 and a doctorate in American history from Washington State University in 1970. A faculty member of the University of Alaska, Fairbanks, since 1969, Naske is a professor in the history department. He has written numerous articles on northern history and worked extensively on contract assignments for various state and federal agencies. He has written three books and co-authored four others. Currently he is preparing for publication a manuscript on Alaska's territorial governor Ernest Gruening. He and his wife Dinah have two children and reside in Fairbanks.

Ludwig J. Rowinski grew up in Passaic, New Jersey. He majored in ornithology at Cornell University, where he received his bachelor of science degree in 1951. After military service, he enrolled at the University of Alaska, Fairbanks as a graduate student in wildlife management, receiving a master's degree in 1958. From 1964 to 1965 he took graduate studies at Cornell University, and from 1970 to 1971 he studied regional museums in Denmark. Rowinski has read numerous papers at professional meetings, conducted workshops, and co-authored two books. He and his wife Christi have three children and reside in Fairbanks. Rowinski retired from the university in 1980 and since that time has become a passionate farmer.